Technical Marketing
COMMUNICATION

Sandra W. Harner
Cedarville University

Tom G. Zimmerman
GE Capital Information Technology Solutions

Longman

New York   Boston   San Francisco
London   Toronto   Sydney   Tokyo   Singapore   Madrid
Mexico City   Munich   Paris   Cape Town   Hong Kong   Montreal

Senior Vice President/Publisher: Eben W. Ludlow
Marketing Manager: Chris Bennem
Supplements Editor: Donna Campion
Production Manager: Mark Naccarelli
Project Coordination, Text Design, and Electronic Page Makeup: Nesbitt Graphics, Inc.
Cover Design Manager: Nancy Danahy
Cover Designer: Caryl Silvers
Manufacturing Buyer: Roy Pickering
Printer and Binder: Hamilton Printing Company
Cover Printer: Coral Graphic Services

Library of Congress Cataloging-in-Publication Data

Harner, Sandra.
    Technical marketing communication / Sandra Harner and Tom Zimmerman.
      p. cm.
    ISBN 0-205-32444-4
    1. Communication of technical information. 2. Marketing. I. Zimmerman, Tom (Tom G.)
    II. Title.
  T10.5 H36 2002
  658.8'04—dc21   2001038967

Please visit our website at http://www.ablongman.com

ISBN 0-205-32444-4

1 2 3 4 5 6 7 8 9 10—HT—04 03 02 01

Dedicated to the
One
who provided these
talents and opportunities!

CONTENTS

CHAPTER 4 ## Strategy Development   50

CHAPTER 5 ## Internal and External Branding   67

CHAPTER 6	Enhancing and Applying Creativity	87

CHAPTER 7	Print Media	101

FOREWORD
by the Series Editor

The Allyn and Bacon Series in Technical Communication is designed to meet the continuing education needs of professional technical communicators, both those who desire to upgrade or update their own communication abilities as well as those who train or supervise writers, editors, and artists within their organization. This series also serves the growing number of students enrolled in undergraduate and graduate programs in technical communication. Such programs offer a wide variety of courses beyond the introductory technical writing course—advanced courses for which fully satisfactory and appropriately focused textbooks have often been impossible to locate.

The chief characteristic of the books in this series is their consistent effort to integrate theory and practice. The books offer both research-based and experienced-based instruction, describing not only what to do and how to do it but explaining why. The instructors who teach advanced courses and the students who enroll in these courses are looking for more than rigid rules and ad hoc guidelines. They want books that demonstrate theoretical sophistication and a solid foundation in the research of the field as well as pragmatic advice and perceptive applications. Instructors and students will also find these books filled with activities and assignments adaptable to the classroom and to the self-guided learning processes of professional technical communicators.

To operate effectively in the field of technical communication, today's technical communicators require extensive training in the creation, analysis, and design of information for both domestic and international audiences, for both paper and electronic environments. The books in the Allyn and Bacon Series address those subjects that are most frequently taught at the undergraduate and graduate levels as a direct response to both the educational needs of students and the practical demands of business and industry. Additional books will be developed for the series in order to satisfy or anticipate changes in writing technologies, academic curricula, and the profession of technical communication.

Sam Dragga
Texas Tech University

PREFACE

IT'S A NEW MILLENNIUM, and this text is as much about the ways marketing communication should leverage technology as it is about applying communication to market a technology. Today's technical marketing communicator (TMC) is much more than a writer. We are deliciously rooted in principles for content development. Communicators should continue to own clarity, concision, and style. But we've also been handed the freedom to deliver our content in boundless ways. The world is indeed our oyster—as are the Web, portals, handheld computers, video, print, audio, and all other media combinations. We are virtually unlimited in options to reach various audiences. If writer's block is best represented by a blank piece of paper, then technical marketing communicator's block includes the visualization of data networks, monitors, audio speakers, and Web browsers.

A successful technical marketing communicator is still part technologist, part interpreter, and part content creator. But add orchestra conductor to the list to indicate the technology instruments and nuances in our hands. Without the TMC's baton keeping tempo, every technical marketing communication endeavor risks the noisy confusion of departments and teams playing to the beat of their own drum and drowning out the overall, objective melody. To round out the TMC's responsibilities, include prophet in light of the inevitable change and choices that literally occur with the latest dot-com start-up or e-business buyout.

You'd need a book to try and explain it all. And that's what we hope to do. This text represents a snapshot taken even as IP telephony and co-located application service providers (ASPs) are entering the TMC lexicon. It's more than a little scary to wonder which terms will have already become obsolete by the time we go to press. But much of what we have to say should be timeless. The basic needs to clarify your objective, identify your audiences, develop strategies, and execute tactical solutions are not going away. We must ensure that our methodologies and processes are dynamic enough to accommodate the pace of change being driven by the very technologies with which we are associated.

We can all remember a time when technical communicators were handed a software package and told to write the manual. However, times have changed. As an industry, we have advocated user-centered design, and today it is often accepted practice for the technical communicator to be a member of the technology team in the earliest stages. The result has been better communication and ultimately increased profitability for the technology organization, institution, or company.

Technical Marketing Communication presents a technical marketing communication life cycle in which TMCs can effectively contribute at every step. That doesn't mean that every organization invites them to do so. In fact, technologists and marketing leaders alike often forget to involve TMCs from the very start of the program. It can be a costly mistake. Technologists can lose sight of the market in their zeal to deliver, just as pure marketing strategists can miss the total impact of a technology. TMCs help them to see both sides of the equation and share it across multiple audiences.

The scope of technical marketing communication, as presented in this text, is extensive and thorough. The text is permeated with real-world examples and situations to give you a look into the life of a TMC. At the end of each chapter, we have included a summary to provide you with a quick reference of the most important material. End-of-chapter exercises give you the opportunity to apply what you've learned. We urge you to complete these exercises even if you are not using this text in an educational setting. Because we believe that effective learning is collaborative, we have provided a small group activity at the end of each chapter.

As you read, you will see the text taking you through a process that results in a plan. In Chapter 1, we begin by laying the foundation for the concepts of technical marketing communication. In the next three chapters, we discuss the importance of developing a process involving needs analysis, audience analysis, and strategy development. In Chapter 5, we provide some brand basics from the perspective of a technical marketing communicator. We believe that creativity should permeate everything a technical marketing communicator does, and in Chapter 6 we discuss what creativity really is and offer suggestions to help you develop your own creative abilities. Then you'll be ready to choose your tactics. Chapters 7 through 10 provide a plethora of choices: print, electronic, personal presentations, trade show exhibitions, and premiums. Chapter 11 offers important advice to help you choose the right tactic for the specific goal you have in mind. We call the process aligning tactics with strategies. Finally, Chapter 12 brings our text to a close by helping you see the importance of evaluating all that you have done in order to make your next effort even more successful. We trust that this text will help you to see the big picture of technical marketing communication as well as the nuts and bolts of producing effective communication to achieve your marketing goals.

As you consider adopting this text for your class, rest assured that the Instructor's Manual (IM) will guide you step-by-step as you prepare your course. Syllabi are included, both for quarter and semester systems, complete with course objectives and a daily classroom schedule. We have worked hard to anticipate your questions and have provided the answers in the section entitled FAQs. Reading quizzes are available for each chapter and can be used to assess your students' reading comprehension, or you can use them as study questions to guide students as they read. If you are part of a well-established technical communication program that does not currently offer a course in technical marketing communication, your first task then is to understand or convince others of the need for such a course. The IM will help you do just that.

When we set out to write this text, it was our goal to speak to our audience in a relaxed, conversational voice. We imagined our readers with a cup of coffee in hand—sharing our thoughts about technical marketing communicators. We hope we have achieved our goal. We hope you'll join us at that virtual café.

This text would not be possible without the help of many people. We were fortunate to share the writing process as co-authors, and through it all our friendship has deepened. But there are others who helped make this possible. We'd like to begin by thanking the staff at Longman for working with us and for patiently answering the many questions only first-time authors ask. We wish to thank our students and colleagues from whom we have learned much of what we have written about. We especially appreciate the help of former students, Angela Pappas Lundquist, Jill Bollman Cassidy, Lisa Van Wormer Hodge, David Kimmel, Cindy Moore, and Peter Chevere, who provided workplace examples for our text. We thank you, our readers, for giving us your time. Love and appreciation to our spouses, Don and Angela, and to our children and grandchildren, Sarica, Scott, Char, Amy, Jason, and Zachary, for exchanging many hours of family time for hours of time spent on task. In all ways we have been truly blessed.

Sandra Harner
Tom Zimmerman

Technical Marketing
COMMUNICATION

CHAPTER 1

Marketing Communication Concepts

Overview

"So what does your company do?"

I was staffing the company booth at a technical exposition, and visitors were beginning to drift in after a keynote speech in the auditorium. Our three-panel booth backdrop featured examples from a cross section of our work. There were screenshots of Web sites and hard-copy brochure collateral samples, while a slide show ran on the laptop off to one side. A few posters hung on the panels added bulleted insights: consulting, technical documentation, and database development.

Like most companies, our management team struggled to find the best way to articulate our core competencies during brief encounters. Our scope of offerings was large enough that it wasn't easy to state them all in a 30-second elevator speech. We were wary of any definition considered too restrictive or conventional. We certainly didn't want to limit any new business opportunities by presenting too narrow a focus. Consequently, our booth didn't really come out and define our target market or dream client.

The prospect was looking at one of the Web-site screenshots, and I explained our capabilities for Web architecture and design.

"So you're a Web development company?"

"Well, not exactly." I explained that Web sites were sometimes the best way to communicate, but we also worked with print solutions. The prospect had turned to the panel with brochure collateral.

"Oh, so you're more like an ad agency."

"Well, not exactly." In addition to the promotional aspects of communications, there were times when in-depth technical documentation was in order, and we even developed online help systems to support complex technologies.

"I see." Unfortunately, my prospect didn't really see. He was struggling with the same issue our management team had struggled with. "What exactly do you do?"

Fortunately, one of his colleagues was watching the laptop presentation as I explained the connection between holistic marketing concepts and communications—all focused on technology organizations and institutions. The colleague casually looked over to the prospect and observed, "They're a technical marketing communication firm." The prospect looked at me hopefully, and I gratefully concurred. A technical marketing communication firm.

In this chapter, you learn what the terms mean: technology, marketing, communication. And then we distill and combine these three areas to show you how they intersect to create a unique discipline.

Tom

Technology

Technical marketing communicators must successfully relate technology across diverse industries and fields of study (see Figure 1.1). What images does the word *technology* conjure up for you? Ask five people that question, and the variety of responses will be based on their personal experience. In our current culture, technology most often means computers and the Internet: modems, disk drives, storage servers, routers, fiber optics, video cards, Ethernet devices, frame relays. But there is so much more to consider.

In the medical field, diagnostic imaging technologies include X-ray images, magnetic resonance imaging (MRI), and computed tomography (CT). The stunning diversity of technical communication in this arena simultaneously encompasses human physiology (biochemistry), software algorithms, radioisotopes, superconductors, mathematics, electrical engineering, and manufacturing processes. It's all related to the technology of diagnostic imaging, but not necessarily to computers.

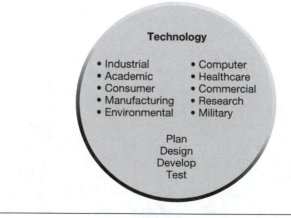

Figure 1.1   Diverse fields of study that relate to technology.

The individual domains within the field of diagnostic imaging own very distinct technical peculiarities. As part of these distinctions, specialists from each discipline develop discrete technical expertise and communication dialects. Facing this truth is both humbling and challenging to technical marketing communicators: humbling to realize how vast the spectrum of technology really is and challenging to know we have the tools to take it on.

We do our best in this text to avoid becoming too technology-specific. By definition, technology relates to things scientific, methodological, and of specialized technique. It's true we devote a great deal of attention to the Web and other online aspects of communication, but we'll do so in ways any field of technology might benefit in marketing communication.

Communicating on Behalf of Technology

The *technical* in technical marketing communication is truly meant to differentiate the subject matter of marketing communication. As stated previously, the t-word covers a lot of territory: robotics, aeronautics, plastics, and chapsticks. From that perspective, think of technical marketing communication as a specialty area of marketing communication.

Consider consumer marketing for a new dishwashing detergent. Many shoppers would be interested to learn of new and improved fragrances or spot-free rinse features. Classic marketing techniques stress the combination of features and benefits to illustrate value. But regardless of how specialized these features are, few people would care to hear of the chemistry or manufacturing processes required to produce them in detergent. In fact, you could actually lose consumer interest if you got too technical. Consumer marketing for them.

But the engineering technology team that just patented these ideas for private label resale has a different agenda. They definitely want to market the details of emulsifiers and formula-specific breakthroughs. They're hoping to attract major manufacturers to their new concept. Billboards and yellow page ads aren't appropriate and are ruled out immediately. Sure, they have a Web site, but what should it say, and how can they drive Internet traffic to it? How can they best leverage communication that *clarifies the value of their technology* without reproducing every detail from their lab books? Technical marketing communication for them.

Communicating with the Help of Technology

We take license with the more classic definitions of technical marketing communication at this point. Clearly, most technical marketing communicators seem to enjoy working with and being around technology. When asked why they enjoy participating in this field, communicators often say they like the complexity of various technologies, and it's always changing.

More and more of those who *communicate* technology are themselves technically savvy. Technical marketing communicators apply scientific techniques and technology tools as part of their own professional methodology. Typewriter, print, and word processor technology saw them through all but a few of the last 133 years (the typewriter was patented in 1868). Then the explosion of desktop software tools and online access in the 1990s prompted the more technical communicators to push the creativity envelope of their work beyond old borders. Technical marketing communication is not just desktop publishing programs and translation software although they also represent important tools of the trade.

You may be able to burn a CD presentation from your own desktop computer today, but it was a much more involved and costly proposition a few years ago. However, once the idea took hold—that we could have direct access to technology as a tool—a new day dawned for technical communicators. Now, we wonder how a video might be streamed instead of shipped. Logging hundreds of people onto a real-time Webinar requires far less energy than herding them through airports and into a convention center for two days. A hot market update can be pushed to your customer's handheld much faster than a telemarketer can dial a cell phone. A personalized Web portal wields much more tracking versatility than a standard HTML site.

These technologies speed communication delivery and broaden audience accessibility. But you have to know how. More importantly, you have to know what's available. Which brings us right back to an increasingly foregone conclusion: Successful marketing communicators in the 2000s aren't just going to be communicators—they're going to be *technical* communicators.

Communication

Almost all of us choose and are able to communicate in some form or fashion. Speech is communication. Sign language is communication. Writing communicates with words. Attitudes convey emotional states. T-shirts shout sports team affiliation. What we wear or drive may communicate our lifestyle. In short, communication sends a message.

We'd like to believe sending implies receiving, but that's not necessarily the case. How many university students have left a lecture either confused or bored after listening to 50 minutes of communication? Some of the more hopeful definitions of communication do, in fact, suggest an exchange of thoughts and ideas. Certainly, that's the ideal. But dialogue and conversation are better words to describe exchanged communication. In truth, most of our communication is simply meant to make known or impart information. We may desperately hope to be understood, but our communication mode is most often *send* and not *receive*. I talk; you listen. Spammers send e-mails you read or delete (Spammers don't accept replies to unsubscribe). People even ask, "Are we communicating?" when they really mean, "Are you getting *my* message?"

Many marketing situations and communication forums are just not set up to accommodate real-time, bidirectional communication (i.e., dialogue). Online Web interactivity usually lacks an immediately responsive human element although faster, more intelligent networks are breaking down those barriers. The size of the audience for business or university presentations may inhibit meaningful interactive feedback until the closing questions and answers. Print communication might simply be left in your dorm mailbox or on your desk at work. These might communicate a message to call a 1-800-number or return a postcard, but interaction isn't happening.

We are forced to ask the question, "What defines **effective** communication?" Is it simply better in the eye of the beholder? It's an important question. For the purposes of our text, **effective communication is communication that is clearly understood by the intended audience.** Asking that question provides a simple test for much of the work technical marketing communicators do in our industry: "Do you understand?" When the answer is "no," we have failed to do our job well, and improvements should follow. There may be complex nuances to this test. The barriers to good communication might simply be murky, boring, or confusing content (not clearly understood). Sometimes we can attribute that to bad writing or poor media work. Or you might have really good content—crisp, clear, and loaded with information—but for the wrong audience. Regardless of anything else we impart in this text about marketing and technology, all you do must be built on a foundation of good communication (see Figure 1.2).

Communication Variety

We write much more about the various means of communication in later chapters, but a summary here helps to build clarity. Not surprisingly, all forms of communication rely on at least one of our human senses: sight, taste, smell, touch, and hearing. Consumer marketers do a wonderful job of appealing to sensual themes. TV commercials combat thirst with sports drinks and bad breath with mouthwash. It's a pretty good trick to have audiences recall a taste (cool mint) or scent (fresh pine) in a communication limited to sight and sound. Technical marketing communicators face the same challenges but with different twists, as we'll see later.

Figure 1.2   Diverse elements of effective communication.

Written Communication

The largest percentage of communication is still written—whether in print or online. To write means to form words and set them down independent of media. This book was primarily composed using various keyboard and monitor combinations (PCs and laptops), but many of the editing rewrites were done on paper. Memorandums, documents, reports, technical manuals, service bulletins, training guides, and quick reference cards—all are written communication. And almost all other communication has integral written components. Videos require written scripts and teleprompter text. Most presenters in public and private situations use written notes and bulleted slides. Even communication plans are written. It is imperative that technical marketing communicators have command of their written communication. You can hire video producers to run with your ideas, and Web designers can imagine your dot-com site architecture, but you won't get far without being able to communicate your ideas in writing.

Audible Communication

Effective communication often originates during conversations at the local coffeehouse or tennis court. Being able to communicate with the spoken word is prerequisite to streaming audio presentations on the Web, CDs, and distributed voice messaging. It's also the foundation of interview techniques and focus group facilitation. Besides spoken words, other auditory cues are critical in different industries. Most airline technicians are keenly aware of a healthy sounding turbine whine. Automotive engineers know the clunk of a well-designed door closing. Technical marketing communicators need to remember that sound helps to send a message.

Visual Communication

Pictures and other visual graphics offer shortcuts to ideas and emotions. They are an excellent complement to written communication. Isn't it more fun to watch a well-done video with special effects than to wade through a poorly written technology monograph (or textbook)? Scanning a simple bar or pie chart is a much faster way to grasp salary comparisons (see Figure 1.3). But beware. Many visual graphics and animations bury a significant message in superfluous background. These graphics may be fun, or they may waste the time of a serious audience. Successful technical marketing communicators know the difference.

Olfactory/Taste Communication

A well-meaning real estate agent suggested a client keep a package of yeast in a warm kitchen oven. The agent had learned the resulting aroma created a homey impression of baked bread. On the other hand, people have come to expect a sanitized, antiseptic smell in a hospital or dentist's office. The smell of baking bread would seem inappropriate if you were about to undergo a root canal. Medical device manufacturers like to give factory tours to demonstrate the large scale and commitment of their technology enterprise. They quickly learned that visiting healthcare specialists were confused by factory smells of machine oil and cleaning

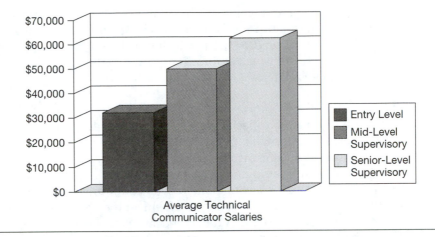

Figure 1.3   Effective use of bar chart for salary comparisons.

solvents. These were foreign odors to their usual patient treatment settings and did not enhance their perception of end-product quality.

As we write this text, a new breed of digital scent machines is being developed that will be compatible with Web-based applications. Technicians will be able to get fast feedback from colleagues and clients at different locations as they develop new scents without the costly delays and processing of physical samples. Technical marketing communicators will need to incorporate this type of communication tool if they intend to be successful in the affected industries. What might be your technology-based analogy to a perfume strip in a fashion magazine?

Technology is just as hard at work to understand and serve our sense of taste. What do the bouquet and body character attributes of a good wine communicate about its age and value? Purists would claim great wine design is more art than science, but the chemically balanced contributions of tart acidity and bitter tannins are manifested in the taste that matters most to the end user. Do you have friends who absolutely cannot drink the diet version of their favorite soda, or eat low-fat ice cream? And how many millions in advertising are spent to boast the home-made taste of soup, crackers, cookies, and bread? Think of how many taste test wars have been promoted over the years. One of Wild Flavor, Inc.'s stated objectives is to "lead the way by supplying its customers with innovative products based on the latest technology and developments." Taste matters and it's quantifiably measurable—a great reason to ponder its role in effective communication.

Attitudinal Communication

"I like your attitude." Technical marketing communicators set the tone for their communication campaigns. You may hear someone refer to the nuance of meaning that was planted between the lines of a presentation or paper. At times it becomes necessary to send an attitudinal message in contrast to past audience experience. For example, a company or department that has become recognized for surly technical service needs to respond with a campaign of very open and accommodating demeanor among employees. Such communication may or may not actually say, "We've changed our attitude," but people will get the message just the same. How that gets communicated is the job of the technical marketing communicators. Much of what we might call attitude is captured in the voice or tone of written content, as we discuss later.

Tactile Communication

The sense of touch is especially prevalent in technical arenas. How easy it is to handle various equipment and technologies is often as important as their design specifications—no different from what we expect from a smooth luxury car ride. And just like luxury automobiles, expensive technology is usually packaged with an appropriate look or feel of quality. Even communication materials themselves can be sensitive to the touch. Clients often feel the weight of brochure paper and worry if it is heavy enough. A flimsy brochure can send a message of cost cutting that attaches itself to product perceptions. How does a free promotional pen feel in your hand? Does it have a nice metallic heft and brushed sheen, or is it cheap plastic? You should select your communication materials based on the message you are trying to send.

Communication Content: What's the Message?

Information content is at the heart of any communication. That's why, as a successful technical marketing communicator, you must also be an excellent communicator. You must be able to craft your message content, or no amount of technology will enable you to prevail.

As we have seen, we deliver content in different sensory packages. Carefully crafted images and sounds can deliver a powerful message in video. A simple slide presentation might convey the elegance and simplicity of a technological solution without glitz and glitter, but the opposite can also be true. An overdone conglomeration of special effects and poorly chosen music might mask and muddy the essential message of a video or Web site. Ten pages of brochure text may never get the same attention as a cleverly crafted tag line. Too many slides and bulleted text points undermine the essential content of a technical marketing presentation. The message can be lost in the packaging.

Ironically, the most obvious negative fallout of the proliferation of online communication is the decidedly bad content prevalent on the Internet and Intranets. It's become so easy for people to publish and distribute Web content that much less thought or editorial process seems to be taking place before pushing the button to publish. In fairness, it may also be true that professionals who now have publishing access are not necessarily professional communicators. They are simply HTML enabled or they are making use of the many HTML editors. While that might sound self-serving in a technical marketing communication text, it is risky to shortcut the communication process. Just as flimsy brochure paper might imply a company's disregard for technical product quality, poor online content may generate the same lack of credibility.

Jakob Nielsen, well-known Internet user advocate, writes, "Hire Web editors. Good content requires a dedicated staff who knows how to write for the Web and how to massage content contributions into the format required by your design standards."[1]

Much of this text is devoted to choosing and organizing content in light of objectives and audience. These are more strategically marketing-oriented concepts. However, your content writing and development skills are crucial to your success, and you should make every effort to develop those skills. You can start by looking for ways to create content with the following characteristics.

Accessible

Simply put, accessible means playing to your audience. Newspapers usually present their vocabularies and content at a sixth-grade reading level. On the other hand, content writers for technical journals and product sheets don't need to worry about audiences who lack a particular grasp of a challenging technology language. From another perspective, the technology content itself must be accessible. For example, a client wished to distribute a corporate message to employees located in multiple retail offices across the United States. He had completed a significant amount of the content to be burned on a CD before he realized that most of their offices had not yet upgraded their computer hardware to include CD-ROM drives. Even with a CD-ROM drive, most of their computer infrastructure wasn't advanced enough to handle the hefty graphics files included with the content. For all intents and purposes, the content was inaccessible to the target audiences.

Well Organized

Regardless of your communication medium, the content must be well organized. Books and technical papers are usually broken into logical chapters and sections. The same is true for online Help and Search directories. We need to understand intuitively the folder names listed on a data CD when we double-click and browse its content.

Effectively Sequenced

Sequencing becomes less important in searchable technologies, but many communication forums still benefit. Training modules are obvious choices for sequencing, so that learning concepts are presented in a logical, progressive order. It's much easier to learn a word processing program if you've first been trained to use a computer mouse. Technology proposals also benefit from sequencing. Readers and listeners grasp concepts more readily when led through a sequence of background information, summary basics, and content that gradually increases in complexity. Even then, searchable technologies should allow aggressive audiences to bypass the logical sequence and speed to the locations of their choice.

Voiced and Stylized

As technical marketing communicators, we can be at our worst when sharing technical content. Dry-as-dust combinations of terms and data are unattractive invitations to our core message content. Breaking through the information overload of our time requires something more imaginative than the basic facts. It's true we can't ignore the way our technology audiences acquire content. They need and want the details in bulleted, no-nonsense fashion. But today's technical marketing communicators should seek fresh approaches that incorporate conversational tones and humor, as well.

We're also communicating with much more technically sophisticated audiences than any previous generation of technical marketing communicators. Incorporating the complex voices of these multigenerational technical experts requires that we immerse ourselves in their culture. Breezy, staccato phrasing for Web site banner advertising may be part of the same marketing communication effort that includes a ten-page detailed spec sheet about machining tolerances. Whatever the chosen voice and style for your communication content, it must be what your target audience needs and expects. We'll explore that in greater detail in the next chapter. Remember to assume that *successful communication content is appropriately packaged to deliver a message that is clearly understood by its targeted audience.* When technology and communication intersect, the result is technical communication (see Figure 1.4). However, when we throw marketing into the mix, the result is quite different.

Marketing

In Nebraska in the early 1900s, farm families consumed much of the food they grew, stored some, and took the rest to market. The point of going to market was to get your produce (products) in front of people who might not otherwise journey out to the farm. The successful purchase or barter transaction required proximity and visual inspection. Otherwise, you might have the best produce in the region, but it could rot waiting for potential customers to venture by.

The public market was ideal in its capacity to match buyer to seller. Buyers knew they could find a mixture of food products to buy based on the regional offerings. Depending on the number of sellers, they might even find differing grades of size and quality (features), leading to competitive price variation.

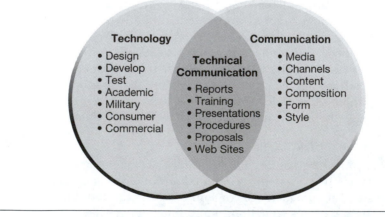

Figure 1.4   Intersection of technology and communication.

You could choose to go somewhere else to get different products, or you could go directly to a seller's location (the farm). But travel and transport came with a cost. Central locations that might house an appropriately named farmer's market also appealed to the farmers themselves, for they could acquire goods and services not immediately available at home. The town square was likely to have a mercantile store for household goods, blacksmith for tool repair, and the professional services of a doctor, lawyer, or optician.

Effective marketing consists of many elements. A marketer has to consider strategy, promotions, public relations, advertising, and branding. The effective mix also includes such things as research, focus groups, distribution, pricing, sales, and creativity (see Figure 1.5).

Defining Market

In the past, the market for farm produce was a literal gathering place where people assembled wagons and baskets. Although today very little produce is delivered to these markets via horse and wagon, today's *super*markets are still the literal distribution points for thousands of products. People are attracted to a supermarket by the location, prices, or unique offerings (i.e., fresh seafood, coupons, and discounts).

In a much broader sense, a *market* is the collection of people or entities that have an interest in or need for a particular product or service. The association of potential buyers, users, and decision makers may have nothing in common other than their interest in a particular technology. Or they may have many things in common across multiple markets. For example, musicians and recording engineers are heavy users of computer technology as well as musical equipment. Both are distinct markets.

Markets are further defined by geography, gender, age, life experience, profession, income, education, industry, technology, or ethnicity—and countless other combinations of buying and decision-making preferences. Our readers probably share interests across more than one of these sample markets:

Figure 1.5   Diverse elements of effective marketing.

- Electronic gaming market includes users of handheld devices, computer software, and TV appliances.
- Sportswear market includes buyers for T-shirts, shoes, caps, and the logo of your choice.
- Fiber optic cable market includes telecommunication companies, corporations, academic institutions, and small businesses.
- Disposable diaper market includes families, hospitals, and daycare centers.
- Denture adhesive market includes senior citizens, specialized care centers, and dental practices.

Consider your own needs for products and services of a technical nature. If you need or are considering the purchase of a laptop computer, you are said to be "in the market" for that type of product, whatever the brand. Your purchasing propensity suddenly combines you with an entire global market of potential laptop buyers. It should be easy for anyone marketing and selling laptop computers to find you, right? But it's not. Among other market attributes are your location, budget, planned use of the technology, and past experience. Market research reveals that most people who do not order computers directly from the Internet or other mail order entities tend to purchase from a local geographical area that includes retail stores. Now the market that includes you shrinks from global to local. If you are involved in the education arena as a student or educator, it is likely you prefer computers with certain operating systems. Beyond this general consumer market, an entire school system might be in the public or private education market for large volume purchase of the same computer.

All of these market differences and divisions interest the technical marketing communicator. Consider our definition again: A market is the collection of people or entities that have an interest in or need for a particular product or service. Note that a market needn't be solely comprised of active buyers. Our definition specifically identifies people and entities with an interest in *or* need for products and services. Your need may or may not be fully realized as a purchase. You could simply choose not to act on your interest or need. Maybe you've got a student loan or car payment to pay and cannot afford to act on your very real need for a computer. You remain in the market just the same.

Still other members of a market haven't yet recognized their need for a technology product or service. It may not have occurred to the person banging out homework assignments on a typewriter that life could be easier with a word processor and printer. Again, they're in the market of people who can benefit from the available technology (they have a legitimate need), but are not aware of the benefits. Raising the collective awareness of these potential users is the responsibility of technical marketing communicators (see Figure 1.6).

Technical Information Markets

We are also concerned with the markets for technical information within entities such as corporations and technology institutions (e.g., universities and research labs). Most large organizations are quick to attribute poor information sharing to

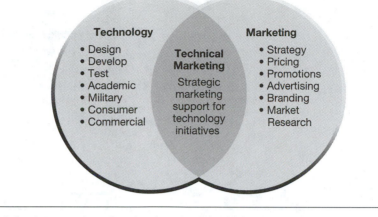

Figure 1.6 Intersection of technology and marketing.

poor communication skills and practices. But as we've stated, plenty of well-meaning technology communication tends to be dry and aimed in one direction.

Poor information sharing particularly plagues information technology (IT) organizations within companies. Every time a company or institution rolls out the latest desktop software, Web application, or e-mail package, it can slow employee productivity to a crawl. Staff members naturally chafe against surprise or unexpected change and can be particularly petulant if not consulted for their own insights and suggestions beforehand. IT technologists have historically been more interested in making new technology work than in educating and informing users of change. More than once, we have been called upon to fix an organization's internal altercations that pit technology users against implementers. Fortunately, if not painfully, some of the more progressive companies have learned their lesson and now deploy technical marketing communication techniques to gauge internal information market needs and incorporate these insights into ongoing strategic marketing communication (see Figure 1.7).

This inward-focused application of technical marketing communication rarely involves specific buyers or purchase transactions per se, but it is true to our definition of market. Throughout this text, we refer to *technical information markets* whose needs and interests are in technology products and services provided by the parent company or institution. As end users or internal consumers, these market audiences pay for products and services with their resulting productivity and participation. We'll discuss internal market audience peculiarities in more detail in Chapter 3.

Technical Marketing Communication

- *Technology:* Any scientific, methodological, specialized work related to the development, sales, service, distribution, application, and integration of technology.

Figure 1.7   Intersection of marketing and communication.

- *Marketing:* The strategically oriented business of understanding markets, aligning products and services with select (target) markets, and coordination of efforts to attract, capture, and fulfill sales to those markets. In our text, we include the practice of marketing technical solutions and programs *within* a company, organization, or institution. These may not involve the actual sale of technology, but rather the funding and application of targeted technology, as might be done by an IT or research department.
- *Communication:* The development (composition), application, and distribution of content across various media to convey information that is clearly understood by a particular audience.

When we distill and combine these three areas, they intersect to create a unique discipline:

- *Technical marketing communication:* Technology-oriented communication created and coordinated in a strategic fashion to accomplish an overall marketing goal (see Figure 1.8). Successful technical marketing communication is clearly understood by a targeted audience (or audiences), valued for its content, and clear in its actionable directions (e.g., buy, learn, prepare, wait, do).

What's Not Included?

Just as content development is a separate subject, many elements of marketing and technical communication are actually tools for technical marketing communicators. For example, technical documentation is a tool of the technical marketing communicator. Public relations announcements are a promotional tool. Focus groups and usability studies are feedback tools. Technical marketing communication strategically coordinates and incorporates the application of these tools, but it is not the discipline of how to create and execute the tools themselves. You can

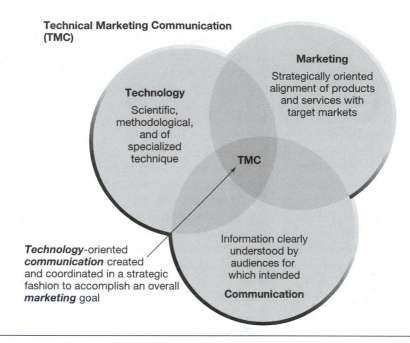

Figure 1.8 Intersection of technology, communication, and marketing.

consult many other books and training forums to enhance your skills in technical writing or presentation development. However, we frequently comment on ways to merge technology, marketing, and communication concepts into a holistic approach.

The Technical Marketing Communication Life Cycle

Whether our focus is on end users or internal consumers, it is easy to see the process of technical marketing communication as a life cycle consisting of seven stages. Let's examine those stages carefully.

Demand

In a free market economy, we are not motivated to develop technology products or services unless a demand exists for them. Demand is one of the parents of invention. And invention, in turn, helps to drive demand. Like it or not, technology development is expensive and someone is always left to ask the basic question, "How much will it cost?" Even philanthropists who provide technology to less fortunate users must somehow fund the technology itself. The eventual product price or other funding allocations bear the cost of technical innovation. Granted, some technologies evolve from other endeavors. Technologist (inventor) Alexander Graham Bell was actually working on technology to assist the hearing-impaired when he happened into telecommunication research. He created his telephone first and found a way to make money later. But that was 1876. Although the demand for voice communication was untapped, Mr. Bell hadn't proactively gone after that market. However, he quickly capitalized on it, and the Bell Labs legacy of ongoing innovation is legendary.

Going back to the farmer's market example, anyone who desired fresh produce demonstrated demand for a product simply by appearing at the market. If no one showed up, you could safely assume demand was down or other compelling market influences were at work (e.g., poor economy, a better or closer market somewhere else, or poor produce available at the previous market gathering).

However, demand for new wireless electronic technologies is breathtakingly powerful across most global markets. Who has not used pagers, cell phones, and personal digital assistants (PDAs)? At first, pagers made it possible to notify someone with whom you needed to speak. Medical doctors were a logical market for emergency contact when conventional phones might not be immediately accessible (e.g., when they were attending theaters, sporting events, or restaurants). Demand for additional information fueled the incorporation of additional pager features but at a higher cost. Soon we had the option to read brief text messages before deciding when to call back and how to prioritize multiple messages stored in pager memory. Since the aura of any page actually representing an emergency has long since worn off, callers have begun to include the numbers 911 in messages just to grab the attention of the person they are paging.

The technology for wireless cell phones took instantaneous accessibility to ridiculous levels as pent-up demand for that access was unleashed. Now any self-respecting technophile family requires at least one cell phone per member. With voice contact virtually assured at all times, we have also demanded wireless access to schedules, e-mail, and stock reports via our handheld PDAs. And the features keep coming. PDAs have digital camera attachments, global positioning devices, voice modules, and dial-up modems.

But how about that chicken and the egg thing? Has it really been demand that has fueled the unending flood of new features for wireless technology? Or have we merely clamored after each new feature as it has been introduced to us? Think about it. Did you really hear any of your friends saying, "I've just got to turn in my analog cell phone for a new digital version—the clarity is really worth it"? Could it be that it's just good marketing compelling us to act?

Many corporations dolefully accuse prominent software companies of introducing new feature sets simply to build grassroots demand to purchase additional software upgrades. This is the corporate version of keeping up with the Joneses. Sure, the features are real, but are they really worth upgrading across an entire enterprise that is paying dearly for licensing? The demand and the debate continue.

In the end, we can probably all agree that demand is pivotal in our overall equation to market technical information, products, and services. Demand arises from one of two directions:

- We respond to and answer market demand with technical solutions.
- We generate and proactively drive additional demand because of technology innovation or enhancement.

We create demand through the three basic components related to technology products and services: features/benefits, price/value, and availability.

Features/Benefits

As we've said, great technology features satisfy demand, especially if they make us more competitive or productive. The most effective technical marketing communication explains both a feature and its benefit to the user: You want this particular feature because it delivers these particular benefits. Sales teams want more features to differentiate their product from a competitor. It's a much easier sale when you offer a feature no one else has developed yet. Internal organization markets want their technology users to accept new changes faster in light of added features and benefits. And when a feature has pent-up demand in the market, like pager text messages or cell phones did, its benefits are easily communicated. Unique, valued technology features with obvious benefits are a technical marketing communicator's best friend.

Price/Value

While it's true that price is a key differentiator, most technology buyers understand there's no such thing as a free lunch. Sometimes the more expensive solution delivers added features and better value than the less expensive alternative. This is the so-called value-add sale. You don't mind paying a little more for a video camera that has a powerful zoom lens and digital effects—if you have use for them. Technical marketing communicators are frequently challenged to clarify value in order to justify higher price. When technology is so similar in nature as to be considered a commodity (like corn or carrots), some companies must compete on price alone. With time, many technologies evolve from unique feature marketing to price-based marketing where profitability is lower. This isn't by choice, of course. As more and more technology suppliers meet the competitive demand for features, we find fewer ways to differentiate value. When that trend continues, price becomes the distinguishing factor.

For example, when ad agencies first made the shift to online graphic design, the systems were complex and expensive. Being an early adopter of technology has its leading-edge advantages, and it has its price. Much of the software was proprietary and not available at the local retail store. Agencies had to purchase service support, customization consulting, and a dedicated hardware staff. Millions of dollars were usually at stake. Still, it was worth it. Agencies valued the speed and flexibility these new systems provided, and the time-consuming drawing by hand was a thing of the past. It was revolutionary, and the ends justified the means. But imagine having just invested in this technology when the first desktop publishing system for personal computers was announced. Now they had to reassess the value of the graphic system in comparison with competing systems.

Personal computers are another example of the price/value component of demand. IBM desktops commanded five-digit prices in the 1980s. Compaq was originally introduced as a portable, but bulky, computer. It was perfect for users who demanded mobility. Since Compaq, Dell, Toshiba, and Gateway have gotten into the desktop game, many other features have become commonplace. Users have gradually come to expect monitor, keyboard, sound card, video board, digital video camera, CD burner, DVD compatibility, and high-speed operating system as minimum features. Competitive pricing for these commodity-like systems is now much lower. The large volume of buyers in this market also makes it possible to manufacture the technology with huge economies of scale. It costs less to produce technology in large quantities. With computer prices this low, profit margins have also shrunk. Now, how do you differentiate the sale? Price or feature? Promotional tools such as price rebates demonstrate that it's more challenging to differentiate in this particular technology market.

On the other hand, the handheld PDA is still in the higher price spectrum of dollar per feature. Monochromatic PDAs with less memory cost much less than thin-profile color graphic versions with triple the memory. Technology manufacturers are still able to justify higher prices for these unique features.

Availability

The flip side to commodity pricing is limited availability. Oil prices go up when supply (availability) slows down, and we all see the difference at the local gas station. High demand in the face of limited availability maintains or increases prices.

In the networking world, companies are scrambling to build business-to-business (B2B) e-commerce. These B2B e-commerce solutions are based on network connectivity hardware (e.g., routers, switches, and hubs) supplied by a very short list of competitors. Much of this hardware technology is similar enough across competing vendors as to be considered a commodity.

At the writing of this book, global availability of the most popular (most in demand) networking hardware is insufficient to meet the ravenous growth this market needs. In other words, supply isn't keeping up with demand. This has caused an interesting twist in the market. Whereas commodity market forces had been driving prices (and profits) down for these products, the limited availability has the opposite effect. Now, distributors who have the most coveted hardware technology on their shelves are in a position to request uplift charges (higher prices) related to "stocking and handling." Have they added value to the technology itself? Probably not. But their propitious position in the demand/availability cycle has worked to their benefit.

At the heart of technical marketing communication is market need or demand. Technical marketing communicators speak to market audiences in voices and styles that recognize and leverage the nuances of demand. They also listen to and interpret how demand should be incorporated into technology design.

Design

Technical marketing communicators facilitate information sharing during technology design efforts. They contribute market research information and support design team communication within an organization. Someone needs to ensure that marketing issues such as features, benefits, pricing, and packaging are consistently incorporated into technology designs. Technical marketing communicators help to bridge this potential gap in information sharing.

Develop

Technology development teams must continue to infuse real-time feedback from the market. Technical marketing communicators participate in usability testing recommendations, focus group reports, and guided discussions with market samples. Technical training and sales documentation also begin to assemble during the technology development cycle. Technical marketing communicators are a voice of consistency between what sales and support staffs design in conjunction with what eventual customers receive.

Differentiate

Promotional efforts such as advertising and public relations are all about differentiating one competitive offering from another. Technical marketing communicators help to identify and articulate the distinguishing technology characteristics as content for various media. Differentiation occurs in collateral material such as brochures, advertising, and Web banners, as well as interactive media such as CD-ROMs and personal presentations (sales).

Theodore Levitt discusses differentiation in his book, *The Marketing Imagination*. He says, "To attract a customer, you are asking him to do something different from what he would have done in the absence of the programs you direct at him. . . . Differentiation represents an imaginative response to the existence of potential customers in such a way as to give them compelling reasons to want to do business with the originating supplier. To differentiate an offering effectively requires knowing what drives and attracts customers. It requires knowing how customers differ from one another and how those differences can be clustered into commercially meaningful segments."[2]

Display

Today we put our technology products and services on display in virtual marketplaces such as the Internet as well as literal marketplaces that include convention exhibits, seminars, and client education centers. Technical marketing communicators have a hand in imagining the display of technology as well as the communication messages that need to be coordinated and shared in the process.

Distribute

Once you've identified a technology market, responded to demand, completed the design of the technology, developed the technology, and created ways to display the product, your products and services have to reach their destination in order to be useful. Our farmer's market distribution point was highly centralized and cost-effective. You simply drove your product to a standard location. Today's technology markets have surprisingly complex distribution strategies. Many local and regional players constantly juggle price discounts against availability.

Technical marketing communicators contribute to distribution in the areas of timing and sequence. They determine what to communicate to each audience and when to do it. Timing is everything. Direct mail letters need to occur in advance of the sales cycle. Telemarketing calls need to be made in the midst of direct mail and other advertising promotions. Actual product availability and distribution follows training for technical support and installation personnel. Technical marketing communicators are involved in all information-sharing aspects of the distribution sequence.

Discuss

Good technical marketing communication is a never-ending cycle. Just as you complete distribution of a new or updated technology, technical marketing communicators begin to collect feedback and facilitate discussion of improvements and follow-up communication. These are combined with ongoing research for market demands to repeat the cycle for the next round of technology development. We describe how these stages in the technical marketing communication life cycle are played out in the remainder of this text.

We could say much more about marketing. It is a science and an industry all its own. However, we are most interested in key marketing concepts that intersect with our shared interest in communication and technology. Keep in mind that technical marketing communicators can effectively contribute at every step of the technical marketing communication life cycle. That doesn't mean every organization invites them to do so. In fact, technologists and marketing leaders alike forget to involve technical marketing communicators from the very start of a program. It can be a costly mistake. Technologists can lose sight of the market in their zeal to deliver, just as pure marketing strategists can miss the total impact of a technology. Technical marketing communicators often see both sides of the equation and share it across multiple audiences.

Summing It Up

We defined technical marketing communication that combines the three areas of technology, marketing, and communication.

- Any form of technology is fair game for technical marketing communicators. In addition, technical marketing communicators as a group have enhanced technical savvy and they can put the tools of technology to work for themselves as well.

- At the heart of good communication is a clear message, our information content. We must discover ways to market technology so the various media do not mask or overshadow the information content we want to convey.
- Marketing is a broad field. Classic marketing techniques involve an entire scope of product design, pricing, promotion, sales, and distribution. For purposes of this text, we have narrowed our marketing focus to elements associated with various fields of technology.
- Technical marketing communication merges elements of technology, marketing, and communication in a very strategic fashion. Technical marketing communicators aren't given static assignments to write a document or a procedure. They are challenged to recognize and incorporate the demands of a technical audience into a variety of communications that accomplish an overall marketing goal.

Applying What You've Learned

1. A new teaching assistant is standing in an empty lecture hall with his professor and 50 sets of blank exam forms. The TA says, "I don't understand; I thought I communicated very clearly. At the end of last Friday afternoon's class, I clearly stated, "Monday's exam location has been changed to lecture hall "B," not "A." The professor smiles knowingly. What went wrong?
2. Describe situations where you have witnessed technical marketing communication in action. Why was it successful or productive? What would you improve?
3. Name three ways you can personally overcome the pitfalls of unidirectional communication in your school or workplace.
4. Find two online examples of marketing promotions: one technical and one nontechnical. Prepare an analysis of each promotion including the following:
   - Why is one technical marketing and the other not?
   - How do they relate to or use technology?
   - Is each piece effective? On what basis do you make that judgment?
   - Does each promotion involve more than written communication?
   - Evaluate the content according to the following criteria: accessible, well organized, and voiced and stylized.
   - Identify the market for each promotion.

SMALL GROUP ACTIVITY

Three university students have attracted the attention of a venture capital (VC) group who may invest in their new start-up business. The students stumbled onto a complicated detergent formula whose main feature is keeping clothes fresh three weeks at a time without having to launder them. The initial student consumer response has been fabulous. However, in order to secure the VC cash, they've been asked to convince a private manufacturing/engineering firm and some university professors that their business concept is viable. Which aspects of their efforts will require technical marketing communication rather than more mainstream consumer marketing? Explain. How will they leverage technology to market their product? What are their target markets? How might they communicate to these markets?

Notes

1. Jakob Nielsen, *Designing Web Usability* (Indianapolis: New Riders Publishing, 2000), 101.
2. Theodore Levitt, *The Marketing Imagination* (New York: Macmillan, Inc., 1986), 128.

CHAPTER 2

Needs Analysis

Overview

"Everyone needs a Web site."

I once had a colleague who worked in the marketing department of a young software development company. The company seemed to have discovered its niche and was doing well in the profit column. One day my colleague's phone rang, and the vice president of development was on the line.

"I've just authorized the development team to start work on the new version of our best-selling software. It should be ready to roll out next summer. I'd like your group to start work on a Web site so we can get the word out to our customers. Everyone I know has a Web site, and it's time for us to get with it! Don't you think?"

"Well, maybe not," my colleague thought, although that was not the response the vice president was expecting. Later that day, my colleague and I discussed the phone call over a cup of coffee. "Of course, it's the twenty-first century; *everyone* needs a Web site," he said.

"Or do they?" I questioned.

While this scenario presents a dilemma for the technical marketing professional, the fact that the vice president of development was talking to marketing before work had begun on the new software version was reason alone to be optimistic. Many unsuccessful technology introductions have waited until the last minute to consider their communication needs. Technical marketers must continually remind themselves (and their clients) to begin as far upstream from actual change and implementation as possible.

Sandi

Needs Analysis Defined

Getting involved early in the development process allows the marketing group to develop a plan. But to plan, you must start by asking the question "What are we trying to accomplish?" When you ask this question, you begin a process called needs analysis, an activity that examines the communication challenge and the intended audience. This analysis will help you to understand the purpose and objectives of your marketing project and then to develop the appropriate marketing

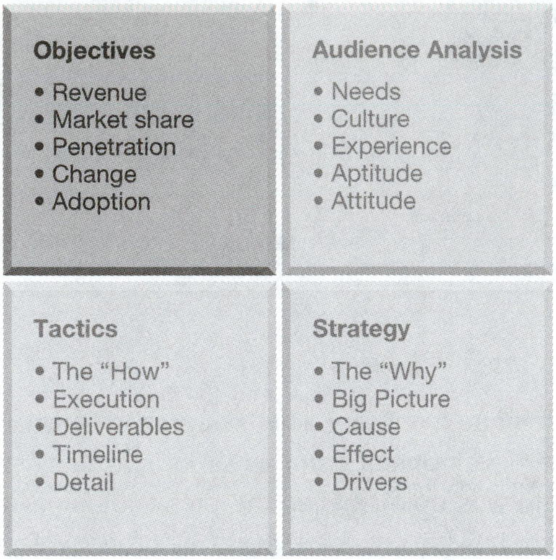

Objectives	Audience Analysis
• Revenue • Market share • Penetration • Change • Adoption	• Needs • Culture • Experience • Aptitude • Attitude
Tactics	**Strategy**
• The "How" • Execution • Deliverables • Timeline • Detail	• The "Why" • Big Picture • Cause • Effect • Drivers

Figure 2.1   Setting objectives, or doing a needs analysis, is the first part of the communication plan.

strategies. We begin by asking the following questions: How will we know if our technical marketing communication has been successful? What will we have accomplished to satisfy the client's expectations? The answers to those questions represent your goal and its related objectives. A goal is the big picture. It's what you're trying to accomplish. For example, the assault on the Normandy beaches at the end of World War II had the strategic objective to enter Germany's European stranglehold, but it was based on a clear, overall goal to defeat Hitler.

Before you can articulate the goal, you must determine why a need has developed. Usually the need arises because of change or impending change. Asking what has changed is a good way to focus your attention on the need. Perhaps, as in the introductory scenario, a new version of software is going to roll out. This change precipitates the need for information exchange. Discovering what you ultimately hope to accomplish is tantamount to the success of your marketing effort.

Getting the vice president of development to back up and determine what he or she really wants to accomplish before jumping to the Web site conclusion may be a challenge. However, taking the time at the beginning of a process to articulate a purpose statement and clear and measurable objectives will pay great dividends as you reach the conclusion of a successful marketing campaign.

To begin a needs analysis, you need to understand the overall technology project goals and objectives. Only then can you determine the role of the marketing communication team. For example, you must understand the purpose of the new software in order to see the big picture. If you do not clearly understand the goals and objectives of the project, you cannot be successful in your marketing effort. Historically, many organizations have experienced tension between the marketing people and other parts of the organization—particularly concerning communication deadlines.

One technical documentation team grew particularly tired of receiving late subject matter content and being blamed for holding up the project completion and technology rollout. They retaliated by refusing to include completion deadlines in their published schedules. Their timelines simply offered drafts and finished products "three days after receipt of content," or "one day after sign-off." It was reasonable from their perspective, but it created a we-them mentality with the technology team who needed to report hard dates for their deliverables. After airing their frustrations, they compromised by publishing dates with asterisks indicating their target deadline was based on receipt of content by a certain date.

TMCs must work hard to foster cross-functional cooperation. When you demonstrate an interest in the overall project goals, others will see that you understand the significance of the project, and you will win respect in your organization. In addition, when you better understand the overall goals and objectives, you can begin to articulate the more specific purpose and objectives of the marketing initiative.

The Needs Analysis Process

1. Clarify goals and objectives to guide the project
2. Understand the audience who needs this information
3. Determine the information to be communicated
4. Determine how to acquire the necessary information

Clarify Goals and Objectives to Guide the Project

The first step in the process is to understand the goal—the one big picture—and the objectives for this marketing endeavor. You should begin by asking what is the desired outcome of this technology project?

It is very possible that as you work through this process of needs analysis, you may uncover otherwise unstated team objectives to articulate for other audiences. Often during the initial process of interviewing team members to assimilate information, you will discover these previously unstated team objectives and subobjectives. The following questions help you and the technology team determine if you have missed a significant piece of the puzzle. Consider them in light of the new software version being introduced to a major client.

Q. What are we trying to accomplish?

A. Successfully deploy a new software version on time, on budget, and to the satisfactory adoption of users.

Q. Why is this work important to the organization?

A. Much of our daily work and production is directly related to this software availability and functionality.

Q. What known barriers are there to resolve?

A. Users are adverse to change and past application rollouts have caused serious downtime.

Q. What other projects must succeed first or in parallel?

A. Users' hardware must be upgraded to the new software.

A marketing department tasked with enhancing the image of the company should also include the following questions:

Q. What image do we want?

A. A technology team that understands user needs, communicates needs, plans, and executes well.

Q. What is our image now?

A. Past technology changes have been rocky, poorly communicated and executed.

Q. How can we change to achieve a new image?

A. Improved planning, user consultation and communication, and execution as promised.

The topic of image is also referred to as brand. Much has been written on the topic of branding, and we will discuss it in greater detail in Chapter 5.

Once you understand your overall goals, you can determine your supporting objectives. Table 2.1 shows you how to pair your goals with your objectives.

TABLE 2.1	Pairing Your Goals with Your Objectives
Goals	**Objectives for Users**
Enhance the image of IT department	Respect and trust information technology (IT) department
	Embrace—do not resist—new initiatives
	Seek IT for future team consultative participation
	Speak favorably of IT to peers and others
	Avoid false or negative impressions
Market new product or service	Participate in training
	Adopt technology or process by chosen target date
	Improve work related productivity and reliability
	Avoid confusion, chaos, and disruption
Facilitate change	Fast, complete, and enthusiastic adoption
	Improved productivity
	Apply related implications of change to other processes
	Embrace change positively
	Avoid confusion, chaos, and disruption

Understand the Audience Who Needs This Information

Understanding the audience who needs this information is critical to your success. Simply *identifying* the audience is not sufficient. For example, when designing a Web site to market a technical communication career, you should avoid thinking of your audience as primarily high school students. You need to *analyze* high school students and people of similar experience to determine everything you can possibly know about them to communicate in a way that meets their needs. The subject of audience analysis is so important to the process that we have devoted the entire next chapter to this subject.

Determine the Information to Be Communicated

In this stage of the process, you must carefully examine your need for information. In our earlier example of the new software version, we would try to uncover all information related to the new rollout. Consider some of the following communication needs:

- Current users need to know that a new release is coming out and what changes, if any, would affect them.
- Prospective customers need to know about the new version and how it will meet or exceed their needs.
- The sales force must understand information about the new release from both perspectives.

Chapter 11 provides an in-depth working example of how information aligns with tactics and other media.

It is always helpful to inform current users what to expect in a new technology version well in advance of its rollout. This information should focus on new features and benefits as well as assure users of continued service and a high-quality product or service. While giving this information, you can also direct your attention to acquiring new customers. For these new customers, your information cannot simply focus on what's new but will need to include the major features and benefits of the technology product or service. And, of course, the sales force will need information on the new release for their own knowledge as well as information to pass on to potential customers.

Some of the more aggressive salespeople we've worked with simply begin calling technologists to get tidbits and insights when such information is not forthcoming from the technical marketing communication channel. That leads to anarchy if some members of the sales team get information and others do not. Technical marketing communicators have to stay ahead of the information curve and help sales teams do the same.

When marketing high-tech products and services with long development lead times, sometimes you will likely have to supply prerelease information to build the attention of potential customers. This information does not need to be as detailed as information for the later purposes of closing the sale.

One old-hand sales professional had a standard line in his bag of tricks to assure customers that the next version of technology would resolve their current issues. "We're working on something that's going to improve that," he'd say, regardless of the specific item. Invariably, that bit of comfort carried the day until he had more concrete information to share.

Prerelease information will help your audience to discover your product or service and potentially stave off competitors' advances. Later your information will become more detailed as you educate your potential customer about your product and company. After getting the customer's attention and supplying detailed information, the information must now become persuasive as you motivate the customer to complete the actual purchase. At this point you might also need to include information about the competition so the customer can make comparisons. Your customers will need ongoing support information after the sale has been completed to affirm their purchase decision. You will also need to keep them apprised of new service programs, products, and upgrades.

Each marketing situation will call for different information to be communicated. Taking time to assess the information you need to communicate helps to ensure a successful marketing project.

Determine How to Get the Necessary Information

To get the necessary information to meet the communication needs, you begin by asking the right people. It is not always an easy job to identify the people who retain or have access to the information you need to know. It is an even more difficult job to get them to share that information. This task requires sleuthing, cunning (not in an evil way), diplomacy, and skill. People who have your information are very busy, and they are not always thinking beyond the scope of their responsibility for this project—which is to say, they may not have given a lot of thought and concern to the marketing efforts on behalf of the product or service. Methods for uncovering or assimilating information include interviewing, focus group, guided discussions, conference calls, Web meetings, and audience questionnaires.

Interviewing

No one has spare time during a technology rollout. Call and make an appointment for an interview. If possible, give them some questions ahead of time so they can be prepared, or at least have gathered the necessary information for you. Be prompt for the interview. Don't waste a person's time by being late or participating in unnecessary chatter. It is acceptable to spend a moment warming up to begin the interview, but stay on track and be professional at all times.

One technical marketing communicator quickly scans an office or cube to identify something non-work related that the occupant has in a place of prominence. It may be a vacation brochure, cartoon, or family photo. She makes a brief observation such as, "Do you enjoy skiing?" People are usually more at ease talking about something they choose to do in their leisure time, and this has served as a productive ice breaker for her. The brief conversation doesn't take much time, and it truly goes to the heart of understanding the interviewee and his or her perspective.

Do your homework before going to the interview. Research if possible. Visit the Web. Ask for technical specifications, white papers, product descriptions, or anything else that would help you become acquainted with the technology product or service.

The time you spend with people who supply the necessary technical information can help in two ways. First, it helps you to obtain the necessary information. Second, your interviewee may discover that the conversation has helped to clarify the purpose of their product or service initiative.

It is also important to ask the right questions. JoAnn Hackos introduces a set of questions that are useful in a software documentation process. Some of these questions would be helpful to most technical marketing communication teams:

- Why is the company thinking of introducing this product?
- What niche will the product occupy relative to the competition?
- Who are the competitors? What are their strengths and weaknesses? What publications do they provide?
- What are our strengths and weaknesses?
- Who are our customers, and what are they asking for?
- Do we have any direct information from our customers? Do we know what they want or how they use or regard our product?
- What have we learned from customer support on previous products?
- Have we held focus groups or used other information-gathering techniques?
- How will the product be marketed?
- Who is most likely to buy the product?
- Are there any problems the new product must overcome?[1]

Ron Zemke and Thomas Kramlinger write the following about face-to-face interviews: "The personal interview is the most common information-gathering technique. Face-to-face interviewing is the primary information source for dozens of occupations. Reporters do it, recruiters do it, trainers do it, managers and market researchers do it. But few do it well. . . . Our tactic is to use the face-to-face interview as a primary information-gathering tool only where we must and then to control as many troublesome factors as we can. When we work in this mode, we refer to what we are doing as a structured interview. When we use the interview process as only part of the information source—for instance, when we *observe* sales behavior and *talk with* a field sales rep—we refer to what we are doing as either a conversational or informal interview."[2]

Many informal interviews take place in technical marketing, and they are usually spontaneous. When you have had an unplanned, but meaningful, conversation about anything that would help you to understand your audience better, record those thoughts as soon as possible. Date them and record the time, place, and participants. That information will be helpful to you as you get to know your audience. Structured interviews take much more time—both before and after the interview.

Zemke and Kramlinger identify four features that characterize the structured interview. The following is a summary of their ideas:

- The interview is the only contact we will probably have with the informant.
- The interviewee is in a unique position and is privy to information we can obtain only from him or her.
- The interview is positioned as a formal, fact-finding affair; it is scheduled.
- The results are formally analyzed in some fashion.[3]

It is a good idea to have a certain set of questions you intend to ask each person you interview, but you should also try to keep the interview agenda open to change. In this way, you can be surprised by the discovery of certain attitudes, opinions, issues, and facts not anticipated beforehand.

The structured interview consists of five steps:

1. *Preparing for the interview:* This preparation time consists of learning the jargon associated with this product or service. Don't structure your interview around yes or no questions. Ask open-ended, problem-solving questions. Try your questions out with a neutral and knowledgeable source before the interview. Cluster the questions topically. Always conclude with an open-ended question such as "What haven't I asked about that I should have?"

2. *Starting the interview:* Because interviewees can be nervous or tense in one-on-one interviewing, don't touch content until you've built an element of trust with the interviewee. Be prepared, but admit to knowing a lot less than the interviewee. The interviewee is the only subject matter expert in your immediate field of focus.

3. *Conducting the interview:* Keep your mind focused. Don't let your thoughts wander while the interviewee is talking. Sometimes we are so intent on our next question, we fail to really hear the answer to the one we have just asked. Sequence your questions from general to specific. Taking notes seems to be the most flexible and usable approach to capturing the data. However, you must be careful not to let note taking get in the way of your interview. Some firms will not allow the use of recording devices for security reasons. Recording the interview may inhibit the interviewee's candor, so record with sensitivity and only if you have gained their permission.

4. *Concluding the interview:* Don't bring the interview to a sudden halt. Ease it to a stop. Summarize what you learned, but emphasize that you will undertake follow-up time to pull everything together. Request the right to call for clarification as necessary.

5. *Compiling and analyzing results:* Look back over your notes and compile pertinent information you have learned. Call for clarification of key points, if necessary.[4]

It is your responsibility to analyze the results. You can analyze by looking at the information collected and by performing the following tasks: comparing, interpreting, inferring, evaluating, judging, and concluding. These activities are conceptual skills. You are processing particulars and producing generalizations.

Focus Groups

Market strategists have long used focus groups to get a sense of direction for a marketing project. During a well-planned focus group, you can elicit valuable content information as well as learn a great deal about your potential customers. When you are dealing with new products, focus groups can also help you to understand the current brand image of a company.

The success of the focus group depends on careful planning. You must carefully plan how you will select your participants by establishing criteria that each participant must meet. You can use one of two approaches: a carefully chosen and well-matched group—considering gender, age, culture, or occupation. In this approach, your aim is to put together a group with similar tastes or interests related to the technology product or service. You may assemble CIOs for an IT focus group or managers for a CAD system focus group. Or you can choose people randomly, resulting in people of diverse backgrounds and interests from your particular market. This is more appropriate for consumer technology subjects such as personal computing. You do risk getting a group of people who are not interested in your product or service. Because the quality of the output from focus groups depends on having the right people in the room, you should take the extra time and effort to choose the right people or hire a service to do so. Participants do not have to be attractive, articulate, and well educated to be effective in a focus group. Regardless of their qualities, they usually have an opinion and can voice it in a way that is beneficial.

In addition, you must carefully plan and create a moderator's guide. You will be deciding about the content you wish to cover. It is helpful to involve the technology team in developing the topics for discussion. Involving them demonstrates that you are clearly interested in meeting their needs—not just your own. It is essential that you create a handbook to lead the moderator through the focus group you have designed.

Success also depends on the moderator; therefore, choose or hire one carefully. The best focus group moderators bring energy, insight, objectivity, and expertise to a project. Effective moderators have the following characteristics; they are

- Able to familiarize themselves quickly with the technology product or service
- Flexible; able to respond spontaneously to new ideas
- Skilled communicators
- Diplomatic; careful not to offend participants
- Objective
- Patient
- Empathetic
- Insightful

One of the most important roles of the focus group team is to provide an interpretation of what happened during the group meeting and to relate those events to the technology project's objectives. The team must be able to communicate the results of the focus group clearly and concisely.

Focus groups enable observers from the technology team to stay behind two-way mirrors. This could include the technical marketing communicator. This real-time observation provides the benefit of seeing and hearing nuances that are not adequately captured by a typed transcript. Videotape delivers the same benefit.

Guided Discussion Groups

A guided discussion group is a less rigorous version of a focus group. For the most part, a guided discussion is a face-to-face meeting with more people. You might even use the same question list. Identify yourself as the discussion facilitator and limit yourself to asking questions and recording responses (including a scribe to take notes is even better). As facilitator, be prepared to let the group run freely. Again, wandering from the exact question posed is fine, as long as you gain insights into the audience profile that will support your communication objective. Do your best to gather input from all attendees. It is perfectly acceptable to address less vociferous attendees and ask them for their insights as well.

Conference Call

Ideally, you prefer to personally interview your intended audiences whenever possible. Time restrictions and locations may pose barriers that prevent in-person interviews. For example, a busy executive may not be willing to sit still for an interview. Harried project leaders may not see the value in communication when so many technical details remain. One of your key contacts is probably in another city, time zone, or country. It's up to technical marketing communicators to suggest and organize acceptable ways for team members to reach their unique audiences.

Conference calls to profile your audience are simply guided discussions with telephony. This technology is an effective way to draw in people who are otherwise too busy to attend a meeting. Assume a similar facilitator's role in conference calls, clearly stating your questions and being as inclusive as possible with all attendees.

Web Meetings

Thanks to inexpensive Web technology, online meetings are quite easy to host. The most effective services allow you to combine audio and online visuals to pose questions and collect information. Questions in these formats can even provide real-time statistical feedback. For example, online attendees might answer a question by clicking one of three choices in their browser screen. Your facilitator's screen can usually calculate simple percentages of respondents' answers. Again, Web meetings are often more attractive and realistic to schedule with technology audiences than face-to-face sessions.

Audience Questionnaires

When it is not feasible to personally interact with your audience, forward a survey or questionnaire. Typically, our experience has been that return rates on questionnaires of this type are notoriously low (3 to 5 percent at best), but you can help to improve upon that.

One of the more interesting survey tools to have emerged is the Web pop-up. A dialog box is designed to automatically open in the browser of a user visiting your targeted Web page. The dialog box questions can be as brief or as long as you believe people will tolerate during their online session. This form of feedback has the advantage of reaching the exact person who has accessed your targeted content. Why are they there? What led them to your content? What would cause them to come back? You have the opportunity to capture their impressions at the same time they are experiencing them. Custom designs for these online questionnaires can vary how frequently someone is solicited (e.g., every tenth visitor) and how registration information is collected. Several research firms offer packaged tracking metric tools to provide this information.

Keep the questionnaire short. Offer a reward on completion. When working with an internal audience, many companies offer cafeteria coupons or even small cash awards for important information. Be sure to call or leave messages for anyone you ask to complete a questionnaire. If possible, solicit and coach internal people who can influence others to participate.

Although face-to-face interviews should strive to include open-ended questions, questionnaires should provide an equal balance of closed and open-ended questions. Questionnaire audiences are much more likely to check boxes than they are to complete narratives. In fact, studies show people with very positive or very negative experiences are much more likely to provide feedback than respondents in the larger midrange of the bell curve. Above all, make sure your questions support a consistent theme related to ultimately achieving your communication objectives.

Stay Focused on the Goal

When you have gathered the information, you must now sift through it to save the best and most useful and discard the rest. Like any research, you will have bits and pieces of information that are accurate but not necessarily pertinent to this project. It's like having the lone note card filled with an especially perceptive quote, but it doesn't fit in the outline anywhere. The note card must be discarded to prevent including information that causes the paper to go off on a tangent. The same is true of the focus group information now gathered. Discernment is necessary to determine what is useful and what is not. In the perspective of this chapter, we are trying to identify technology project objectives.

For example, an organization was merging two regions and administration asked a technical marketing communicator to make a marketing presentation to the joint sales teams. Her job was to explain the newly combined market focus based on strategic information she gleaned from both teams. After she did her homework and interviewed most of the key players identified for the task, one of the regional vice presidents instructed her to emphasize some services that were really quite specific to his team alone but not necessarily relevant to the newly combined strategy. Sensing something was wrong, she circled back and recontacted some of the other team members. She learned that the regional vice president had a strong preference to promote these services, but his peers did not. They helped her work through the awkward situation, and she avoided making a presentation based on biased interview information.

While focus groups are productive, they are also expensive to prepare and execute. Guided discussions also rely on a facilitator but have less rigor and formality. They can be carried out on a conference call or as a "break-out" session at a larger meeting. The resulting information collected may have less structure but is no less valuable.

If planned well, you can use focus groups to measure the effectiveness of your marketing efforts (see Chapter 12). Our purpose in this chapter is to focus on articulating the goals and objectives. For evaluative purposes, a focus group can be used effectively to determine if, in fact, you met your goals.

After you have gathered your information and identified a clear, measurable goal, you must determine your strategy. But throughout a technical marketing communication project, it is essential that you not lose sight of the goal. If your strategies and tactics do not contribute to the accomplishment of your goals, your endeavors will be fruitless. For example, in 1963, President John F. Kennedy challenged NASA with an outrageous goal: Land a person on the moon by the end of the decade. There were countless strategic missions and tactics along the way, but the end goal was clear. Any interim objectives that did not advance NASA in the direction of the moon landing were superfluous. That is the kind of clarity technical marketing communicators must distill from the needs analysis. If you've interviewed and assessed your communication customers without discerning when and where you're supposed to land the rocket—there's still more work to be done.

Summing It Up

The process of needs analysis takes time, and many people make the mistake of failing to see its importance. When the vice president of development says she needs a Web site, you should not go forward with the project without first doing a needs analysis. It may be that a Web site is exactly what she needs. But it is equally possible she needs something entirely different. It is not an easy task to complete the needs analysis. But without it, you simply have someone saying "We need a Web site," or "We need a newsletter," or "We need a brochure." The requirement being demanded may have no bearing on the true technology needs. If the needs analysis is flawed, then the project plan is flawed; if the plan is flawed, then its implementation is defective. It is worth the effort to work your way through the following steps:

1. Clarify goals and objectives to guide the project
2. Understand the audience who needs this information
3. Determine the information that needs to be communicated
4. Determine how to acquire the necessary information

Applying What You've Learned

1. A member of the sales staff calls the marketing department and tells you he has just returned from a big sales convention. He explains that everyone there had multipage, slick brochures to market their products. He wants one and asks how soon you can get it to him. What will you say to him? How will you proceed?

2. You are aware that tension exists between the IT department that is installing a new e-mail system and the marketing department. IT has the information marketing needs, but in the past it has never given marketing the time or respect needed to get the information. How can you work to solve this problem? How would you proceed?

3. You have been asked to help your university market the technical communication major to high school students. State the goal and write the objectives for this endeavor. Save this assignment because you will be adding to this project as you progress through the text.

SMALL GROUP ACTIVITY

You work in the marketing department for a major telecommunication company. The manager of the Intranet comes to you and says, "I've made a decision to change our e-mail system. I know people are going to complain, but our new system is a much better system. Once they get used to the idea, I'm sure they'll like it. I was just thinking—you're in the business of motivation—could you help me motivate them to accept this new system?" How would you respond? How would you proceed? Assuming you have convinced the manager of the Intranet to give you enough time to market this change, begin the needs analysis by generating the objectives to guide the project. (Use the e-mail system you are currently using in your own place of business as the new system to be installed.) Without doing a complete audience analysis, make a list of the different people who must be convinced to accept this new e-mail system. Determine how you will get the necessary information you need for this marketing campaign.

Notes

1. JoAnn Hackos, *Managing Your Documentation Projects* (New York: J. Wiley, 1994), 113.
2. Ron Zemke and Thomas Kramlinger, *Figuring Things Out* (New York: Addison-Wesley Publishing Company, 1982), 99.
3. Ibid, 101–104.
4. Ibid, 105–111.

CHAPTER 3

Audience Analysis

Overview

"Give me your wallet."

In which situation are you more likely to comply with a stranger's request for your wallet?

a. Standing in a well-lighted, crowded grocery store checkout lane
b. Sitting in a first-class airline seat
c. Walking alone on a dark, deserted street at 3:00 A.M.

Most people desperate enough to take a wallet from a stranger would have innately judged the most compliant audience category for this request as *walking alone on a dark, deserted street at 3:00 A.M.* At one time or another, we have all adapted our communication approach to the audience at hand.

When my daughter was a toddler, she had already mastered some of these skills. She would ask for candy treats from her grandparents because she knew her requests would earn an emphatic "no" from her parents. I have seen sheepish fathers indulging the smiling request of a daughter who has just been turned down by her mother. When I was a university student, I spoke more deferentially to my professors during conversations about grades than I did during debates about sports teams. I'm sure you can imagine many other instances.

Tom

Who's Your Audience?

According to dictionary descriptions of *audience*, the *readers* of printed material are not the most important subject definition. *Spectators* and *listeners* at performances are more common examples of audience, with readers listed as secondary meanings.[1] In our multimedia technical marketing communication world, we must always consider our audiences from multiple communication angles and not just the printed or online word.

In this chapter, we consider the incredible insight and communication power we gain by understanding our audience.

Figure 3.1   Audience analysis is the second stage in the communication cycle.

Asking who your audience is should be one of your first tasks for the rest of your days in technical marketing communication. In fact, it is much more effective to ask, "Who is *our* audience?" In this consultative fashion, you immediately become part of the team and part of the pending solution. Of course, in individual situations, the question more appropriately will become "Who is *my* audience?" Even more prevalent, complex communication begs the question "Who are our *audiences*."

When you ask these questions, you take the first step to adapt and accommodate communication content. Conversely, when you seek the identity of your audiences, you combat any notion that you can prepare communication in a content-centric fashion. As a technical marketing communicator you are often the one to uncover and identify your key audiences. Ask these questions of yourself and anyone else involved in a communication initiative:

- Who is helping to establish the objectives of this communication initiative?
- Who must make decisions based on this communication?
- Who will use this content to teach, learn, or act?
- Who will benefit from the outcome of this communication?
- Who must reapply this information to other related activities?

These questions will usually uncover other "hidden" audiences as well. Whether to include or exclude audiences in your communication is much easier to decide once you have identified them all. It is much worse to forget an audience than to inform them of their exclusion.

When J. C. Mathes and Dwight Stevenson write about audiences, they suggest you "forget the faceless blocks on the organization chart and the great pyramid of the company's theoretical organization. Think instead of the communication situation and of the roles you and your readers have in it."[2]

How Many Different Ways Can You Look at Your Audience, Really?

It isn't enough to answer the question, "Who is your audience?" That is merely audience identification. Now, you must analyze the audience you have identified. You do that by examining the audience to determine its distinguishing characteristics. No two audiences are alike.

In the past two decades, we have become increasingly aware of audience diversity. People sharing common interests, traits, heritage, or belief systems react to and assimilate information in increasingly segmented ways. By some accounts, people of color, women, and immigrants account for 85 percent of the net growth of the U.S. labor force.[3]

Regardless of this impressive growth in diversity, it has always been, and will continue to be, incumbent on the technical communicator to recognize and accommodate audience characteristics, preferences, and motivators. Because of the daunting scope of diversity, some might argue that this concern could lead to communication paralysis. Still, we have plenty of opportunity to accommodate the needs and very real benefits of audience diversity without reaching a limit of diminishing returns.

For example, a large information technology organization had expanded significant portions of their operations to several Asia-Pacific countries. Within weeks of their initial contact, the U.S.-based teams quickly adopted a self-imposed policy to eliminate contractions, jargon, and slang from their communications. Sometime later they cheerfully acknowledged that the changes had not only helped their transcontinental colleagues, but communications seemed clearer to U.S. associates as well!

Although you cannot address every possible combination of communication diversity, you should consider the following ways to look at your intended audience. The characteristics listed are not exhaustive. Rather, you should consider them as starting points to help you become more aware of your audience and, therefore, more aware of the communication options posed by your own audience analysis.

Hierarchical

Where is your audience on the organizational chart? In technology businesses, one of the easiest ways to characterize an audience has traditionally been hierarchical. The higher they are on the chart, the busier they are and the less likely they are to read long, detailed accounts of anything. Today, senior executives tend to request the bulleted lists or drastically reduced versions of complex content. They are often reading to make decisions or to approve budgets. For example, e-commerce technology details may be much less important than the increase in revenues that should result.

One business division became accustomed to presenting executive summaries on one slide with four equally sized boxes of information. The cultural premise was that you didn't have to flip through a lot of pages to get to the detail. A technical marketing communication colleague, new to the organization, drafted a presentation that summarized his points on several slides. True to his training, there were only five to seven bullets per page and plenty of white space. But before the slides were able to make it past the draft stage, his fellow associates convinced him that the executives reading the summary would have no patience for multiple charts when one would do. Dutifully, though doubtfully, he converted the content to a single slide with four segments. To his surprise, the feedback from the executives was, "Great chart!"

The reports or presentations to department managers in the hierarchical technology chain we previously described may include increasingly technical information about e-commerce infrastructure, software, and equipment decisions. The technical marketing communicator must determine what information to reserve or include at each level of interest.

Use of Technology

In a careful audience analysis, we determine how our readers relate to and use technology. Technology managers and leaders are often most interested in schedules, personnel, and costs. Hands-on technology developers and implementers instinctively need to access technology details right down to the architecture, software code, and hard drive location. Not surprisingly, the beneficiaries and users of technology most often want to know how it will help them do their jobs. This concept is better known in the technical marketing communicators' vernacular as WIIFM, or What's in it for me? We'll learn ways to accommodate these perspectives in later chapters.

Indigenous Languages or Dialects

Even when English is the chosen corporate language, it may be a second language to the indigenous people at any given location. When targeting multilingual audiences, it's absolutely mandatory to write and diagram in straightforward language, without slang or euphemisms. On the other hand, local variations in language (dialects) can include references and euphemisms that will actually make your local communication more effective and easier to understand. Heavy use of corporate or industry-based acronyms is the most commonly encountered form of dialect. As with other dialectical nuances, you cannot assume all audiences will understand an acronym's meaning without additional explanation. When in doubt, spell the acronym out.

Skill Level

Education, training, and skill levels are particularly important to understand for technical marketing communication. If language is too simplistic or laden with elementary definitions, highly technical people can become bored, and even insulted. Imagine how you would feel reading a third-grade science book while trying to study for an organic chemistry test. But your communication content can also become stilted and inaccessible if it resembles a doctoral thesis. Technical marketing communicators are most often challenged to distill and interpret highly technical information for a less technical audience. It is vital to honor the essence of the content and keep the attention of your audience.

Experience

A bright, young product manager, who had clear command of his high-end computer technology, had produced Web sites, given seminars, and was a self-proclaimed e-mail communication junkie. However, when he was asked to develop a direct mail letter to customers, he sheepishly admitted that he had never had to write a *business letter* and was unfamiliar with the basic layout and formatting involved.

Similar to past education and training, a person's work or life experience influences his or her audience persona. It is not surprising to have a technology audience described as a team of *experts*. But compared to what? With today's dot-com frenzy of new companies and technology, experts may have simply released a new application language a few weeks in advance of the next wave. *Experienced* teams may have lived through several iterations of such technology releases. Our own culture sometimes decries speaking of age in relation to experience. However, technical marketing communicators will want to know as much about the experience level of their audience as possible, whether they are driven by life experience (often age related) or other signals of specialized knowledge. If it helps you to communicate more effectively, it's relevant.

Culture

It is amazing how many different cultures spring up within countries, companies, industries, and departments. One industry insider reminds us, "Ethnic marketing means more than placing an Asian or African-American in your brochure photos"[4] (see Fig. 3.2). Even campus cultures may be different among athletes, artists, or graduate students. In student cultures, clothing, food, music, and study habits differentiate membership. Some students move easily among various subcultures. In many companies, corporate culture takes on attributes of the most highly visible leaders. In such cases, people may say they have a corporate culture of learning or teaming, or even acquiring other companies. Patterns and traits exhibited by cultural differences are additional clues to the technical communicator. It's important to look for and incorporate cultural elements not merely because they are there, but also because of their intrinsic value to enhanced communication.

Inclusion

Be sure to account for the special needs of your audience and their ability to access information. Not everyone can hear, see, and touch. Although every brochure you print cannot be produced in Braille, making provision for that is ideal. Audio conversions are relatively inexpensive, as long as the original content didn't rely heav-

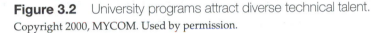

Figure 3.2 University programs attract diverse technical talent.
Copyright 2000, MYCOM. Used by permission.

ily on visuals. But what if the technology you are marketing is targeted at producers or consumers of special needs products? Digital hearing aid technology might
benefit from marketing efforts that include statistical audio comparisons so that
people *without* hearing loss will understand the significance of improvement for
people *with* actual loss. Similarly, technology for someone *with* hearing loss would
benefit much more from actual product demonstrations than from graphs or
statistics.

One large multistate nonprofit organization was trying to raise awareness for
inclusion by expanding their communications into the technical arena of the Internet. Their biggest challenge was not how to get people with special needs to use
technology, but how to have people with special needs *included on the committees* to
plan and strategize for inclusion within the community. Technical marketing communicators can help to bridge these gaps.

What Comes After Identification and Analysis?

Mathes and Stevenson believe, "Once you have identified and characterized your
audiences, you have to classify them in terms of their importance in regard to your
purpose. Not only are your audiences diverse, they are of unequal importance.
Particularly, be aware of these differences so you . . . address, primarily, the correct
subgroup of readers among your total group of readers." Mathes and Stevenson
have classified audiences for technical reports into three types:

- Primary audiences
- Secondary audiences
- Immediate or nominal audiences

As technical marketing communicators, we should give some thought to this classification system. According to Mathes and Stevenson, "Primary audiences are those persons and groups who will act out and/or make the decisions necessary for you to accomplish your purpose. . . . Secondary audiences are those persons who have to implement the recommended decisions or who will be affected by the recommended actions. . . . Immediate audiences are those persons who transmit and route your report through an organization. They are typically the first-level and second-level managers who have a responsibility to review and sign or initial reports before they are released for distribution. These readers may have no other use for the reports themselves; they merely act as quality controls and as administrative gateways for information on the move."[5]

How does this concept apply to technical marketing communicators? We must think of our audience in terms of those who make decisions (primary audiences), those who implement the decisions (secondary audiences), and those who act as quality controls and administrative gateways (immediate audiences). The primary audience decides to purchase the latest version of an important technology tool for his or her company. The secondary audience will be responsible to install the new version, and the immediate audience may follow-up to see if it will accomplish the purpose intended.

What Happens When You Do Not Understand Your Audience?

Without dwelling on negatives, you must recognize that overlooking or ignoring the characteristics of your audience causes communication to be deficient. Especially in the technical marketing arena, we often help to influence or convince in relation to purchase or other budgetary decisions. If we alienate one or more members of our target audiences by our communication diversity choices, we may not earn the right to have them consider our content. If I don't see or hear myself in a communication addressed to me, many times I simply will not engage in the content. With all the avenues available to receive information, yours may simply fall by the wayside.

A very entrepreneurial firm was off and running with its new technology. Unfortunately, the technical marketing communicators had not gotten out in front with their Web site or collateral material. They knew their target audience would expect some technically packaged information, especially a Web site, but they had funneled all their energy into the technology itself. One of their first salespeople relayed the prickly conversation he'd had with a potential client. The prospect had been amenable to learning more about the technology and asked that the salesperson send him some literature. "Well," the salesperson explained, "the collateral material isn't available yet." The prospect replied that it was not a problem and asked if the salesperson could send the URL so he could look at the Web site. Unfortunately, the salesperson had to admit they were not quite ready with the Web site. "Then let's do this," the now unlikely prospect suggested, "when you *do* have something, why don't you call me back?"

How Can You Learn About Your Audience?

Learning about your audience is an ongoing process. Many technical marketing communicators have been stung when they thought they already knew the audience, only to miss a significant shift in culture or motivation. If at all possible, plan a face-to-face meeting with the targeted recipients of your marketing communication. That is always the best way to discover what you need to know about your intended audience.

But face-to-face meetings with the intended audience of a technical marketing piece are no less daunting than face-to-face meetings with users of technical documentation. JoAnn Hackos, director of the Center for Information-Development Management, wrote in her monthly newsletter column for the center, "Getting close to the customer takes effort and time and travel. I've had many writers quit their jobs over the years when we asked them to travel because no one was going to infringe on their personal time."[6] The same is true in technical marketing communication. We need to get out of our comfort zone and meet our audiences where they are. We are quick to say we represent our audience. But when asked, "How do you know your audience?" we must be able to do more than return a blank stare. We must be able to do more than simply identify the audience. When personal contact is impossible by phone, e-mail, or travel, we must research related information. Internet searches, public or corporate library research, and other media can help to build an audience profile.

Use an Audience Profile

How you organize or categorize your audience profile is less important than the capture itself. Many times a simple table will suffice, with additional tiers recommended for subaudiences. Table 3.1 provides a sample audience analysis form. The grid in Figure 3.3 is also an effective way to capture the information about your audience.

With experience, most communicators will be able to ask questions directly from their chosen audience profile. Other questions are specific to the technology initiative at hand. Record these questions separately from the audience profile. How to choose and pose questions is a consulting field all its own. Your best question resource is your own curiosity. Ask yourself these questions:

- How must I communicate with this audience in order to accomplish my overall communication objectives?
- What do they know that will help me develop communication for other audiences?
- What can I learn from them that I won't learn from the project sponsor?

Visualizing Your Audience

After you have interviewed your audience, held a focus group, or received survey forms, what do you do with all this data you have gathered? Of course, the obvi-

TABLE 3.1	Simple Audience Analysis Form
Clearly identify this audience	Use an audience descriptor that will be meaningful to you at a later date. "VP North American Sales" is better than "Sales Executive." Also list phone numbers, e-mail addresses, and other available information.
Is there other audience interaction?	What other audiences interact or blend with this audience? Are your technology users reporting to this audience? Is this audience a decision maker for an audience that executes against their decisions?
What is the audience size?	How many people comprise this audience? Does it fluctuate? Is it seasonal? What is the industry or company revenue?
Locations?	Are members of this audience co-located?
Communications access?	How do members of this audience prefer to communicate? Do they read their e-mail? Will they actively engage the Intranet? Is voice mail more effective in their culture? Professional journals? TV? Trade shows?
Key elements of diversity?	Take note of ethnic, hierarchical, linguistic, experiential, cultural, and educational diversity.
Key motivators?	Are they motivated by performance goals, quality measures, knowledge acquisition, or hierarchical influence?
Who influences them?	Are they influenced by other audiences, teams, or individuals?
Whom do they influence?	How will your communications indirectly influence other audiences?
Past issues with communications?	Have they had any past issues with this subject matter that must be overcome before they can "hear" it? "Old tapes" are often the bane of technical marketing communications. Learn whether or not there are existing barriers to communications.
Other special communications needs?	Are there any other special communications needs? Before committing to specialty media for your content delivery, be sure that your audiences have the proper hardware, memory, and software.

ous goal is that the information you have gathered will have an effect on your communication decisions. Sometimes communicators are so busy in the task of audience analysis that it becomes an end in itself. You must learn who your audience is so you can make appropriate decisions as you develop your marketing communication.

While Marie Floyd Tahir was an employee at Lotus Development, she was asked to help create user profiles of prospective customers for a new software product. The design team needed data about these customers quickly in order to make their product plans. They didn't have the time or the desire to wade through

AUDIENCE ANALYSIS			
	Writer	**Audience**	**Document**
Knowledge	*What do I know about this project?*	*What does my audience know about this subject?*	*What content (verbal and visual) should I include?*
Attitude	*How do I feel about this project?*	*How does my audience feel about this subject?*	*How should I present the information?*
Needs	*Why do I need to communicate this information?*	*Why should my audience need this? What does my audience need to know?*	*How does this information meet the needs?*

Figure 3.3 Grid for audience analysis.

lengthy reports on site visits, but they wanted data from real people. Tahir and her group gathered the data and, after analyzing the data, presented it to the design team in the form of audience posters.[7]

Recently, while developing a Web site to market the profession of technical communication, we adapted Tahir's idea for presenting audience information to our design team. We had already identified the primary audience as high school students, and we knew we wanted to market this Web site, and eventually a CD-ROM, to high school guidance counselors. But identifying our audience was not enough. We could all sit around and talk about the characteristics of our intended audience because we all knew some high school students. We could have surveyed high school students, but we wanted more. We wanted information about our audience, but we also wanted a way to help us stay focused on our audience and their needs all the way through to completion of the project. And the posters seemed to be the answer.

The Process

We invited seven high school students to meet with us. In preparation for their visit, we had a brainstorming session and came up with the following questions:

1. Do you have a computer at home?
2. Do you have access to the Web?
3. How many of your friends have Web access?
4. What kinds of things do you look for on the Internet?
5. How much time per day/week do you spend on the Internet?
6. What kind of sites do you like to visit?
7. In your opinion, what makes a good Web site?
8. What things frustrate you as a Web user?
9. Do you use the search function when you go to a Web site? If so, how often?
10. Do you like to surf when you go to a Web site?
11. How much time do you stay at one Web site? Why would you leave that site?
12. Have you decided where you want to go to college? Where? Why?
13. What are your tentative career plans?
14. How did you get the idea for that career?
15. Where do you think you can go to get information about a specific career?
16. What do you want to know about a potential career?
17. Have you used the Internet to search for information about careers? If so, how did you search for information?
18. What college major will best prepare you for your anticipated career?
19. Do you know what you need to do to get started in the career you are interested in? (What classes you must take? What degree you should earn? What training is necessary?)

When the high school students arrived, we assigned members of the Web design team to pair up with a visiting student for the interview. After asking permission, we took a picture of each high school student. The design team took careful notes during the interview. In the days following the visit, the design team worked together in groups of three to analyze the data gathered and to create the audience posters (Fig. 3.4 shows a sample poster).

We displayed the posters around our work area. In the weeks to come as we designed the Web site, we referred to the posters. As manager of the project, I often saw one or two team members consulting the posters as a reminder of the audi-

MEGAN

DEMOGRAPHICS:
Age: 17   Female   Cheerleader   Senior

QUOTES:
I use an HTML Editor, and I am on the Web team at school.
I also have my own homepage.
I own a computer and have web access.
I email the majority of my friends.
I spend 1 hr/day online, sometimes more.   I'm not a big web surfer.
I use search engines a lot (Infoseek or Lycos).   I visit my karate site and my HS site most often.
I don't like to have to read a lot of text.   It's easier to use the internet than to use books.
I spend 10 minutes max on one page.   I'm not real big on going to the library.
I like centered text, very organized info, a very neat/clean page design, and color & excitement.

VALUES:
Useful search function/engine   Finding info about various jobs
Clicking around on her own   Ease of use
Efficiency (being able to find the right info fast)   Info about job placement and specialization

Figure 3.4 Audience analysis poster.

ence we were striving to reach. And when we made certain design decisions, someone would say, "That will work for Joe," or "That's just what Megan wants." It really did help to create a bridge between gathering raw data about an audience and making every effort to apply what we learned to our design decisions.

Leveraging Audience Information

Even if you don't make audience posters or use a similar device, your audience information is a valuable reference library. Keep it in mind as you develop your technical marketing communication.

Attached or pull-through technology products and services are an example of leveraged audience information. For example, if you have a long list of customers who have historically purchased your technology product, you will want to know who has been conducting the installations. Some customers will do it themselves; others hire someone to do that for them. New wireless computer networks pose multiple opportunities for manufacturers who had previously marketed the initial network hardware. Can we expand your network to other floors or buildings with wireless? Do you have someone to install the antennae on your building? Has anyone walked through your building to identify any wireless dead spots? Same audience with new opportunities to leverage.

Remember to compare and test content against your audience knowledge. Where you sense potential conflict in acceptance or understanding, develop parallel communication targeted specifically to different audiences. Where there is shared audience perspective, economize with more singular communication.

Summing It Up

The first step toward effective communication is to discover the identity of your audience. But identification is not enough. You must analyze your audience as you look at the following characteristics:

- Where are they in the hierarchical scheme of things?
- How do they relate to and use technology?
- What is their first language? Second language? Technical dialect?
- What are their education, training, and skill levels?
- What is their experience level?
- How would you describe their culture, both geographic and corporate?

Learning all you can about your audience is extremely important. It is helpful to use some form of audience profile as you gather data through interviews, face-to-face meetings, guided discussion groups, conference calls, Web meetings, audience questionnaires, and audience posters. Always compare and test content against your audience knowledge.

Applying What You've Learned

1. Why are audiences important to the outcome of technical marketing communication?
2. List the different ways you can look at your audience?
3. What role does diversity play in understanding audiences?
4. You have been asked by the human resources director (HRD) of your company to announce and explain the new e-mail software being introduced by the chief information officer (CIO) and her information technology (IT) staff. You're aware that the company president and most of your co-workers prefer the old e-mail software. Who are your audiences and how are they different? What else would you like to know about each audience? What specific questions would you like to ask in an interview with each? In a survey?
5. Locate a brochure or newsletter that markets a technical product or service. Brainstorm a list of characteristics you can assume about the intended audience. Does the marketing piece adequately meet the needs of that intended audience?
6. Locate a technical marketing piece you believe adequately addresses the issue of diversity in audiences. What does it do well?
7. Locate a technical marketing piece you believe does not address the issue of diversity in audiences. In what ways does it fail?

SMALL GROUP ACTIVITY

Your university has asked you to help market the technical communication major to high school students. Identify the different audience groups, other than high school students, who would have an interest in this major. Have one member of the group role-play a person from one of those audience groups. The rest of the group will gather data about that person by interview, survey, questionnaire, or any other creative means. After the data is collected, create one audience poster for each person represented. Share the posters from each group.

Notes

1. *Webster's New World Dictionary,* 2nd ed., s.v. "audience."
2. J. C. Mathes and Dwight Stevenson, *Designing Technical Reports* (Boston: Allyn and Bacon, 1991), 32.
3. *Congressional Record.* Daily ed., Feb. 6, 1996, 142: S91–S94.
4. Donna Banks, "Advertisers Are Urged by P&G to Connect with Ethnic Markets," *Wall Street Journal*, May 26, 1999, B13A.
5. Mathes and Stevenson, *Designing Technical Reports*, 42–44.
6. JoAnn Hackos, "From the Director," *Best Practices*. 2(4) (August 2000): 62.
7. Marie Floyd Tahir, "Who's on the Other Side of Your Software: Creating User Profiles through Contextual Inquiry." In *The Art of Seeing, Conference Proceedings of the 6th Annual Conference, Usability Professionals' Association*, Monterey, California, 1997, 19–26.

CHAPTER 4

Strategy Development

Overview

"What kind of strategy was that?"

I learned to play chess in grade school and enjoyed teaching the basic concepts to family and friends so we could play together. At that beginning level, I enjoyed modest success and liked the variety of moves represented by rooks, bishops, and knights. However, I played less and less over the years, partly because of a progressively poor win-loss record. My opponents often anticipated my moves and seemed much bolder as they decided to advance or retreat in an organized fashion. In short, I never really knew how to position my opponents for checkmate, and I was constantly on the run.

Eventually, a college friend coaxed me into a game at the student union. I could tell she was excited and she asked me what my favorite offense was as we set up the pieces. I was at a loss as she mentioned a few of her favorites by name. Halfway through our first game, I was happily removing her pawns and a few other pieces. But she was shaking her head and smiling after each of my moves—right up until she announced, "checkmate."

"What kind of a strategy was *that*?" she asked as we set up the board again.

"Strategy?" I replied.

"You know, your plan. How were you planning to get to my king?"

There, in a nutshell, was the explanation for my previous ten years of dismal chess play. I didn't have a plan. Instead, everything I did was tactical—dealing with the very next move. While I was greedily taking her knight with my rook, she was carefully laying a framework to get to my king. With her eyes set on the goal, she wisely allowed me to take a series of pieces on one side of the board just as she opened a road to my king on the other. Eventually, with my attention sufficiently diverted, she simply moved in and trapped my unprotected king. Checkmate.

She was thinking strategically.

Tom

Strategy Development

The most important differentiator between simple communication and more complex marketing efforts is strategy development. Strategic marketing communication creatively applies cause and effect relationships wherever possible. Strategies inform and educate to spur early adoption and enthusiasm. They influence in order to garner endorsement. Unlike my chess loss, most technical marketing communication strategies do not require a diversion. But they usually involve a series of carefully calculated steps. This chapter demonstrates a variety of ways to fulfill marketing communication objectives with well-positioned strategies based on target audience profiles (see Fig. 4.1). Ultimately, we're going to build an example of an entire strategic framework in Chapter 11. The generic strategic technology framework depicted in Figure 4.2 illustrates how strategy germinates in the immediacy of competitive market forces. From there, each step of brand building, customer definition, engagement, and sales relates back to strategy. Let's begin with the basics and build a better understanding of this critical concept.

Why Versus How

Even seasoned technical marketing communicators struggle over the difference between strategy and tactics. In fact, it is sometimes easier to understand strategy by clarifying what it is *not*.

　　When you ask *what*, the answer is the overall objective for your technical marketing communication. To be successful, what must have occurred? When you speak of the outcome itself, you refer to the *result* of sound strategy, not the strategy itself. When you ask *who*, the answer is the combination of targeted audiences

Figure 4.1　Determining strategy is the third stage in the communication cycle.

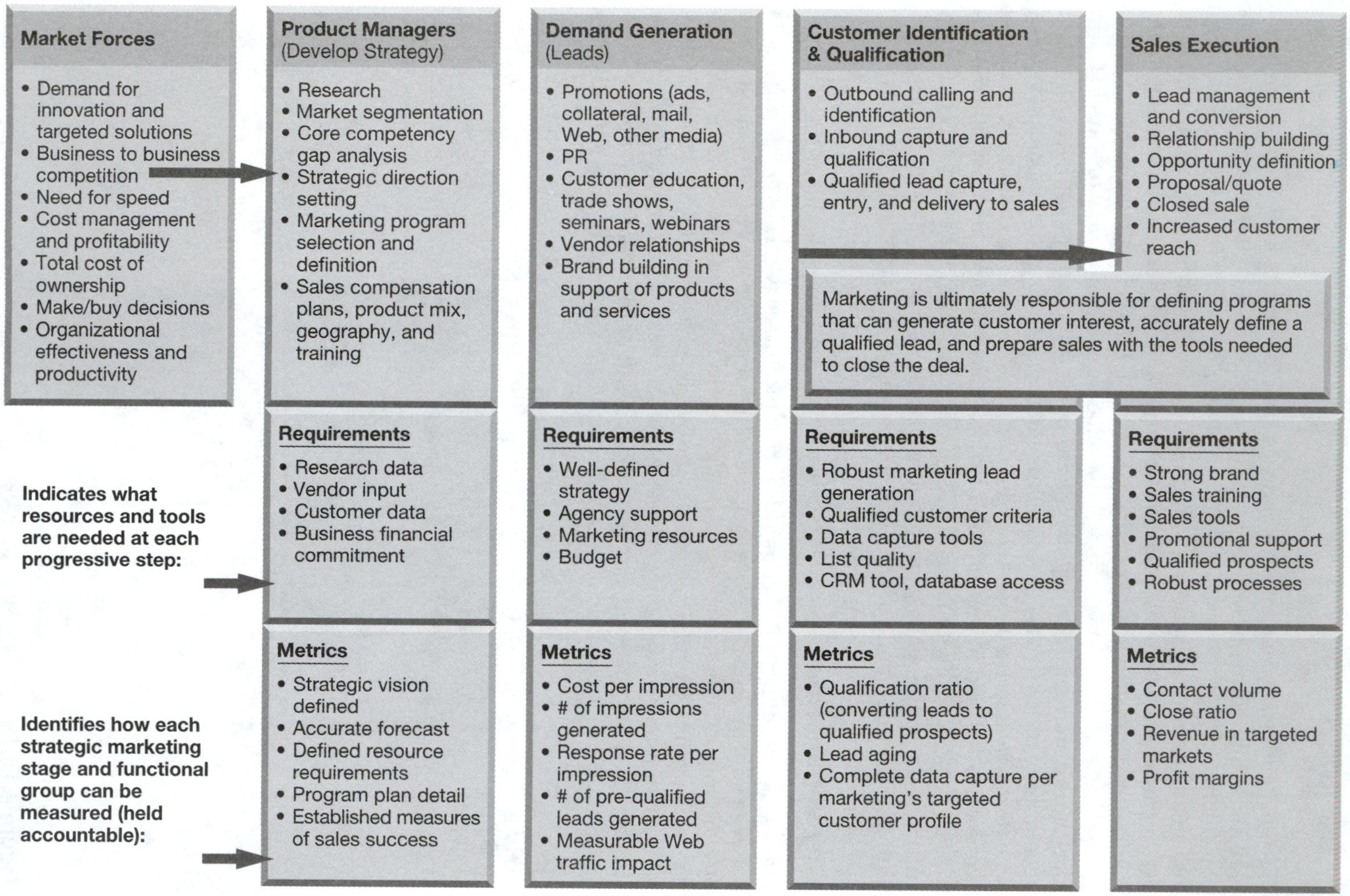

Market Forces
- Demand for innovation and targeted solutions
- Business to business competition
- Need for speed
- Cost management and profitability
- Total cost of ownership
- Make/buy decisions
- Organizational effectiveness and productivity

Product Managers (Develop Strategy)
- Research
- Market segmentation
- Core competency gap analysis
- Strategic direction setting
- Marketing program selection and definition
- Sales compensation plans, product mix, geography, and training

Requirements
- Research data
- Vendor input
- Customer data
- Business financial commitment

Metrics
- Strategic vision defined
- Accurate forecast
- Defined resource requirements
- Program plan detail
- Established measures of sales success

Demand Generation (Leads)
- Promotions (ads, collateral, mail, Web, other media)
- PR
- Customer education, trade shows, seminars, webinars
- Vendor relationships
- Brand building in support of products and services

Requirements
- Well-defined strategy
- Agency support
- Marketing resources
- Budget

Metrics
- Cost per impression
- # of impressions generated
- Response rate per impression
- # of pre-qualified leads generated
- Measurable Web traffic impact

Customer Identification & Qualification
- Outbound calling and identification
- Inbound capture and qualification
- Qualified lead capture, entry, and delivery to sales

Requirements
- Robust marketing lead generation
- Qualified customer criteria
- Data capture tools
- List quality
- CRM tool, database access

Metrics
- Qualification ratio (converting leads to qualified prospects)
- Lead aging
- Complete data capture per marketing's targeted customer profile

Sales Execution
- Lead management and conversion
- Relationship building
- Opportunity definition
- Proposal/quote
- Closed sale
- Increased customer reach

Requirements
- Strong brand
- Sales training
- Sales tools
- Promotional support
- Qualified prospects
- Robust processes

Metrics
- Contact volume
- Close ratio
- Revenue in targeted markets
- Profit margins

Marketing is ultimately responsible for defining programs that can generate customer interest, accurately define a qualified lead, and prepare sales with the tools needed to close the deal.

Indicates what resources and tools are needed at each progressive step:

Identifies how each strategic marketing stage and functional group can be measured (held accountable):

Figure 4.2 Technical marketing strategic framework.

or markets to be addressed. Each may warrant a unique *strategic* approach. When you ask ***how, where,*** and ***when,*** the answer will be tactical considerations to be made *based on* strategy. But when you ask ***why,*** the answer should describe your strategy.

Beginning with a how, where, or when question is one of the most common planning errors for technical marketing communicators.

- How should we create the Web site?
- Where should we locate the billboard?
- When should we distribute the direct mail piece?

All of these *tactical* questions can be challenged from a more *strategic* perspective.

- *Why* are you creating a Web site?
- *Why* have you chosen to include billboards in your media choice?
- *Why* will direct mail help to achieve your overall marketing communication objective?

If these *why* questions cannot be answered with a cohesive and comprehensive explanation of the overall technical marketing communication approach, then you should go back and focus your attention on strategy development before taking any further tactical steps. *"Why are we doing this?"* is a strategic question. *"How should we do this?"* is a tactical question. Tactics are used to execute the strategy.

At a major corporate presentation for a new marketing campaign, a vice president carefully explained the inviting market dynamics of several targeted regional locations. Each held huge percentages of untapped clients. Market research and customer surveys had shown that people wanted access to the company's new technology services and that their pricing structure was probably about right. At the end of the presentation, someone asked how they specifically intended to market to those prospects and how they would fund it. The VP confidently responded that the team didn't have all those answers yet. The tactics would follow now that they had determined a workable strategic direction.

Deadlines and Other Tactical Distractions

Technology-oriented individuals and organizations often leave communication to the last minute. In these cases, communication clients drive toward tactical efforts without including technical marketing communicators in their earlier strategic thinking. As a result, the technical marketing communicator is likely to receive a request beginning with, "I know we don't have a lot of time, but. . . ." By definition, an immediate deadline precludes strategy development because no one has time to plan—only time to do. In these instances, your only available alternative is to react with tactical solutions.

- We need a Web site.
- We need a logo.
- We need a brochure and direct mail campaign.
- We need . . .

But part of the technical marketing communicator's ongoing job is to drive toward strategy development by saying, "Of course, I can help with that, but help me to understand why it's part of your plan. How does it help to accomplish your objective?" It may be too late to develop strategy for the tactical situation at hand (create a newsletter), but most clients are interested to hear how strategy development will make their next marketing communication effort more successful.

One technology team published an annual projection of the latest and greatest technologies likely to affect their business over the next 18 to 24 months. They meant this report to help other technical associates look to the future and not be caught off guard by unforeseen change. The first time they simply published a very thick document and were disappointed by the low readership. Still, the organization saw value in the effort and decided to try again the next year. The following year they called on a technical marketing communication team at the last minute *to build their brand identity* and managed to generate additional interest in the remaining time available. Finally, the next year, they planned and executed a strategy to build awareness and demand for their communication *product* well in advance of its publication. They also added a much shorter summary addendum to the main document and included an audiotape version for people who simply did not have the time to read another document. The resounding success of their program was not due to any change in the actual content they created but in their overall strategy *to market* their product.

Strategic Cause and Effect Nuances

Technical marketing communicators want to understand *why* in order to plan strategic *cause and effect* relationships for their communication. We want to communicate our information in a certain way so we can achieve a specific outcome. At the onset, we can do this without feeling constrained by time or budget because we aren't yet interested in the tactical questions of "how, when, and where?"

We must consider important nuances among causal strategies because they lead directly to the desired communication content. The following list describes strategic terms you can use to articulate causal strategies. The first three terms are similar in nature but distinctly different in their strategic application. To understand the causal strategies *inform*, *educate*, and *train*, consider the following content nuances.

1. **Inform—Impart information and make the audience aware of, or acquainted with your subject.** Informing someone is usually more benign than trying to influence them. From a strategic standpoint, you are more likely to inform a

key audience in advance of a subsequent milestone or event. For example, keeping a management team aware of the progress of developing technology does not require that they become educated in that technology. You may want to keep an audience or market of technology users informed of planned improvements well before there is enough information to actually educate or train them on those improvements. Keep the information high level and devoid of technology specifics. When informing users of a pending Microsoft product release, you are more likely to highlight several new features and benefits without explaining how to actually access them in the software.

2. **Educate—Develop the capabilities of your audience and provide them with the knowledge they need.** Educating them requires you to present a deeper level of information content but not necessarily in a way that results in the ability to perform a task or procedure. Whereas a leadership team needs to be informed, a technology development team must be educated as they progress. This education requires more specific information about the technology or process without actually training them. Students who are educated in communication may require additional training to perform a specific task. A technical sales team wants to be continuously educated on their competition and other market factors in addition to learning about their technology product or service.

3. **Train—Enable people to be proficient in a task.** Support staff and technology users must be trained if they are to become proficient in a task or procedure. Training generally represents a much more detailed body of information and coordination, whether it is developed for online access, instructor-led sessions, or on-the-job formats. You should have a much more outcome-oriented approach that includes accountability for the instruction and the learners.

The content nuances of *influence* and *motivate* have different strategic applications:

4. **Influence—Position your communication to influence people when you need to sway or incline their thinking concerning a particular subject.** If you must trigger a budget appropriation before you can begin work on a new technology, your strategic communication content will need to positively influence those involved. Influencing them doesn't mean you are driving toward an immediate tactical response. You are more likely to be preparing them with information to position a future response or action. Political teams are notorious for disseminating information in advance of partisan votes in order to influence public opinion. By strategically influencing constituents, they may in turn motivate their elected officials to support a specific issue.

5. **Motivate—Choose a motivational strategy when you must move someone to action or a series of actions.** You may need to offer an incentive or compelling consequences (positive or negative). Grades only serve as motivation for people who recognize certain outcomes related to those grades. At some level, you need to have been influenced to recognize the strategic value of good grades in obtaining scholarships, job opportunities, or self-esteem. Motivation is more

action oriented than influence. You may influence people's thinking in advance of future events, but you want to motivate their actions for near term results. Strategically, a technical marketing communication plan states your intention to motivate a certain audience or market to try a new technology. "*How* will we motivate them?" That will be left to your tactical solutions.

The content nuances of *introduce* and *implement* also have distinctively different strategic applications.

6. **Introduce—Establish or bring forward for consideration.** We introduce new technology initiatives to an audience or market to establish their place as part of change. In a social or professional setting, you often introduce acquaintances or colleagues. This introduction bridges the unknown and provides a cursory overview of names and backgrounds. From that point, the people involved will begin to form their own impressions and opinions. A lot can be inferred from the manner in which you introduce someone. "I'd like you to meet my good friend," or "I believe you two share an interest in this new technology," pose a much more compelling introduction than, "Mr. X meet Ms. Y." The same is true with the introduction of new technology or changed technology. Stimulating an audience or market to visualize value at the point of introduction will strategically speed and enhance ongoing communication.

7. **Implement—Bring things into practical effect.** Having been introduced to technology products, services, or processes, a technology team can more comfortably move toward implementation of their features. Try the opposite. Bring in your colleagues and simply begin working without having introduced them. It makes for an awkward, even rude situation, doesn't it? Similarly, learning that an audience is offended shouldn't surprise us when we didn't introduce them to a new technology or change before asking them to implement it. Our technical marketing communication strategy should call for implementation communications to follow a strategic introduction. How exactly will you conduct the implementation? That is a tactical question for another chapter.

Targeted Effects

The targeted effect of the causal strategy, that is, the effect you want your strategy to have on the targeted audience, is equally important to understand. You choose a particular causal strategy so that your targeted audience will respond in one of the following ways:

- *Act:* Carry out a function (respond). More often than not, a technical marketing communicator is trying to stir up action. Clearly understanding and wisely choosing that action is part of your strategy development process.
- *Wait:* Watch for and anticipate (prepare). If your strategy doesn't seek immediate action, it should integrate some form of nonaction, including a request to

wait for more directions or instructions. Waiting is an especially important strategic result if you have time to inform and influence your audience. Their natural inclination is to ask, "what now?" Be prepared to communicate "wait" to your audience when it's appropriate.

- *Change:* Cause to be different, exchange or replace, lay aside and leave for another. Asking someone to change is one of the most frequent, and most difficult, things to communicate. Informing and educating your audience make it easier for them to embrace change.

- *Adopt:* Take into your family, take and follow by choice, choose as a standard, take up and make your own. Adopting a technology or change initiative means taking it up as your own. You can force the elements of change, but they are ineffective until people actually adopt and take it into their "family." The tone and voice of adoption communication must be much more sensitive to culture and past experience than aggressive "change or else" communication. Knowing your audience is essential to knowing what will help them adopt your ideas.

- *Endorse:* Give approval and support to, especially by public statement or action. Having a third party endorse your communication initiative is an excellent strategic choice if your intended audience respects or values the opinion of the person you've chosen for the endorsement. A sports star may not be the right celebrity endorsement for an infrared-tracking device. And a lower level manager may not have the celebrity reach to endorse an internal corporate initiative. Choose wisely and refrain from using endorsement as intimidation to the neglect of a clear, substantive connection to your communication objective. An executive endorsement can be as subtle as well-timed praise for a project during a regular staff meeting.

- *Learn:* To acquire experience, ability, skill, knowledge, and become informed. Earlier in this section we differentiated between the strategies to inform, educate, and train. Similarly, the technical communicator must strategically guide the intended audience either to learn enough for personal application or to simply be informed.

- *Understand:* Perceive and comprehend, grasp significance. Understanding subject matter does not require that you have mastered it. Again, put your intended audience at ease by clearly stating that what you wish them to understand is related to a targeted strategic outcome.

- *Participate:* Be part of, take part in (attend). Participate is a cousin of *act*. A call-to-action strategy might seek participation in a series of meetings, training classes, process change initiatives, or other specific events. Participation could strategically lead to becoming informed, learning more, endorsing a concept, and ultimately adopting it.

- *Contribute:* Help bring about a result. Contributing knowledge, information, time, or budgets is strategically less demanding or confrontational than participating. Your communication strategy should differentiate between people who should contribute from a distance and those who should be hands-on participants.

Linking Cause and Effect Strategies

Once you have a grasp of cause and effect nuances, it is much easier to link them as part of your strategic framework. For example, in Table 4.1 you can see how linking certain causes to certain effects works with a generic technology rollout to a Fortune 500 company. Later, you will determine the tactics for implementing these strategies.

Technical Marketing Communication Strategies

Technical marketing communicators must consider causal strategies in order to achieve a specific outcome related to their product or project initiative. A generic technology maturity curve is one of the best ways to visualize key communication opportunities in a technology's life cycle (see Fig. 4.3). These life cycle phases ap-

TABLE 4.1	Linking Causes to Effects for a Technology Rollout
Communicate This (Cause)	**So That (Effect)**
Inform the CIO of how the new technology will help to improve productivity and add a competitive edge to the company.	Gain the CIO's **endorsement,** budgetary support, and influence across all departments.
Introduce the technology's basic features and benefits to a broad managerial representation of business functional groups whose staffs will utilize the technology.	Obtain the leadership team's ongoing support and permission to distribute information that will **prepare** their staff **for change.**
Educate a core group of technology support leaders who will help to maintain and manage the technology.	Ensure that communication content is developed and delivered in time for them to **learn** and **share** with other associates.
Invite and motivate actual end users of the new technology (they should be considered "customers") to provide input to the technology development, testing, and deployment process.	Begin early enough in the technology cycle to ensure that end users can **participate** and offer feedback before deadlines eliminate that offer.
Train service staffs, trainers, and end users in the deployment, support, and use of the technology.	Build enthusiasm during the entire rollout process so that people welcome training and become **proficient, early adopters** of the technology.
Implement processes and procedures to ensure that the new technology becomes standard and that legacy technology is transitioned out.	Follow through to ensure that the organization as a whole, and individual audience niches in particular have robustly **understood, valued, and embraced the change**.

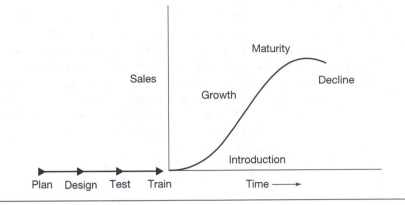

Figure 4.3 Technology maturity curve.

ply whether your organization uses a technology internally or whether your customers purchase the technology externally. And before you can introduce the product, you should be considering strategic communication in the planning, designing, testing, and training phases as well.

Consider what happened when a small software firm with a great idea and great people spent years and millions in venture capital funds to develop a desktop applications interface. Unfortunately, desktop application technology was changing so quickly that the team's design had to evolve and reinvent itself several different times *before* it could even hit the introduction curve. Many of their technical marketing communication strategies had to wait patiently while the product cycled in its prerelease phase.

Plan

Technical marketing communicators should ask to be included in the process long before the company introduces a technology to the end users. We need to begin strategic communication planning for a technology rollout as soon as the product plan has gotten under way. Our purpose is to ask the following questions:

- Who is the audience?
- What do we want them to do?
- Will we need to integrate training?
- Are there budgets available to influence or approve?
- Why are we doing this in the first place? What's the big picture?

Asking these questions early will also help the technology design team to maintain focus on their objectives and audiences.

Design

Preparation for a communications rollout continues during the technology design phase, but we should also make sure that the right people are receiving up-to-date information about the design progress itself. Technology teams can become so engrossed in the detail that they forget to come up for air. It is best to get the design team to commit to a strategically scheduled series of information updates for various audiences. Communications preparation is also a good time to involve end users of technology and continually affirm that they are willing to adopt a design once it becomes available. If you strategically distribute the available information, you will begin building enthusiasm about features and benefits within the user community without giving away competitive tips.

Test

Even as design and testing are taking place, advance communications for training should reflect your strategy of motivation, timing, and preparation. We need to convince busy service and sales people to schedule another training class. We need to ask the following questions:

- What makes this technology initiative different?
- How will sales teams and their internal or external customers benefit?
- What must these support teams know and when will they need to know it?

Train

Multimedia training materials are often left to the technical marketing communication team, especially if they develop a strong understanding of the technology along the way. Make sure your strategy framework allows time to integrate the emerging technical information into training plans and materials.

For example, one technology rollout team was caught off guard when their training peers were inadvertently left out of the loop on a new product. With an immediately impending product release and a very unhappy sales vice president looking at them, they turned to the technical marketing communicator who had created an internal slide presentation. The presentation's original objective was to detail the project for executives who had budget approval. With some quick response and insight from the training team, the presentation was quickly repackaged and expanded into training modules. It was a good catch (recovery), but you want to avoid such highly reactive situations as much as possible.

Hitting the Maturity Curve

Introduction Phase

The introduction phase of a new or changed technology calls for a promotional strategy of high activity. You must update and inform all audiences frequently.

Your strategic goal is to build broad awareness and adoption. Now is the time to air a commercial of the Rolling Stones playing "Start Me Up."

Strategically speaking, you need to be tactically active during an introduction. One manufacturer of a technology component knew his firm had to overcome a competing company who enjoyed well-entrenched market share. The challenger identified some of the market's largest customers and aggressively pursued them during an introductory burst. They made liberal expenditures in trade ads, distributed promotional materials to resellers, and offered sales incentives to telemarketers. But beyond that, their technical marketing team made themselves readily available and accessible to their resale channel partners and evoked a contagious, fun esprit de corps. Not surprisingly, they also made excellent market share inroads, thanks to their strategic grasp of the introductory phase.

Growth Phase

During the growth phase of technology use and evolution, you must aggressively identify and resolve any information barriers that arise, including product problems and competitive misinformation. This phase is also the time when users and support staff experience first hand how the new technology affects linking technologies and processes. Strategic communication should influence your users to expect ongoing change and updates and at the same time help them to appreciate expanded features and benefits.

During the growth phase, some of the frenetic energy and expense of introduction gives way to steady information-based activity. As we write this, mid-range storage servers are poised to become one of the fastest growth segments of the information technology market. Watch for an avalanche of growth-oriented support information throughout that industry.

Maturity Phase

Once a technology service, product, or process has matured, change will be less frequent. Strategic marketing communication needs to balance ongoing awareness with an eye to replacement technologies that lurk on the horizon. This strategic need also drives the budget planning for technical marketing communication. Microsoft Windows products have had a lot less promotional splash since its introduction of Windows95®. The Windows operating system is a mature product, and we generally understand what it can do for us. It's ubiquitous to our technology culture.

Decline

Eventually, as a technology product or service is on the way out and a replacement is on the way in, technical marketing communicators should help to redirect attention, educate the user, and urge them to adopt the next phase in a carefully orchestrated manner. Many times end users simply abandon a legacy technology and demand the new. However, unless budgets, training, and product availability have kept pace during transition, that can be a recipe for disaster.

Although Microsoft Windows operating system is mature, it is still highly supported and continuously adding new features. However, it's fair to say that the earlier 3.1 version has declined in relative popularity. Many other companies' custom mainframe applications are not as robustly supported. Professionals in corporate operations frequently lament that older mainframe legacy applications lack funding and even trained professionals to maintain and support them.

Technology users are not the only ones who abandon current technology. CIOs or other functional leaders may succumb to business demands for new technology before their organization is really prepared to deliver the next generation. In either case, technical marketing communicators play a key strategic role to keep everyone informed and prepared.

Strategic Drivers

Along the course of the typical sales maturity curve, there are a multitude of other competitive situations or industry activities that drive specific approaches to strategic communication. Here are four of the most common strategic drivers.

Differentiation

The most commonly heard plea from technical sales teams is "help us to distinguish what we do compared to our competitors." This task is easy when you have a technically superior or innovative service, product, or process at a reasonable cost. However, it becomes increasingly difficult if you are late to a particular market space or an aggressive competitor has posed a challenge. It often requires the creativity and cool head of a technical marketing communicator to sift through all the features and benefits of an offering and reveal its unique value.

When established companies are challenged to defend their turf and articulate a value proposition, they can also leverage their unique brand strengths. More than one technical marketing communicator has decided to lead with, "We're [insert name], and it's a name you can rely on." Any benefits related to a proven brand experience, like quality and innovation, absolutely help to differentiate it from the start-up company who just might be a flash-in-the pan.

Leadership

It is more fun to devise and execute marketing communication strategies when you are clearly in the lead rather than saddled with a "me too" program. Once in the lead, continue the perception by being a visionary fountain of information. Continuously gather customers and market representatives in virtual and location-specific forums to share ideas and plot the future together.

Cisco Systems, Inc., a model of leadership in the internetworking arena, continuously sends messages to reinforce that cutting-edge image. Their user summits, funded market studies, Web functionality, and technical support contribute to fuel a winner's image. In addition, they've thrown energy and employee commitment behind community initiatives. They are relentless and highly focused in their zeal to continuously expand the Internet economy.

As leaders, technical marketing communicators should steadfastly avoid portraying any appearance of arrogance or complacency in their messages. Technology users want to know you're constantly listening, innovating, and looking ahead. Don't brag or boast—lead.

Come from Behind

As many sports teams know, it's often easier to be the underdog. People tend to root for you, and if the front-runner exhibits any hint they are arrogant or complacent, you'll have the opportunity to prove yourself worthy to compete.

We've also heard wisened technology entrepreneurs look back and observe, "We were at our best when we were hungry. The team was seizing every opportunity, and there was something to prove." Technical marketing communicators need to harness that type of unique energy to their strategic advantage.

Again, the most important strategic communication messages of the underdog emphasize a fresh approach and the distinguishing features, value, enhanced quality, market responsiveness, and unique service offerings that may have lost the attention of number one.

New and Improved

New and improved feature strategies can also successfully propel a mature product right back to the high growth stage. New and improved claims make it much easier for technical marketing communicators to differentiate a value proposition. Faster, longer, cleaner, brighter, louder, and tastier are all new and improved descriptors. But new improvements have to matter to the audience. How fast do users really want to go? Does research justify the cost of louder or brighter? In business-to-business situations, how does it make us more competitive? It has to matter. What's in it for me?

New and improved is often the fastest, most cost-effective way to reemphasize the original value of a technology while incorporating the latest competitive features. This is especially true if the first edition of the technology was a winner. Customers can immediately grasp the favorable implications that the new technology is all that and more.

Ethics and Compliance

Strategically applying ethical considerations to technical marketing communications is really no different than any other aspect of life. In fact, it can usually be boiled down to two key guidelines:

- Don't lie.
- Don't steal.

We'd like to think both tenets are universally recognized and agreed on, but unfortunately that is not the case. Like any form of commerce or trade, technical marketing communication can harbor the temptation to distort the truth or use someone else's ideas. Both practices are morally wrong. In most business cases, they're also illegal.

Don't Lie

The easiest way not to lie is to tell the truth. Describe the actual features and benefits of a technology rather than the ones you wish were available to market. Don't promise the introduction of added functionality six months before it's actually available just so you can close a deal. And don't compromise your own integrity along the way.

For example, many years ago a technical marketing team worked with a technology solution that had a three-month construction cycle after designs were approved. Team members were often in fierce competition with the number-two rival to quote the fastest delivery. The sales team would ask the product manager what to tell the potential customers about improving delivery dates. His answer was to simply, "tell them whatever the factory schedule and some extra overtime will get you." One day a senior manager pulled the product manager aside and suggested he find out what delivery the competition was promising and at least offer to beat it. The senior manager said, "You know the competition is lying just to steal our business. It can't hurt to even the odds."

But it didn't take too many failed deliveries by the competition for their major clients—who placed multiple multimillion-dollar orders each year—to learn that this company stuck by its schedules. One of the company's unscripted marketing benefits became, "You can believe our delivery dates." And that led clients to believe other business commitments the company made would be true as well.

The lines of truth in marketing sometimes seem grayer than they really are. People wink and say, "Oh, we're just embellishing the truth with a little smoke and mirrors. That's what marketing is." But honest marketing isn't just a good idea. Not delivering on the promise of a technology can also be called fraud by anyone willing to sue. It's an expensive and resource-consuming risk to take—and it's not worth it.

Don't Steal

Some technology theft is obvious. You can't walk off with someone's formula card or patented design and market it as your own (although some countries have been lax to protect U.S. intellectual properties). And you can't steal registered trademarks or taglines either. That's why the ® and ™ symbols are used to protect products and technology brands whose image is what helps to set them apart from the competition.

Other technology brand attributes are tougher to protect. So-called generic brands are a good example. Go to your favorite drugstore and scan the shampoo aisle. It won't take long to see a few private-label bottle designs that mimic a national brand's shape and color. In some cases, consumer product companies have successfully sued to have imitators removed. But not always.

For most ethics and compliance issues, let an honest, objective, moral compass be your guide. But be sure to get good legal advice too. Healthcare, environmental, and defense technologies have a myriad of compliance issues to observe. Confidential disclosure agreements (CDAs) are de rigueur in the information technology industry before any intellectual property sharing takes place. You can't necessarily use competitive information in a marketing campaign if it didn't come from a public source. It's illegal to set prices in cooperation with competitors.

We've only touched the surface of the important ethics issue here, and we encourage you to carefully establish a personal standard of ethics and integrity long before you're challenged to test it.

Summing It Up

As a technical marketing communicator, remember you are well within your rights to ask strategic questions beyond the immediate tactical task at hand. It is always appropriate to seek background information and insight about how your communication fits into the bigger picture. That should naturally lead you to ask "why?" as you look for strategic threads between your communication and any other aspect of the project, process, or product.

Questions That Represent Strategic Thinking

Why are we doing this? or What's the plan? These are good ways to determine if a functional team or client has thought beyond the immediate tactical task at hand. Don't be surprised to hear technology people answer, "to meet the deadline." It's often up to the technical marketing communicator to look and plan beyond that deadline. If there is no plan, offer to develop one.

- *What's your market?* Understanding your market helps you to position your communication within the framework of the market audience. If this market has certain expectations, budgets, or competitive focus, your communications need to reflect that.
- *What's been done before, successfully and unsuccessfully?* Learn from the past and improve on it, especially if you have time to plan. Internal communication will benefit as will external customer or market communications.
- *What are your competitors doing?* Visiting a competitor's Web site or searching for their press releases provides a mirror to other industry ideas of which you may not be aware. If you are working on a corporate product, the same is true for internal communication sources and approaches.

Applying What You've Learned

1. What causal strategies would be involved in the following projects?
   - Development of an e-commerce Web site
   - Converting all hard-copy manuals to online documentation
   - Installment of new equipment to perform laser surgery
   - Rollout of the upgrade to the e-mail system
2. Choose one of the projects in Exercise 1 and make a table similar to Table 4.1, linking cause and effect.
3. What causal strategies would be involved in marketing the university's technical communication major? How do these causal strategies affect content nuance? What targeted effects do you want your strategy to have on the targeted audience? Make a table similar to Table 4.1, linking cause and effect.

SMALL GROUP ACTIVITY

A university has hired you to develop a strategic communication plan for their new grade tracking technology. All students will have their own bar code imprinted on a large roll of stickers. They will affix a bar code sticker to every homework assignment and test. Professors will have laser wands to scan the codes and enter grades. Student grades will then be automatically updated and posted on the school's password-protected Intranet throughout the semester. It's April, and you have six weeks before the spring semester ends and students depart. The university plans to have the technology installed in time for the fall semester.

Without resorting to tactical detail, anticipate some of the following strategic issues:

- What do you recommend as the overall marketing communication objective?
- Who might your key audiences be besides students and professors? (Name at least three to five.)
- What potentially negative issues can you anticipate for each of your key audiences and how might you strategically defuse them ahead of time?
- What strategic communication should you immediately tackle before the end of the semester? How might you proactively link a communication strategy that begins now and picks up again in the fall?
- What risks are there if you wait to share some of your communication content in the fall versus having it forgotten over the summer break? What strategic opportunities does the summer break provide?
- Make a list of five causal strategies and five strategic effects you would present to the university to demonstrate your grasp of the situation.

CHAPTER 5

Internal and External Branding

Overview

"Did I have a positive brand experience? You bet."

Like most college undergraduates, music was an integral part of my life outside the classroom. At the prodding of my resourceful roommate, I decided to invest some of my hard-earned summer income in an upgraded sound system. At the time, speaker manufacturers were involved in a highly publicized technology war. I eagerly consumed product sheets that pictured and described the competing brands in exquisite, glossy detail. Admittedly, I also diverted serious study time to listening excursions at the local stereo store. One of the emerging brands at the time touted a full-frequency sound range in a smaller than expected package. The upstart company differentiated their technology with a ported bass feature so the speakers didn't have to be big to have a big sound. Their product line was easy to understand: small, medium, and large; college budget, home budget, or professional musician. The smallest version even had a directional treble reflector—perfect for bouncing the sound off the cramped walls of a dorm room. After carefully studying my options and verifying that the speakers would not crack at warp five-volume levels in the store, I committed my funds.

Twenty years, four moves, three jobs, and one child later, the dorm speakers were still doing fine. In fact, the upstart speaker company had also proved to be a winner. Their brand name became synonymous with innovative sound technology and quality. So when the left speaker of my matched pair finally developed a slight rattle, I immediately consulted the Sunday paper for a stereo store carrying my favorite brand. Unfortunately for me, 20 years of brand recognition also brought price inflation. The replacement set for my model (you had to buy the matched pair) had more than doubled in price. Ouch. Still a great value, but not in my immediate budget plans. I decided to delay my purchase decision and think about it some more.

A week or so later, I heard a nationally syndicated radio host promoting one of the brand's products with an easily remembered 800 number. 1-800-their-name. I started wondering if I might benefit by calling them for a mail order price comparison. Later that week I saw a newspaper advertisement similar to the radio host's pitch and again the 800-number was clearly posted. I had nothing to lose by trying. After a few minutes with a friendly customer service representative, she asked me why I didn't just replace the faulty speaker itself?

"Well, it's 20 years old; I didn't know if you'd still carry the parts. And I don't know how hard it is to service."

"No problem." After checking the serial number, she confirmed my speaker insert had been upgraded over the years but was still designed to fit in the same wood cabinet. I had only to remove a few screws and two wires. Replacement cost? One-fourth the cost of a new matched set.

"By the way," the customer service representative asked, "how do the speaker grill covers look?"

"Fine," I said, "but some of the foam rubber edges seem to be crumbling a bit. Sometimes they rain a fine dust onto the carpet when the speakers are moved."

That's exactly what she expected according to their age and a technical bulletin she was reading. Would I like to order replacement covers as well? Of course. You never know when I might be playing some cover-shaking warp five music again.

Did I have a positive brand experience? You bet. Would I recommend this brand to my friends? Absolutely. Think about everything I now associate with the brand name of my favorite speaker company:

- Their technology designs stand the test of time.
- They evolved their technology without rendering my original technology investment obsolete (compatible upgrade strategy).
- Their product quality is excellent and long lasting.
- Their customer service staff is easily accessible when I have questions (I only have to remember 800 and their name).
- They have friendly, knowledgeable customer service representatives who proactively profile my needs.
- You probably pay more, but it's worth it (reasonable value).

It seems so simple. Yet many technology organizations would gladly pay five points of margin to understand how this company accomplished the feat. We'll use this chapter to study brand basics from a technical marketing communicator's perspective. Keep in mind that brands aren't just for consumers or business-to-business commerce. In-house, intraorganizational technology programs also benefit from brand use for the same reasons.

Tom

What Is a Brand?

Originally, a brand was the distinctive mark that the cattle ranchers burned into the hide of their cattle to designate ownership. Whoa, the cattle really had to be on board with that program, didn't they? It was permanent but not foolproof. Enterprising rustlers were known to burn alterations onto an existing brand and try to pass the beef producing product off as their own. But for the honest folks, brands sent a clear, distinctive message. From that one visual image, you could imagine the ranch owners, their facilities, the hired help, even how they conducted business. Good or bad, you could associate the brand with the people wielding it.

We still associate brands with tangible and intangible qualities of a product or service. Think of your favorite brands, whether consumer or otherwise. Cars, blue jeans, fragrances, lawn mowers, computers, bottled water. If you say, "I bought a car," we usually ask "what kind?" before we ask about the color. We don't just wear blue jeans; we wear *designer* blue jeans. That's because we're brand conscious. Pick one or two of your favorite brands and ask yourself what led you to choose them? What made you a repeat customer? What would make you switch brands? That's what technical marketing communicators want to know about their brand users.

Whether you are aware of it or not, you associate your personal product and service experiences with a brand name. If you're a long-time brand user, you've balanced the good with the bad to formulate your overall impression. If you're a relatively new brand user, your initial impressions carry a lot of weight. You also integrate what you've heard about brands from friends, family, co-workers, and news reports. If people you respect have made a particular brand decision, it influences your own view of the brand. And when the brand owner spends budget money on advertising and promotion, you sift through these paid messages and incorporate some of them into your brand consciousness as well. When enough people develop an impression of a product or service, they *collectively* define the brand image. That image, coupled with actual customer buying trends, is crucial to brand owners. Brand owners can only cultivate and support the image they earn by consistently acting on their brand, but they can't define it. Only customers can do that.

Lynn Parker and Joe LePla, authors of *Integrated Branding*, define brand as how people feel about an organization based on their actions and communications. They often say that brand is the promise you keep. Put simply, brand is the intersection of an organization's strengths and what its customers or members value.[1] Internally, it will keep everyone on the same page, and it will help the company develop meaningful relationships that their customers can trust.

For example, Volvo has a strong brand. According to them, their name is synonymous with *safety*. Safety is a prominent word on their Web site. It boasts, "Beneath its curvaceous silhouette lurks the mind of a safety fanatic." But Volvo goes beyond words in its commitment to safety: Volvo's new, $81 million Volvo Safety Center 2000 is unique in the automotive industry. People join their Volvo Saved My Life Club and tell their stories on the Web site. They clearly know their brand and act on it.

Microsoft also has a strong brand. They are all about *access*—access to knowledge, information, and power. Their brand is well supported in their tagline: "Where do you want to go today?"

Yellow Springs Instrument (YSI) is a developer, manufacturer, and marketer of high tech solutions to the global biosystems market. Their mission statement is to ensure YSI's sustainability as the recognized leader in selected technology solutions that enrich life and protect the world's resources in the global biosystems market. They reflect their brand in their theme statement: "Sensor Technology Dedicated to an Ecologically Sustainable World." Their tagline or slogan also reflects their brand: "Who's Minding the Planet?" (See Fig. 5.1 for YSI's introduction to their Web site.) This theme and tagline are used consistently on the Web site and on all their publications, including employee business cards (see Fig. 5.2).

Sakson and Taylor is a Seattle-based firm that provides online information systems, Web site development, product documentation, process analysis, and training, either through consultants or through placing on-site contract and direct-hire employees. Their mission statement is "We work for the thrill of the match between people and jobs, and people and information." They capitalize on the concept of the "thrill of the match" and use it liberally on their Web site. To further their brand recognition, they incorporate a significant part of their logo in a

Who's Minding the Planet?™

- **Environmental**
  Water Quality
  Data Acquisition Systems

- **Biotechnology**
  Industrial Analyzers
  Medical/Clinical Analyzers

- **Precision™ Temperature**
  Medical Sensors/Probes
  Industrial Sensors/Probes

Sensor Technology Dedicated to an Ecologically Sustainable World.

ISO 14001 Certified

800 765-4974 ~ 937 767-7241

YSI Employment Opportunities

| About YSI | Hot Topics | FAQ | Feedback | Search | Year 2000 |
| Environmental Home | Biotechnology Home | Precision Temperature Home |

Figure 5.1   Yellow Springs Instrument home page.
Courtesy of YSI Incorporated, Yellow Springs, Ohio.

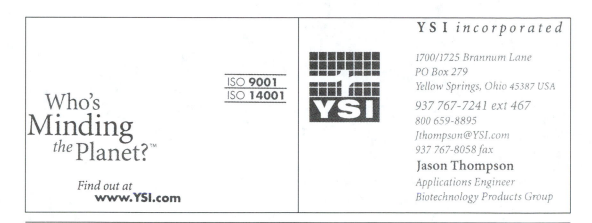

Figure 5.2 Yellow Springs Instrument employee business card (front and back).
Courtesy of YSI Incorporated, Yellow Springs, Ohio.

graphic that illustrates a nontechnical *match* everyone is familiar with. Each page of their Web site features *another perfect match* (see Figs. 5.3 and 5.4).

As part of an initiative to better serve its members, the Society for Technical Communication (STC) initiated a process to reveal and develop its brand—the meaning and personality behind the name STC. The first phase was research that involved a number of interviews with representatives of every group involved with the organization—from management and staff to current, former, and potential customers and members. They interviewed a total of 95 people, asking questions such as the following:

- What do the members value?
- What are the strengths of the organization?
- What are the unique benefits?

With a brand firmly integrated with your organization, you can more effectively communicate your values, purpose, and history to both internal and external audiences. You can also act more effectively on your values. When your organization's actions match your communications, you have an integrated brand (See Figs. 5.5 through 5.8 for STC's branding tools).

Ultimately, brands are marketing shorthand for the distinguishing product or service attributes they represent. Once you connect with the brand, you have fewer qualifying questions to ask about technology brand products or services themselves. Even new products to the brand line are accepted with less scrutiny—as long as the brand track record continues. Otherwise, if even one product in a brand group stumbles, all the other products may be suspect. With a successful brand track record, decision makers are inclined to support ongoing brand purchases.

Of course, not everyone is brand conscious. When all other decision criteria are equal, some people decide to purchase based on price or availability alone. A

SAKSON & TAYLOR

Contact Us

- Looking for Help
- Looking for Work
- Current Employees
- Job Search
- About Us
- Contact Us

another perfect match

Seattle Office
Sakson & Taylor, Inc.
4300 Aurora Avenue North,
Suite 100
Seattle, WA 98103-7390
Ph: (206) 632-6931
Fax: (206) 632-6927
Directions to our office

Boise Office
Sakson & Taylor, Inc.
3150 North Lakeharbor Lane,
Suite 254
Boise, ID 83703-6242
Ph: (208) 853-0335
Fax: (208) 853-0226
Directions to our office

Fort Collins Office
Sakson & Taylor, Inc.
131 Lincoln Avenue
Suite 200
Ft Collins, CO 80524
Ph: (970) 472-9500
Fax: (970) 472-9536

Singapore Office
Sakson & Taylor, Inc.
7 Temasek Bld., Penthouse
#44-01 Suntec Tower One
Singapore 038987
Ph: (65) 430-6645
Fax: (65) 430-6647

Helpful E-mail Addresses:
General information: info@sakson.com
Submit a resume: onsite@sakson.com
Benefits: benefits@sakson.com

Contact Form
If you would like further information about Sakson & Taylor and our services,
please complete the following:

Name:
Email:
Company:
Address:
Address 2:
City:
State:
Zip:
Phone:
Fax:
Questions
or comments:

I would like more
information about:
☐ Staffing services
☐ Consulting services

Submit Form

Figure 5.3 Sakson & Taylor: another perfect match (milk and cookies).
Sakson & Taylor brand information used with the permission of Sakson & Taylor, Inc.

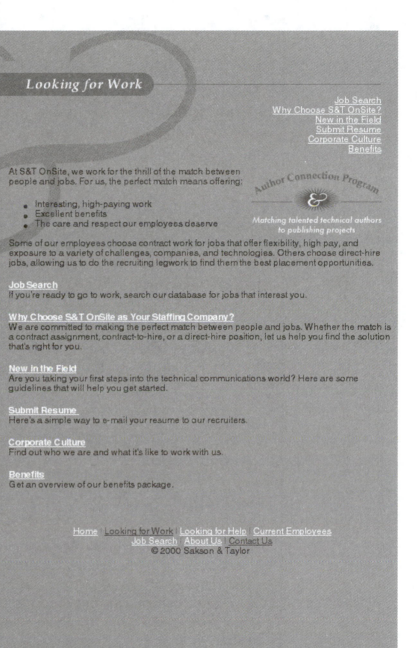

SAKSON & TAYLOR

- Looking for Help
- Looking for Work
- Current Employees
- Job Search
- About Us
- Contact Us

another perfect match

Our specialists include:
Technical Writers
Technical Editors
Web Designers
Web Developers
Programmer Writers
Training Writers
Instructional Designers
Localization Specialists
Graphic Designers
Illustrators
Indexers
Producers

Our expertise includes:
Technical documentation
Hardcopy & electronic books
Software & hardware guides
Online Help
Electronic Performance
Support Systems
White papers & case studies
Multimedia presentations
Interactive Web-based training
Web & intranet development
Documentation
process analysis

Looking for Work

Job Search
Why Choose S&T OnSite?
New in the Field
Submit Resume
Corporate Culture
Benefits

At S&T OnSite, we work for the thrill of the match between people and jobs. For us, the perfect match means offering:

Author Connection Program

Matching talented technical authors to publishing projects

- Interesting, high-paying work
- Excellent benefits
- The care and respect our employees deserve

Some of our employees choose contract work for jobs that offer flexibility, high pay, and exposure to a variety of challenges, companies, and technologies. Others choose direct-hire jobs, allowing us to do the recruiting legwork to find them the best placement opportunities.

Job Search
If you're ready to go to work, search our database for jobs that interest you.

Why Choose S&T OnSite as Your Staffing Company?
We are committed to making the perfect match between people and jobs. Whether the match is a contract assignment, contract-to-hire, or a direct-hire position, let us help you find the solution that's right for you.

New in the Field
Are you taking your first steps into the technical communications world? Here are some guidelines that will help you get started.

Submit Resume
Here's a simple way to e-mail your resume to our recruiters.

Corporate Culture
Find out who we are and what it's like to work with us.

Benefits
Get an overview of our benefits package.

Home | Looking for Work | Looking for Help | Current Employees
Job Search | About Us | Contact Us
© 2000 Sakson & Taylor

Figure 5.4 Sakson & Taylor: another perfect match (pen and ink).
Sakson & Taylor brand information used with the permission of Sakson & Taylor, Inc.

Figure 5.5   STC branding tools 1.

STC Brand at a Glance

Values

➤ Open-minded.
This means being open to new ideas and ways of doing things—open to mavericks and the diversity that comes from an organization composed of so many different people.

➤ Member-focused.
This means empowering the members within the organization as much as recognizing their role in the success of STC.

➤ **Effective.**
This means ensuring that all actions and communications are effective, and that processes and methodologies will be timely and useful—not a hindrance to the mission of STC.

➤ **Ethical.**
This is self-explanatory.

Positioning Statement
STC helps you design effective communication for a technical world through information sharing and industry leadership.

Figure 5.6   STC branding tools 2.

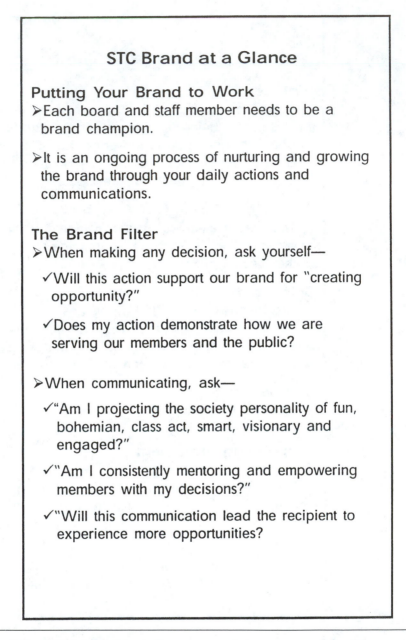

Figure 5.7   STC branding tools 3.

STC Brand at a Glance

Brand Story

Through information sharing and industry leadership, STC helps professionals design effective communication for a technical world. Because technology touches everyone, STC promotes public welfare by encouraging the development of better-educated professionals whose jobs are to make complicated information usable by many.

The organization's growth has mirrored our growing dependence on technology. Initially, STC was primarily made up of engineers who, among other activities, wrote instructions and descriptions of how electrical and mechanical products worked. A profound change took place as the pervasiveness of technology and the need to understand it became an integral part of our everyday lives. With the emergence of the Internet and online communication, our members now focus on supporting all aspects of the rapidly evolving world of technology.

The organization began because those working in the field recognized themselves as professionals with unique training and career issues. Today, STC is nearly 50 years old, with 145 chapters and 25,000 members worldwide. It is the largest international organization for technical communicators. STC offers industry leadership and the education, networking, and information required in a world where change is "the way it is."

Figure 5.8   STC branding tools 4.

brand owner's worst fear is the commoditization of their products—the loss of differentiating features. If all brands are identical, it takes a great deal of expensive promotional work to guide customers in your direction. That's why it's incumbent on brand owners to continually, tirelessly distinguish and differentiate their product with extra value, features, or services, so the customer decision will not be left solely to price or availability.

What Distinguishes a Brand?

Aside from the burning cattle iron, brand use isn't all that different today. Brands are brands because they can be distinguished from other competitors. Leading technology brands are known for the following:

- *Technology leadership*: If the market is watching your brand to see what's new and innovative, you're a technology leader. By definition, people seeking cutting edge technology will be drawn to your brand.
- *Customer focus*: Technology leadership isn't as important if it can't be put into practical use. The brands that develop a habit for interacting with and listening to their customers also build brand loyalty.
- *Value*: If users seem to get more technology or service support for their dollar, your brand adds or delivers value.
- *Quality*: Consistent quality makes a technology more reliable, which leads to less downtime, which improves productivity and lowers costs.
- *Service*: Everyone appreciates and respects a brand team that stands behind its technology with excellent customer service.
- *Availability*: Technology brands that build huge demand they can't fulfill will damage their brand identity. Some brands may purposefully be the second to market with new innovations so they can carefully build a supply channel, and thus strengthen that brand attribute.
- *Longevity*: Being a survivor, despite bumps in the road and market swings, builds credibility. It demonstrates financial stability and commitment. Sales teams love to point out the other casualties and say, "you know we'll be in it for the long haul."

The easiest way to attract loyal customers is to design great products and then stand behind them. Your customers will figure it out and keep coming back. But how do you make sure they remember to associate the technology product or service with you? And how do you make it easy for new customers to discover you? An integrated brand initiative will help you gain brand recognition.

Once you have identified your brand, you can begin to act on it, developing it consistently throughout the company. If you consistently act on a particular brand, over time, your customers will associate that brand with you and your product or service.

How Do You Recognize a Brand?

Once you firmly understand your brand as your customers understand it and as you desire it to be, you can use cues to help your customers recognize or reference your brand. The following sections help you drive your brand home in the minds of your customers.

Brand Name

The easiest way to recognize or reference a brand is by its name. You can create brand names specifically for a technology product line, or you can brand products by the company name. Consider the 3Com Corporation. Some of their early products were Ethernet PCI adapter cards plugged into the sides of laptop computers. These cards had brand names like Etherlink XL, but many people we worked with in the industry simply referred to them as 3Com cards. The 3Com Corporation name itself had brand recognition, and everyone associated rapid card development with the company name. Then 3Com created a handheld personal digital assistant (PDA) that became branded as the PalmPilot. Eventually, the PalmPilot brand evolved and needed more than one model. Each had different features and price points. These became the Palm III, Palm IV, Palm V, and Palm VI, and at the writing of this text, the new Palm VIIx. Later, other companies created their own brands of PDAs. For example, Handspring created the Handspring Visor brand of PDAs. Now, if someone asks you what kind of PDA you have, you'll say, Visor, or PalmPilot, or whatever else you've chosen. That's your PDA brand. Eventually, 3Com separated the PalmPilot business, now called Palm, Inc. The *brand* was movable because it had a name clearly recognized in its own right. It didn't have to be known as the 3Com PDA.

Two weeks after the separation, 3Com issued a press release to announce "3Com Launches $100 Million 'Radically Simple' Brand Campaign to Support New Focus." In the press release the company explains that this campaign "captures the networking company's focus on delivering functionally rich yet radically simple network solutions for businesses and consumers."

"This campaign powerfully illustrates what 3Com is all about," said Bruce Claflin, 3Com president and chief operating officer. "Our ads present real-life problems and simple solutions. 3Com helps people accomplish more through functionally rich yet radically simple network solutions. Our ads clearly demonstrate the value we bring to customers."

One television spot for 3Com's wireless solutions portrays a worker rushing to finish a project who is distracted by a coughing, throat-clearing colleague at a nearby desk. The spot poses the question, "Wireless network anyone?" and a narrator provides 3Com's solution to the busy executive's problem: "3Com lets you get up and work where you want while still connected to the network." The "anyone" theme is continued in the print advertisements, which demonstrate an everyday networking problem and provide 3Com's solution to security, wireless, and Local Area Network (LAN) telephony needs.

The first phase of their integrated brand campaign initially targeted U.S. business markets, with consumer and international advertising to follow later. (See Chapter 7, Figs. 7.11 and 7.12 for samples of their ads.)

Brand names are powerful marketing shortcuts. If a technical marketing communicator can develop a creative, recognizable brand name, it becomes much easier to introduce new features and versions. The PalmPilot name describes a device that can be held in your *palm* to *pilot* through information. It's easy to understand and visualize. Great brand recognition.

Now that the different Palm models within the brand have different price points and features, shoppers have to ask a few differentiating questions: Do I want an entry level, basic feature device (lower cost), or a sleek looking, low profile version with extra memory? Color screen? Each brand has different solutions (models) for an end user's needs. And each technical marketing communication team hopes their brand identity will influence that selection.

Logos and Looks

Next to brand names, logos are the most common brand cues. Technology teams wring their hands endlessly over the design of a new artistic rendering to represent their brand. Should it include the brand name? Its initials? No text at all? Edgy or conservative? Some of the most well-known logos simply feature the brand name in a distinctive font or signature-like flair. Think of running shoes and a swoosh. A colorful fruit with a missing bite represents a computer. A blue globe for a telephony carrier. Logo design is one of the things technical marketing communicators should absolutely, positively outsource to an agency or graphic artist.

Your logo should reflect verbal brand messages, should be unique, should be strong and memorable, and should have style. When STC began the branding initiative, they wanted a new image. They actually started the process a few years prior to the branding initiative. Their search for a new logo was not successful, and soon they realized they were starting in the wrong place. After completing a branding initiative, they realized their current logo was not strongly on brand, it was hard to read, it was not up-to-date for attracting younger membership, and it did not evoke brand personality attributes. The consultants believe the new logo manifests STC's brand tools, has a contemporary feel, is timeless, is clean, stylish, and precise, is designed to appeal to a younger age group, and contains all of the most important logo attributes.

Sakson and Taylor's ampersand in their logo illustrates their *matching* theme, manifesting their brand tools. (See Fig. 5.9 for the logo after branding.)

Sometimes you must consider more practical aspects of logo design. For example, the more complex and colorful the logo, the more expensive it is to reproduce on paper and other physical items. Printers charge you for each color they use. That's why so many brand logos have only two or three colors. Technical marketing communicators choose printed colors that also reproduce well on a computer monitor (for Web sites) so they do not confuse users across various media.

Figure 5.9   Sakson & Taylor's logo after the branding initiative.
Sakson & Taylor brand information used with the permission of Sakson & Taylor, Inc.

Conversely, a very cool, three-dimensional spinning image on a Web site may not translate well to print media. Ideally, a logo should also make it through the copy machine without becoming a single black smudge.

Other brand themes go beyond the logo itself to have a coordinated visual *look*. The look might pick up a color from the logo and apply it to the product itself or its Web site. Technology products or services that have a distinctive letterhead color may actually consider it to be part of their overall brand look, like an interior-decorating theme for logos.

Tagline or Theme Statement

Also known as slogans, taglines, and theme statements provide another brand cue beyond the brand name and logo. These textual cues help to explain and reinforce what the brand stands for. They coax your brand impressions in the right direction. Taglines are built for speed. Expect them to be grammatically incorrect sentence fragments—skipping the subject and going right to the action verb.

- Designing Technology with Your Future in Mind
- Helping Biologists Make the Chicken Come Before the Egg
- Making E-Commerce E-Z for the E-Challenged

Even though we've poked a little fun at the concept, theme statements are extremely productive tools. They're mini-billboards that can show up regularly on Web sites, business cards, letterheads, polo shirts, and advertisements. Other brand elements must be used frequently and consistently to be effective.

Sensory Elements

It doesn't hurt to have a unique sensory cue as part of your brand identity. Remember, not everyone can see or hear. And for those who can, one sensory stimulus may be more effective than another. Close your eyes and see if you can hear the musical tones from the Intel microprocessor TV ads. First, you see a computer board, and their circle logo that reads, "Intel inside." Their logo is in lowercase letters, and then you hear four pleasant musical tones (ta-ta-ta-tum!). If you can image those four notes, then they have done an excellent alternative-branding job, haven't they?

Just imagine you are one of millions of people who know the jingle for a technology product you will probably never actually see. Software companies have even licensed well-known rock songs to associate with and promote their brands.

Using a mixture of emotions, music, and visual cues, e-toy Company took a different turn with their highly effective series of TV ads. Each vignette depicted a parent and child enjoying a magical moment of fun with nature, like autumn leaves and daddy's big wheelbarrow. Then, as the child slept and catchy theme music played in the background, we saw the parent scanning e-toy's Web site. You couldn't help smile as they located the perfect toy to augment the memory. Browse, click, ship. And the commercial ends as the little girl giggles behind her brand new mini-barrow—just like daddy's. What a powerful tug of the heartstrings, just as the parent-friendly functionality of the technology was so clearly depicted. Ironically, many of the most prominent Web brands have invested heavily in traditional media like magazines and TV commercials—for added promotional clout.

Distinctive Designs or Services

Technology *designs* and services are so unique or distinctive they actually help to define the brand. They are said to be *signatures* or *signature elements* of the brand. Most of the handheld computer brands we described have signature designs. Their curved edges and colors can be recognized from across the conference room table. As for services, Dell turned the personal computer industry upside down with their signature online procurement model. Once you and your brand users are able to associate the essence of a product or service with its various brand cues, you've defined a brand identity. Technical marketing communicators take the lead in articulating the brand identity and composing the brand elements. With an established brand identity, your long-term goal is to *build recognition* for the brand. That is where you really begin to see the return on your brand investment. Sometimes technical marketing communicators and their sales teams lament, "We've got no brand recognition in the market." They mean audiences don't have enough exposure to or experience with the brand to draw favorable shortcut conclusions. Build it!

Building Brand Recognition

Establishing a brand isn't necessarily easy (name, logo, look, or tagline), but *building* a brand (broad recognition and understanding) is the real challenge. Technical marketing communicators contribute to building brand recognition in three important ways:

1. Applying the brand as frequently as possible
2. Applying the brand consistently and correctly
3. Fostering brand integrity

Applying the Brand

The easiest way to promote a brand is to apply it. You should apply brand cues such as logos and theme statements to everything a technical marketing communicator distributes: presentations, public relations announcements, letterhead, promotional gifts, incoming phone greetings, Web sites, literature, sponsored events, and advertisements. Ideally, you should promote your brand most heavily during its introduction phase. Your clearest brand-building marketing strategy is to get brand cues in front of the target audiences as frequently and as memorably as possible. Anything even remotely related to a brand is worthy of a press release or Web news update.

Applying the Brand Consistently and Correctly

Most corporations have very strict guidelines for using their brand logos and theme statements. You can use only specific colors and backgrounds. They regulate the position on the page and distance from other text. For example, one technology company requires a single logo's width of space between the logo and the left margin. That way, all brand literature is easily identifiable. Another firm absolutely refuses to allow any background colors to appear behind their logo. Fonts are also carefully matched and specified. Some companies go so far as to commission their very own font designs to make sure they're controlled and consistent. Technical marketing communicators can help lead in developing brand policy—and reinforcing it. People tend to poke fun at the rigor applied by "brand police," but it's really no joke. Part of the power of the brand is how easily recognizable it is. The more variations of a brand there are, the harder it is for a customer to make the mental shortcut. The best way to help your team apply the brand consistently is to keep the rules simple.

Fostering Brand Integrity

Once a particular brand becomes synonymous with quality or value, you have to remain true to the brand. The entire technology team must be committed to preserving the qualities customers associate with your brand identity. Technical marketing communicators have to stay connected to their customers with surveys and focus groups and aggressively address any hint of identity slippage. One technology firm we worked with had become known for their robust designs and workmanship. Their brand identity left the impression nothing ever broke. Imagine the crisis when a particular model suffered a stress crack in the field. To their horror, the engineers quickly uncovered a design flaw. However, rather than cover it up, the company wisely launched a comprehensive (and expensive) effort to repair every item at the customer site, and extended the original warranty. What could have severely threatened their brand identity became a strength. Just as few competitors enjoyed their previous track record of high quality—no competitor had ever undertaken such a comprehensive field retrofit. Their new brand identity carried a strong perception that they would always stand behind their product. Obviously.

When Do You Brand?

Just because you have a technology product or service doesn't mean you have to brand it. Brands are most valuable when you're in it for the long run. It takes time and money to create a brand and build awareness for it. If your technology product or program is going to be short-lived, there's little benefit to branding it. Private label products or so-called generic products may not choose to brand.

In-house technology programs (like information technology [IT] department projects) also benefit from *internal* brands. Desktop computer support teams' help desks are a prime candidate for branding. IT organizations typically get a bad rap for changing the e-mail system (we just got used to it) or implementing a different Web browser. So some IT groups have downplayed their users' overactive perception of change by applying a single brand name to aggregate all desktop services. That way, they're not changing the e-mail system; they're just upgrading the desktop service *brand*. It's not a totally new Web browser; it's an *enhancement* of your desktop services brand. The brand approach works, and IT teams are grateful for the relief.

But what about business-to-business branding scenarios? Let's say you have a single technology product called an electrical oscillator. It gets distributed through manufacturers' catalogs and is quite successful. Your company name has never been attached to the product in the catalog because customers either need the electrical oscillator or they don't. But before long, some of your new customers are asking you to add some features. They like your quality and service, but they need additional functionality. You're worried about raising the price too dramatically because not everyone will want the extra features. Instead, you decide to offer two different electrical oscillators. So what do we call the new one?

Now your technical marketing communicator has a question. Will you be adding any additional products in the future? That hadn't really been a consideration until now, but it's obviously possible. Why not build some notoriety as an electrical oscillator manufacturer? You agree, but wonder what to name the brand. The company name is Smith Products, which seems an unlikely brand for electrical oscillators. Instead, you agree to develop a line of electrical oscillators under the EO brand name. Each with an EO-related name. Before long, EO electrical oscillators have their own page in the original catalog, a Web site, and an annual EO user conference. When you think of high quality, innovative electrical oscillators, you think of EO.

The point of this example is that the lone electrical oscillator could probably have survived without a brand or simply applied the Smith corporate identity. But with the prospect of a growing line of products, the benefits of a brand (enhanced market visibility, broader customer base, repeat business, customer design interaction) outweighed the efforts to create and support it. Let's hope they can keep up with all the additional production and distribution!

Don't forget technology services in your branding efforts. You can't actually put your finger on a service, but it can still be *productized* for branding purposes. Take our EO electrical oscillators, for example. Let's say we've decided to offer an installation package. For $5000 (plus travel expenses) we'll unbox, install, and set

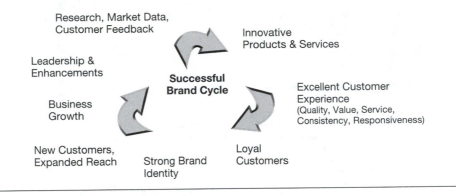

Research, Market Data, Customer Feedback

Innovative Products & Services

Leadership & Enhancements

Successful Brand Cycle

Excellent Customer Experience (Quality, Value, Service, Consistency, Responsiveness)

Business Growth

New Customers, Expanded Reach

Strong Brand Identity

Loyal Customers

Figure 5.10   Successful brand cycle.

up your new electrical oscillator. Our installer will also spend half a day training your operator. Our EO-branded service is called EO-Plus. It's part of our EO family of products and services.

Technical marketing communicators also have to weigh the commitment behind proposed branding efforts. To successfully build brands, organizations have to support graphic design, creative development, and promotional efforts—forever. Weak brand support is a self-fulfilling prophecy. If the brand work is mediocre, the technology will appear mediocre, and the program will struggle. Brand naysayers will then say branding doesn't work. Challenge your decision makers to invest in their brands with the same commitment they invest in research and development. Everybody, including the customer, wins.

The Brand Cycle

In the end, brands are part of an ongoing technical marketing communication cycle. Great products and services help to attract loyal customers. Loyal customers define and honor brand identity. Brand identity attracts new customers and feeds growth. Growth funds innovation and enhanced services. Enhanced services and innovation keep the brand competitive and strengthen customer relationships. Strong customer relationships promote and advance the brand. And the cycle continues (see Fig. 5.10).

Summing It Up

Your brand is the promise you keep to your customers. It is important to understand your brand and work consciously to integrate it into all you do. It is manifest in the following tools: your mission statement, values, story, principle, personality, and association. Your brand is communicated to your customers through your name, your logo, sensory cues, and all you do. Always apply your brand in a consistent manner.

Applying What You've Learned

1. Write a brief e-mail message you would send as a response to someone who wants to use your company logo on a Web site.
2. Locate a Web site owned by a corporation that sells a technical product. See if you can locate any of their branding tools on the Web site. Can you determine their brand personality and other tools that are implicit?
3. What would you do if your manager thought loyalty to your technical product was slipping?
4. Find a logo for a technical company and determine if that logo adequately represents their brand visually.
5. As you prepare to market your university's technical marketing communication major, what aspects of your endeavor will help to build brand?

SMALL GROUP ACTIVITY

Find a Web site for a high tech company and evaluate their brand. If they need any tools redesigned, as a group develop new branding tools. Make a list of possible projects that would be consistent with their brand. Make a list of projects that would not be consistent with their brand. In both cases, give the reasons for your decisions.

Notes

1. F. Joseph LePla and Lynn M. Parker, *Integrated Branding* (Westport, Conn.: Quorum, 1999), 1–12.

CHAPTER 6

Enhancing and Applying Creativity

Overview

What kind of person do you think of when you think of creativity?

I met Czan when she was a freshman in a nationally known art school. Her hair was inky black and fastened into a ponytail high on her head. Below her ponytail, her head was shaved and covered with colorful tattoos. Her clothes were an assimilation of castoffs typically found in a local thrift store. They neither matched nor fit well. She was the picture of a young artist striving to communicate her uniqueness.

Scott was also an art student but in his fifth year. He was featured on national television talk shows to discuss one of his creative projects. He had built a box, equipped it with sound, lights, and a video camera, and climbed in. He shipped himself by freight to his friend's house. He was in the box 26 hours as he traveled on six different semitrucks. When the trip was completed, he made a short video of the experience complete with music and narration.

My friend Kathy was known as the crafty lady. She was always making things: clothes, curtains for her house, a knitted baby sweater set for her new grandson, pictures for the wall, an afghan for the back of the couch, or a cross-stitched picture for a friend.

I knew Paul when he was an executive in a large company. Dressed in his navy suit and white shirt, he sat at the conference table with his colleagues and met the demands of a growing business. Often when no one else could solve the problem, Paul had a suggestion. It was always cutting edge and required a great deal of courage to implement. But most of the time, it was right on target—just what the company needed.

What kind of person do you think of when you think of creativity? Czan? Scott? Kathy? Or Paul? We all know creative people. We view the products of their creative endeavors, sigh, and wish we, too, were creative.

Perhaps you believe only a few are born with creativity, and they are the lucky ones. However, when you have finished this chapter, you will know what creativity really is and have a better understanding of how to exercise your own creative abilities. We've strategically positioned this chapter because many of our remaining technical marketing topics traditionally emphasize creativity as a key factor of success. It's important for TMCs to realize that this poses no barrier to their individual success, and in fact, they can be encouraged by the concepts shared in this chapter.

Sandi

Creativity Defined

Creativity has been defined as "the ability to fashion continually fresh and new responses to problems presented by the available body of knowledge."[1] Creativity is solving a problem in a way unknown to you when you were first confronted with the problem.

The process of creativity includes, implicitly or explicitly, the following five components:

1. Recognition of a problem
2. Definition of the problem to be solved
3. Generation of alternative possible solutions
4. Testing of alternative possible solutions
5. Selection of the best solution[2]

If we accept these definitions of creativity, we must dispel the myth that creativity belongs to the privileged few. It is not a rare or magical process. *Anyone* can "fashion continually fresh and new responses to problems," and *anyone* can solve a problem with a solution unknown to that person when first confronted with the problem. Can it be true *anyone*—including yourself—can be creative? If this is true, why is it that so few people are specifically known for their creativity?

Origins of Creativity

Neurologists tell us the cerebral cortex of the brain is divided into two hemispheres that are joined by a large bundle of interconnecting fibers. To learn how these two hemispheres of the brain function, neurologists studied stroke victims. By studying people whose brains had been damaged when a stroke left them with only one functioning hemisphere, doctors determined that the right side of the cortex primarily controls the left side of the body, and the left side of the cortex largely controls the right side of the body. In addition, they learned that the left hemisphere is predominantly involved with analytic thinking, especially language and logic. The right hemisphere, by contrast, appears to be primarily responsible for our orientation in space, artistic talents, bodily awareness, and recognition of faces. Simply put, the left brain processes information primarily in words, while the right brain processes information primarily in pictures.[3]

Most of the researchers believe that creativity comes from the right hemisphere of the brain. However, if we examine the five components of creativity, we can see that Steps 1 and 2, and perhaps Steps 4 and 5, require logical, rational, analytic thinking, while Step 3 definitely requires you to be intuitive and holistic.[4] If this is true, throughout the creative process we need to access the left hemisphere sometimes, and at other times we need to access the right hemisphere.

Studies have shown that traditional schooling caters to activities requiring left-brain functions. As a result, the majority of people have dominant left hemispheres. This could be the answer to the previously posed question: Why do so few people demonstrate creative abilities? The right hemisphere desperately needs exercise to bring it to full capacity. Psychologists have suggested several strategies to strengthen right hemisphere processing. Some suggest doing exercises that enable us to suppress the left hemisphere long enough to let the right hemisphere's productions come through.[5]

The secret of right hemisphere access seems to be the ability to suspend judgment. That is very difficult for many of us. "Failure to suspend judgment while brainstorming is like trying to get hot and cold water from one faucet at the same time: the ideas are not hot enough; the criticism is not cold enough; so your results are tepid."[6]

When you observe creative people, what do you see? In Czan, you see the courage to look different. In Scott, certainly the courage to try something different. Kathy is clever and talented with hands-on projects. And Paul is effective and original in his ideas. Words such as unique, inventive, unusual, eccentric, confident, versatile, fearless, fluent, original—all bring to mind creativity.

Strategies for Enhancing Creativity

Technical marketing communication demands creative solutions. Your audience has been bombarded with messages to buy the latest software, upgrade to the fastest hardware, and sign up with the most popular Internet provider. It takes a creative approach to reach this media-saturated audience.

Theodore Levitt gives us insight into how creativity is crucial in marketing. He writes,

> Nothing drives progress like the imagination. The idea precedes the deed. . . . Ideas can be willed, and the imagination is their engine. . . . The marketing imagination is the starting point of success in marketing. It is distinguished from other forms of imagination by the unique insights it brings to understanding customers, their problems, and the means to capture their attention and their custom. By asserting that people don't buy things but buy solutions to problems, the marketing imagination makes an inspired leap from the obvious to the meaningful. "Meaning" resides in its implied suggestion as to what to do—in this case, find out what problems people are trying to solve. . . . It is characterized by Leo McGinneva's famous clarification about why people buy quarter-inch drill bits: "They don't want quarter-inch bits. They want quarter-inch holes."[7]

Later, Levitt explains that "imagination means to construct mental pictures of what is or is not actually present, what has never been actually experienced."[8]

To exercise the imagination is to be creative. It requires intellectual or artistic inventiveness. Anybody can do it, and most people often do—unfortunately, however, only in daydreams and fantasies, when they're not constrained by convention or conviction. To do it in business requires shedding these constraints but also discipline, especially the discipline of disassociation from what exists and what has been."[9]

So, how do you enhance your creative abilities? First, concentrate on the characteristics we have associated with creativity. Let's discuss versatility, fluency, and originality in detail.

Versatility

The heart of versatility is the attitude that there is more than one right answer. Versatility is especially important at the beginning of problem solving. It permits you to look at things from a different perspective while it prevents you from seeing the problem in the same stereotyped ways. Albert Szent-Györgyi, a noted biochemist says, "Discovery consists of seeing what everybody has seen and thinking what nobody has thought."[10]

When you exercise versatility, you increase your chances of generating fresh, new solutions. Versatility not only helps you solve the problem, but it also helps you discover the concept or theme for the final product. In the early stages of problem solving, you should break the pattern—do everything in your power to think of a unique way to solve the problem.

Rules tend to make us inflexible. We tend to impose imaginary boundaries that keep us from breaking out of the old pattern—the old way of doing things. The rules and restrictions that we unconsciously carry with us can prevent us from solving the problem. Just as children often color beyond the lines of the figures, we should strive not to be intimidated by boundaries—either real or imaginary. As you foster the characteristic of versatility, throw in a bit of fearlessness. Have the courage to color outside the lines.

Fluency

Creative people exhibit fluency—the ability to freely produce ideas while suspending all judgment. As a technical marketing communicator, you will often participate in brainstorming sessions. These sessions are usually done best in a small group of three to five people. Write all ideas down. Use flipcharts, blackboard, overhead transparencies, computers, or individual pads of paper. The most important thing is to follow the rules:

- Postpone and withhold your judgment of ideas.
- Encourage wild and exaggerated ideas.
- Quantity counts at this stage, not quality.
- Build on the ideas put forward by others.
- Every person and every idea has equal worth.

Brainstorming is probably the most familiar activity in searching for new ideas. The problem comes when you hear that little voice within you whispering in your ear "that was a really stupid idea," or "what makes you think that will work." The next time that small voice whispers in your ear, command it to be still. Right now, you don't need its help. (Later you do. It is always important to evaluate and bring critical judgment to a solution. You just shouldn't do it when you are exploring all your options.)

Another way to develop fluency is to try nonstop writing, the practice of writing without lifting your pen from the page. Nonstop writing can help you become more creative even in the planning stages—when you are just trying to come up with ideas. The very act of nonstop writing requires you to think as you are moving the pen or typing words on a keyboard. And that helps you develop the ability to think quickly—to have a steady stream of ideas coming into your head.

This activity, perfected by Peter Elbow, especially requires you to suspend judgment and to forget rules. That means don't worry about spelling, proper syntax, punctuation, cohesion, or coherence. So rid yourself of rules and restrictions and concentrate on getting words on paper. Elbow explains, "If you do free writing (nonstop writing) regularly, much or most of it will be far inferior to what you can produce through care and rewriting. But the good bits will be much better than anything else you can produce by any other method."[11] Again, just the act of nonstop writing will help you to develop fluency and your ideas will flow much faster.

You can seriously hinder the fluent flow of ideas if your mind is preoccupied or overly focused on anything. The idea is to loosen up, let go, and allow ideas to flow as freely as possible. You must make a conscious effort to prevent the censors from screening your ideas at this time. So relax and take several deep breaths. And then let the words and ideas flow freely.

Originality

Imagination and courage are important in originality. You need to develop the ability to originate ideas—which is the opposite of doing the same old thing. Originate means doing something that's never been done before or giving a new twist to the old way of doing things. And that's where the courage comes in. It takes courage to suggest a new way of doing things—to say nothing of the courage it takes to actually implement that new idea. When you are faced with a problem to solve—a new product to market—train yourself to think "every idea is a good one." As you develop this mind-set, you will begin to unlock the creative ideas that have lain dormant for so long.

Knowing Where to Apply Creativity

To say technical marketing communication should be permeated with creativity is not an overstatement. Because the world is saturated with both technology and communication, your message demands creativity to push through the deluge of other messages vying for the attention of your intended audience.

As you have read in the previous chapters, you begin your project by understanding the needs, the audience, and the strategy. Many times the technical marketing communicator will be working with a creative staff who take the plans and create the final project. It is important that the creative staff understand all that has gone into the planning. It sounds easy. It all depends on communication between the technical marketing communicators and the graphic designers. Right? But is it really that easy? Many a project has gone sour in the hands of the graphic designers—not because they are not good at what they do, but because they were not given the necessary information and background.

Dudnyk Advertising & Public Relations, located in Huntington, Indiana, uses a creative brief to communicate the important information to those who will be designing the project (see Fig. 6.1). This additional step is one that will help to ensure a successful project.

Creativity in the Planning Stage

Think outside the lines. Be courageous; don't be afraid to implement the unusual. If creativity is absent in the planning stage, all the creative content, images, and design will not be effective. It starts here—when creative ideas are most valuable.

One of our clients needed a limited set of individuals to participate in multiple projects, requiring careful time management. In order to plan for the next wave of project teams, leaders wanted to track the available skill sets and experience of all available co-workers. A complex—and very expensive—software database was created to track individual skill sets, training, and experience. Ironically, the system worked great, but individuals refused to take the time to enter their personal updates, and therefore, there was no information populating the database. When asked why, the employees said, "Too time consuming"; "We don't understand the process"; or "Too confusing to get passwords." The information technology developers thought it was intuitive and self-evident. The internal manager realized there was a communication breakdown and decided to try traditional marketing methods to promote the process and system to the employees. The company's own technical marketing communicators were called in to solve the problem.

This certainly called for a creative approach. After brainstorming, the group seized on the database acronym that sounded like an ocean sport and decided to base communication efforts on that theme. They used a water sport theme and graphic depiction across all aspects of the rollout. They placed surfboards and beach balls in the lobby to raise awareness and build interest. They announced that the first 20 employees to input their information into the database would receive tickets to the nearby water theme park. For two weeks before the rollout date, the system team made announcements at meetings wearing Hawaiian shirts and sunglasses. They created a quick reference card with the water sport theme and dropped it off at all computer monitors the day of the rollout. As each employee signed on to the system to input their information, they received a desktop premium related to water sports. The result: A 60 percent increase in skillset registration within one day of the promotion and a steady stream thereafter. Creativity brought results.

Dudnyk Advertising & Public Relations
Creative Brief

Date:	**Job #:**
Client:	**Product/Division:**

Job Description:

LONG-TERM DIRECTION   **Long-Term Position** (*How do we want to be perceived relative to competition?*)

Communications Strategy (*How will we create that perception?*)

SPECIFICS FOR THIS PROJECT   **Objective of Project** (*What is the specific purpose of this project?*)

Target Audience (*To whom are we talking? What behavior do we need to change?*)

Demographics

Psychographics *Values, attitudes, lifestyles, seasonality?*)

Purchase Behavior

Unique Buying Proposition *Relate what we know about the product to what we've learned about the target. What is the one most compelling reason for the target to change its behavior?*)

Support (*Clear, sharp, specific statements that support the proposition, i.e., product facts, research data, emotional data, unique benefits, and favorable market conditions.*)

Brand Personality

Call to Action

Mandatories

Media or Budget Considerations

Measurement

Figure 6.1 Creative brief.

Copyright 2000. Dudnyk Advertising & Public Relations. Used by permission.

Creativity in the Content

Find an original way to express your message. It is especially important to implement a creative concept that will attract the attention of your audience, enable them to clearly understand the message, and motivate them to take the desired action.

A creative concept is the approach used to package and present the message. It is evident in the content, images, and design.

Often when we speak of content, we are referring to the copy or text. Because text is made up of words, it's the choice and order of the words you use to convey your message that make up this part of the creative concept. For example, if your task is to create a technical marketing brochure or Web page, the following guidelines can help you develop a creative concept:

- Develop a theme that is specific to your product or service.
- Develop a theme that is specific to your audience.
- Make a list of words or phrases that reflect the theme.
- Determine the tone and nuances you want your audience to perceive through your marketing efforts.
- Make a list or sketch out rough graphic elements to compliment the choices you have already made in theme, words, phrases, and tone.
- Write a sample headline and a call to action to reflect the theme.
- Write other headings, to reflect the theme as much as possible.

Once you have completed this process, you have a creative concept. It might not be the *best* creative concept, but at least you have begun the process. Now, set that one aside, and start the process again with a totally new theme and carry that concept through to completion. Many marketing copywriters create three or four creative concepts to submit for approval before generating the actual piece itself.

Let's examine three brochures to illustrate the previous concepts. Datastream Systems, Inc., a South Carolina–based software firm, created a series of brochures

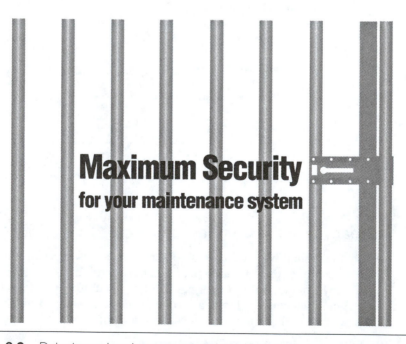

Figure 6.2   Datastream brochure cover marketed to prisons.
Copyright 1999. Datastream Systems, Inc. Used by permission.

S U R V I V A L   K I T

Figure 6.3   Datastream brochure cover marketed to hospitals.
Copyright 1999. Datastream Systems, Inc. Used by permission.

to market their database maintenance software application. Because a variety of audiences can use their application, they created each brochure specific to a particular audience niche.

Figure 6.2 shows the front of the brochure marketed specifically to prisons. Figure 6.3 shows the brochure cover aimed at hospitals, and Figure 6.4 shows the

Figure 6.4   Datastream brochure cover marketed to airlines.
Copyright 1999. Datastream Systems, Inc. Used by permission.

cover of the brochure directed to the airline industry. In each case, the cover copy makes use of words and graphics aimed specifically at the intended audience.

In Figures 6.5, 6.6, and 6.7, you see the inside of the brochures. Notice that the word choice and the graphics are also audience specific. The creative concept is carried through to the call to action. Each of the brochures has a tear-off reply card (not shown). The call to action in the prison brochure reads "Secure Your Future";

Peace of mind for your maintenance staff

If your system is handcuffed by inflexible practices, **Datastream's MP2** is the answer for you. We offer the most effective, results-producing computerized maintenance management software on the market - at prices that are a steal.

MP2 lets you keep track of your maintenance costs without the shackles of endless paperwork. MP2 can free you up for more important things. **Let the computer do the hard time.**

Would you expect any less from the World Leader in Maintenance Solutions?

You have the right to:

- Reduced downtime
- Computerized work/purchase orders
- Easy-to-use, graphic-based software
- Quick and easy set-up
- Automatic preventive task generation
- Streamlined maintenance operations

You are entitled to one phone call.

Use it wisely. Contact Datastream at **1.800.328.2636.** Visit www.dstm.com

Do you understand these rights as they've been given to you?

Datastream and MP2 are registered trademarks of Datastream Systems, Inc. Microsoft is a registered trademark of Microsoft Corporation. Oracle is a registered trademark of Oracle Corporation.

Figure 6.5   Datastream brochure inside copy marketed to prisons.
Copyright 1999. Datastream Systems, Inc. Used by permission.

"Datastream's MP2 Enterprise offered us the functionality and adaptability we needed and the sales and management team we demanded. The seamless integration of MP2 Enterprise into our existing facilities package will make the hospital even more responsive to maintenance-related needs and issues.

WE'LL TAKE CARE OF YOU!

With 14,800 inventory items and nearly 38,000 issued work orders to date–over 100 per day– the MP2 Enterprise and APRP link is invaluable to our hospital's success."

Dave Spurlin
Support Services
Network Manager
Huntsville Hospital

If you are interested in reducing downtime and increasing your profit margin, take a look at Datastream software. Datastream offers computerized maintenance management software at affordable prices... would you expect any less from the leader in maintenance software? Call Datastream to find out what our software has to offer!

For a Software **Emergency** Call **1.800.955.6775** or Fax **1.864.422.5000.**

Figure 6.6 Datastream brochure inside copy marketed to hospitals.
Copyright 1999. Datastream Systems, Inc. Used by permission.

the call to action in the hospital brochure reads "Prescription For Software," while the reader of the airline brochure is implored to "Test-Fly Our Software."

While these brochures are excellent examples of creativity in the printed word, we must not forget creativity is applied in all stages of technical marketing. As you exercise your creativity, you will begin to believe in ideas you previously would have discarded. You will find yourself suggesting a new approach, an original design—all with a touch of confidence.

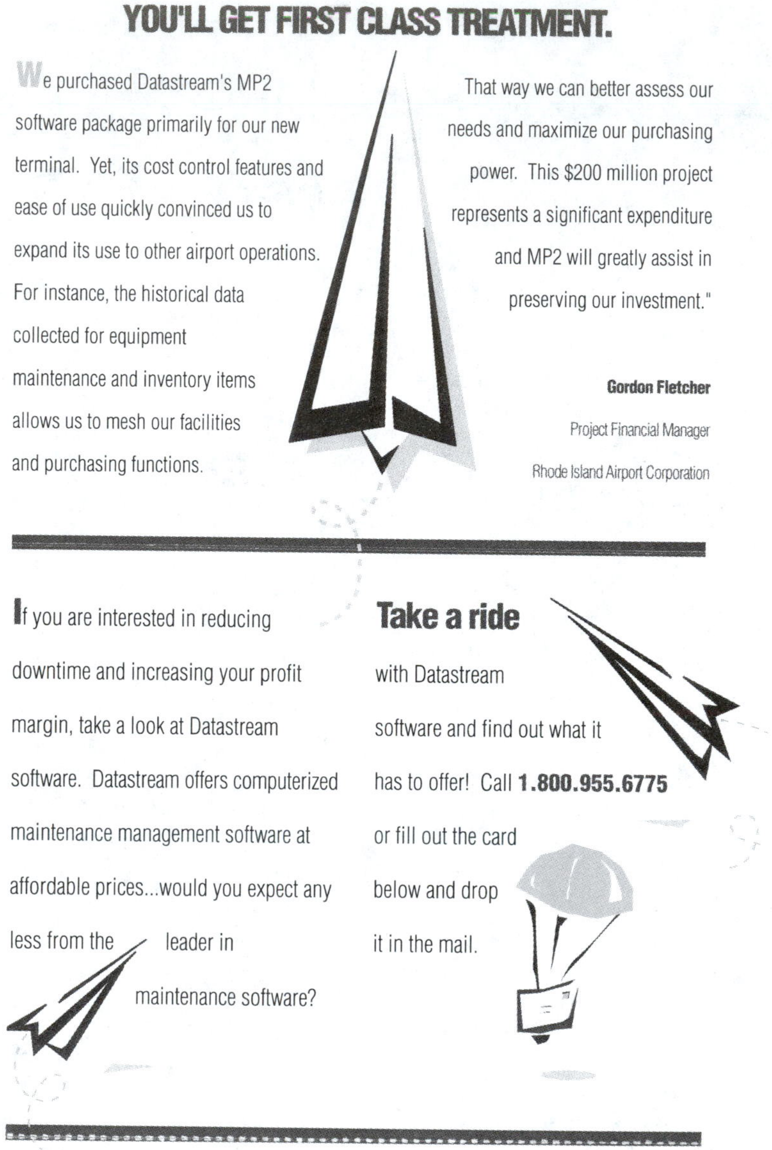

YOU'LL GET FIRST CLASS TREATMENT.

We purchased Datastream's MP2 software package primarily for our new terminal. Yet, its cost control features and ease of use quickly convinced us to expand its use to other airport operations. For instance, the historical data collected for equipment maintenance and inventory items allows us to mesh our facilities and purchasing functions.

That way we can better assess our needs and maximize our purchasing power. This $200 million project represents a significant expenditure and MP2 will greatly assist in preserving our investment."

Gordon Fletcher

Project Financial Manager

Rhode Island Airport Corporation

If you are interested in reducing downtime and increasing your profit margin, take a look at Datastream software. Datastream offers computerized maintenance management software at affordable prices...would you expect any less from the leader in maintenance software?

Take a ride

with Datastream software and find out what it has to offer! Call **1.800.955.6775** or fill out the card below and drop it in the mail.

Figure 6.7   Datastream brochure inside copy marketed to airlines.

Copyright 1999. Datastream Systems, Inc. Used by permission.

Summing It Up

- Anyone can be creative.
- The task is to access the right hemisphere of your brain and be versatile, fluent, and original.
- It is important to apply creativity throughout the technical marketing process, both in planning and implementing.

Applying What You've Learned

1. Define creativity in your own words.
2. How do you know when someone is creative?
3. Who is the most creative person you know? Why?
4. What puts you in a creative state of mind? Why?
5. What paralyzes your creative process? Why? How can you change or manage that?
6. Sit in front of a computer and write five sentences about the monitor. Then set a timer and write again for five minutes. Do no planning. Write nonstop.
7. Write five sentences about a PalmPilot. Now set a timer and write for five minutes. But first, take one minute to plan. Which activity was easier—Exercise 6 or Exercise 7? Why? Which produced the best material? Why?

SMALL GROUP ACTIVITY

Your company offers an excellent series of online training modules for most of the major software packages. Business has been slow. The manager pulls together a team of technical marketing communicators and tells them to come up with a creative approach to marketing these online modules. In your small group, hold a brainstorming session. One person should keep notes. Your task is to record as many solutions to the problem as possible. Remember, don't allow anyone to squelch the creativity of the group.

Notes

1. Paul Joseph Burgett, "On Creativity," *The Journal of Creative Behavior* 16 (1982): 239–49.
2. Roger Gehlbach, "Creativity and Instruction: The Problem of Task Design." *The Journal of Creative Behavior* 21 (1987): 34–47.
3. John T. Myers, "Hemisphericity Research: An Overview with Some Implications for Problem Solving." *The Journal of Creative Behavior* 16 (1982): 197–211.
4. Ibid.

5. Ibid.

6. Alex F. Osborn, *Applied Imagination*, 3rd ed. (New York: Charles Scribners, 1963), 156.

7. Theodore Levitt, *The Marketing Imagination* (New York: Macmillan, 1983), 127–28.

8. Ibid., 130.

9. Ibid.

10. J. D. Bernal, "The Place of Speculation in Modern Technology and Science," in *The Scientist Speculates: An Anthology of Partly-Baked Ideas*, ed. I. J. Good. (New York: Basic Books, 1962), 15.

11. Peter Elbow, *Writing Without Teachers* (London: Oxford University Press, 1973), 9.

CHAPTER 7

Print Media

Overview

"Something is wrong with this communication scheme," I thought.

It was my first day on the job at a mid-sized company specializing in technical marketing communication. Of course, I was nervous. But everyone was friendly and helpful as they showed me to the desk where I would spend the next ten weeks. And it was just that—a desk. No computer. No phone. Just a desk.

The human resource person in charge of my onboarding explained that I needed to fill out forms for employee benefits, personal information, and request forms for a computer, a password, a phone, a voice mail account, and just about anything else I would need. Smiling, she turned to leave. "Excuse me," I called after her, "where do I get these request forms?"

"Oh, we've just put them all online. You'll find them on our Intranet. We've just finished the process; you're the first one to use it," she called over her shoulder.

I sat there staring at my empty desk. "Something is wrong with this communication scheme," I thought. Everything is on the Intranet, and I have no computer. The solution was simple: their high tech, online process was going to have to start with good, old-fashioned paper.

Sandi

Why Choose Print?

Since 1993, futurists have predicted the demise of print. They told us technology would change forever how we communicated. It was obvious we wouldn't need the large four-drawer filing cabinets because we would save everything on disk. However, since that time one of my colleagues has purchased three new filing cabinets for her office, and each one is full of computer printouts. The technological revolution is in large part responsible for the growth of print rather than its projected demise. We still use print to push electronic media as you see dot-com companies advertised in magazines such as *PC World, Internet World,* and *Fast Company.*

One computer executive told of an expensive TV commercial shoot. The company was touting their electronic connectivity for people and businesses. At the climax of the commercial's story line, an office worker learned of a crucial, last minute date change for the big meeting, thanks to an electronic conference call connection. Then, as this executive explained the story, to the horror of the marketing team watching the finished video clip, the actor in the commercial dutifully wrote down the new meeting date in her paper calendar book. So much for a paperless society!

A word of caution is in order. Although print media has enjoyed a great measure of success, in the age of information glut it is critical that unannounced print media messages finding their way into mailboxes do not simply end up in the wastebasket. All the glitzy design features in the world will be wasted if the pieces are never read, to say nothing of the many dollars spent to create them.

After you have determined your needs, targeted your audience, and created a strategic marketing plan, you can determine the value of print media in the particular marketing endeavor facing you. You should use print media for the following reasons:

- To complement other media choices
- To reach audiences who have no other media access (i.e., Internet connections)
- To place information pointers and talk sheets in the hands of your sales teams

If print media is the answer, then you need to plan carefully to ensure that the piece will be read and not tossed in the wastebasket. In this chapter, you will discover how to create some of the more popular tactical tools in the marketing field, attracting readers and accomplishing your purpose in the process.

Brochures

Why choose a brochure? What will a brochure do for you that another marketing tool will not? If you are going to be successful in your marketing effort, you need to know the answer to these questions. It all goes back to the plan: what are your goals and purpose? Who is your audience? What is your strategy?

If your purpose is to inform, educate, or motivate and you need to provide important or critical information in a compact form, your tactic of choice could be the brochure. For many technical sales teams, having a brochure is still as important as having a Web site. Not everyone outside the dot-com and information technology industry is anxious to search down your company profile online. And from a sales standpoint, it never hurts to have something sitting on a procurement manager's desk, even if it's only for a few hours after your meeting. A brochure could be just the thing needed.

One technical sales team's primary brochure objective was simply to brandish their partnership with a leading telecommunications firm. Skeptical prospects would otherwise doubt their claim to be playing in the telco's space. The team's technical marketing communicators took great pain to gain approval to use the telco's name and logo in close proximity to their own company logo on the brochure page. There was much less attention paid to the rest of the brochure's layout and copy!

After you have determined that a brochure will help you to accomplish your overall goals, you need to get specific about the subobjectives you want to accomplish with this particular brochure. Your stated objectives should be measurable. If possible, include weighted criteria by which you can measure your success. If your objective has a measurable result, it should be specific enough that people will recognize its outcome. For example, if you print and distribute 10,000 copies, how many sales calls will be generated? Of these, how many will result in quotes? In closed contracts? How much revenue could potentially be generated by this effort or in combination with other parts of your communication plan?

The Content

It is not unusual that you would want to jump right in and begin designing a brochure. It is tempting to sit down at the computer and play with different looks. Perhaps you will use a creative shape. Resist the urge to design your brochure before you have determined the content. Design is important but the primary purpose of the design is to make content accessible. Substance comes before form. In fact, let substance drive your design decisions.

Text Versus Graphics

Graphics and the brochure's look are your palette to portray strength, vision, stability, flair, edge, and style. Yet white space—the unoccupied part of your canvas—is equally important to build drama and breathing room for your chosen message. Inexperienced technology teams are continuously tempted to fill that space with text. "We have so much to say!" But sage technical marketing communicators will preserve the space and the impact of the piece. Just scan a top-shelf ad agency's own corporate brochure. Expect to see single sentences or phrases on a page, coupled with perfectly matched images.

Substance ultimately drives design decisions. When dealing with *technical* marketing, you have to be very sensitive to information best communicated in graphics rather than in text. Explore the possibilities of delivering your content via graphs, tables, charts, and other elements. Charts, graphs, and diagrams are especially effective when you are presenting numbers and statistical data. Pie charts are used when presenting percentages. Your readers would prefer to view a figure than to read a paragraph full of numbers. Numerical data is more easily remembered in graphical form. Keep the graphic as simple as possible and don't forget to include a caption under the graphic to tell readers the significance of the data.

Features and Benefits

In *The Marketing Plan: How to Prepare and Implement It*, William Luther explains the difference between features and benefits as follows:

> Features are special characteristics that make one product different from another. These features include what the product is; how it is made; how it is used; its history, appearance, merchandising plan, or service. Benefits are the end results—what the

Figure 7.1   eFunds brochure copy.
Copyright 2000. eFunds Corporation. Used by permission.

product will do for the customer. Customers don't usually buy products. They buy ideas—mental pictures of results, such as saving time or money, convenience, pride, prestige, less work and worry, or pleasure. Retailers look for products to increase their sales and profits.

Your company manufactures products but sells benefits. One salesperson expressed it this way: Don't only tell your customer how good (*sic*) you make your goods, tell him how good your goods make him. Unless the customer already has had some experience with the product, it is not safe to assume the customer knows the benefits of each product feature. What is quite obvious to the salesperson may not be so to the customer.

The more product knowledge salespeople have, the more careful they must be to slow down sales conversation enough to include a benefit at the end of each feature. Benefits and product features go together. Neither can stand alone. Both are necessary in every sales presentation.[1]

For example, *conditional text* is a **feature** of Adobe FrameMaker 5.5. The **benefit** is that you can prepare multiple variations of a document in a single file, thus

How will you **respond** to these **marketplace demands...**

while still **maintaining control** of your ACH business?

Capture the potential of the new economy - Spearheaded by the phenomenal growth of new payment options, eCommerce, Internet banking and emerging applications, ACH is rapidly becoming a preferred transaction method for individuals and businesses alike. Does your in-house ACH processing system have the capacity to accommodate this explosive growth – and not become obsolete overnight?

Contain costs - In-house ACH processing systems represent fixed costs... that are rising. And upgrading existing systems often requires extensive lead time. Do you have the time and resources needed to upgrade technology, staff operational and maintenance facilities, and invest in costly software licenses?

Manage the evolution of the revolution - ACH processing continues to evolve to meet emerging payment needs, including new forms of debit transactions like electronic checks, re-presented checks and lockbox check truncation. As online commerce and electronic payments continue to grow, will your ACH processing system be responsive, boost profitability and deliver first-rate customer care?

Enhance Risk Management - Along with skyrocketing ACH growth comes increased exposure to financial risk, especially for those transactions you originate for your corporate customers. Can you identify your exposure for the total corporate relationship relating to return items, items originated but not yet settled, or aggregated risks?

eFunds can help!
Our comprehensive, flexible ACH solution helps you reduce costs and increase revenues – without compromising quality.

Figure 7.2   eFunds brochure copy.

Copyright 2000. eFunds Corporation. Used by permission.

maximizing efficiency. Notice when expressing a benefit, the word *you* is extremely important. It tells the reader *what's in it for me*. This concept is often referred to as the *you attitude*. You need to focus on clear benefits and not just features.

If your copy is not sprinkled with the words *you* or *yours*, it will be full of *I*, *we*, and *our*. The latter is writer centered, but the copy sprinkled with *you* and *yours* is clearly written with the customer in mind. Writer-centered writing sounds like this: We are a full service agency dedicated to doing much, much more than simply making your airline reservation. We take care of the planning, including airline, hotel, and car rental arrangements, quickly and efficiently. The same idea in *you attitude* reads like this: We think you're too busy to spend time standing in line at the airport. Let us take care of your complete planning, including your airline, your hotel, and your car rental arrangements. And you'll get results quickly and efficiently.

The two-page spread in Figures 7.1 and 7.2 illustrates how eFunds, located in Minneapolis, Minnesota, presented the features and benefits of their ACH Processing Services. Notice on the left page, the following features are highlighted:

- Accelerating
- Expensive
- Ever-changing
- Subject to risk

Opposite those features you will find the benefits with details about each one:

- Capture the potential of the new economy
- Contain costs
- Manage the evolution of the revolution
- Enhance risk management

Later in the same brochure, eFunds effectively uses the you attitude (see Fig. 7.3).

The Creative Concept

After you have determined the message you wish to communicate in the brochure, it is important to develop a creative concept. Some refer to the creative concept as the *theme*. Allen M. Cobrin refers to it as the *treatment:* "It's a term used by scriptwriters to describe the flavor and content of a proposed script. The *Dictionary of Film and Television Terms* defines treatment as, 'a written summary of a film script that includes brief descriptions of the characters and the principal sequences around which the plot will be developed, as well as some action and dialog.'"[2] The treatment, the theme, or the creative concept is the idea that the brochure is designed around. It determines the cover design as well as the cover headline. It drives the decisions about headings, body copy, and graphics. In Chapter 6, we looked at a set of brochures designed by Datastream Systems, Inc. (see Figs. 6.2 through 6.7). Notice how the headings and the text change to meet the needs of the particular audience.

A student in a technical marketing class created a brochure to advertise a popular help-authoring software program. Recognizing that creating an effective help system can be a painful experience, she chose a creative concept that was brilliant in its simplicity. In Figure 7.4, you see the cover of the brochure. The understatement and the simplicity of the graphic draw the reader to open the brochure. Figure 7.5 shows the next page the reader encounters. On the next page, the reader sees the package of a familiar help authoring tool and the text reads simply "This will." On the final page, the student provides features, benefits, and an effective call to action. Who says today's universities aren't producing bright, young talent?

Call to Action

Because you are writing towards a goal—to inform, to educate, or to motivate—you need to call your readers to specific action. Exactly what is it you want them to do after reading this brochure? Your list of specific, measurable objectives should tell you. Do you want the readers to call, to attend, to purchase? If so, then ask them to do exactly what you want them to do. For example, a college textbook

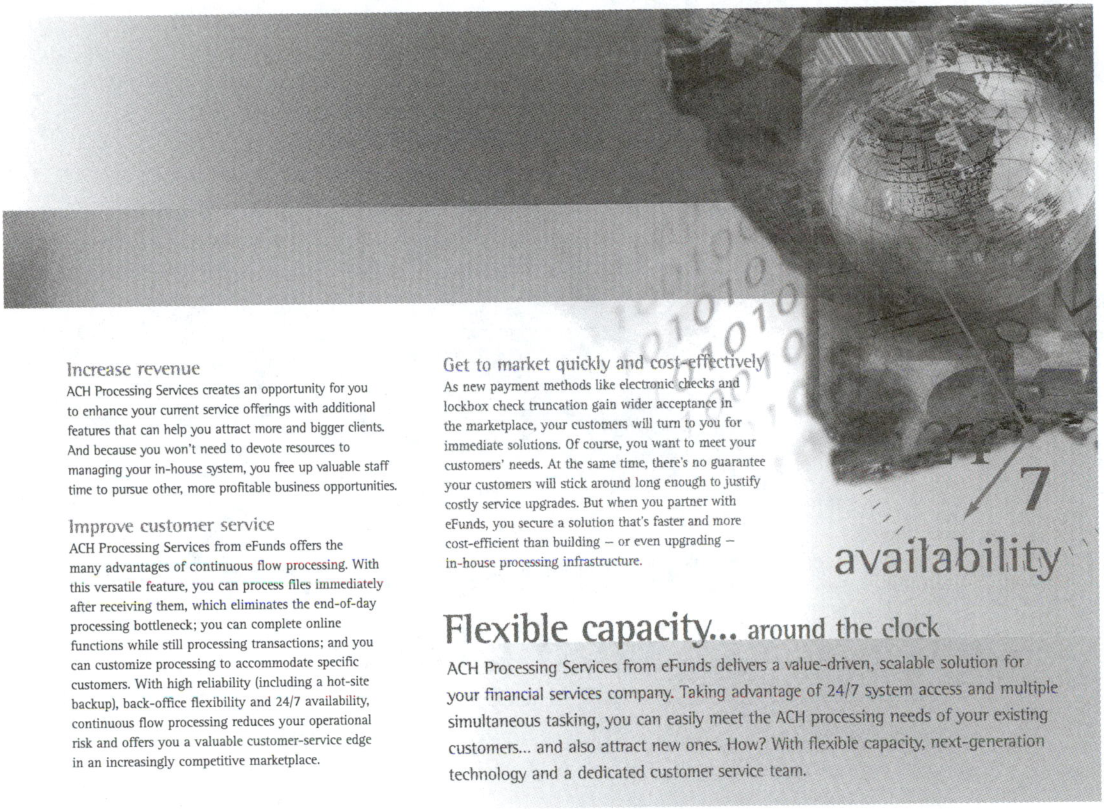

Increase revenue

ACH Processing Services creates an opportunity for you to enhance your current service offerings with additional features that can help you attract more and bigger clients. And because you won't need to devote resources to managing your in-house system, you free up valuable staff time to pursue other, more profitable business opportunities.

Improve customer service

ACH Processing Services from eFunds offers the many advantages of continuous flow processing. With this versatile feature, you can process files immediately after receiving them, which eliminates the end-of-day processing bottleneck; you can complete online functions while still processing transactions; and you can customize processing to accommodate specific customers. With high reliability (including a hot-site backup), back-office flexibility and 24/7 availability, continuous flow processing reduces your operational risk and offers you a valuable customer-service edge in an increasingly competitive marketplace.

Get to market quickly and cost-effectively

As new payment methods like electronic checks and lockbox check truncation gain wider acceptance in the marketplace, your customers will turn to you for immediate solutions. Of course, you want to meet your customers' needs. At the same time, there's no guarantee your customers will stick around long enough to justify costly service upgrades. But when you partner with eFunds, you secure a solution that's faster and more cost-efficient than building — or even upgrading — in-house processing infrastructure.

Flexible capacity... around the clock

ACH Processing Services from eFunds delivers a value-driven, scalable solution for your financial services company. Taking advantage of 24/7 system access and multiple simultaneous tasking, you can easily meet the ACH processing needs of your existing customers... and also attract new ones. How? With flexible capacity, next-generation technology and a dedicated customer service team.

Figure 7.3   eFunds brochure copy.

company created a brochure to market a new text for teaching WordPerfect for Windows. The brochure was mailed to college professors who teach the courses. The cover headline read, "If you could visualize the perfect windows treatment, this would be the book." The creative concept played on the words *Perfect* and *Windows.* They used the following headings throughout the brochure:

- A Clear View for Your Students
- A Keen Perspective on Pedagogy
- The Perfect Visual Aid
- The Perfect Tools for You

The call to action was strong and fit well into the creative concept: *Don't miss this window of opportunity for your students: Send for your complimentary copy of this text today!*

Following the call to action, the publisher provided a tear-off, self-addressed, stamped return card to make that action easier for the reader. The call to action

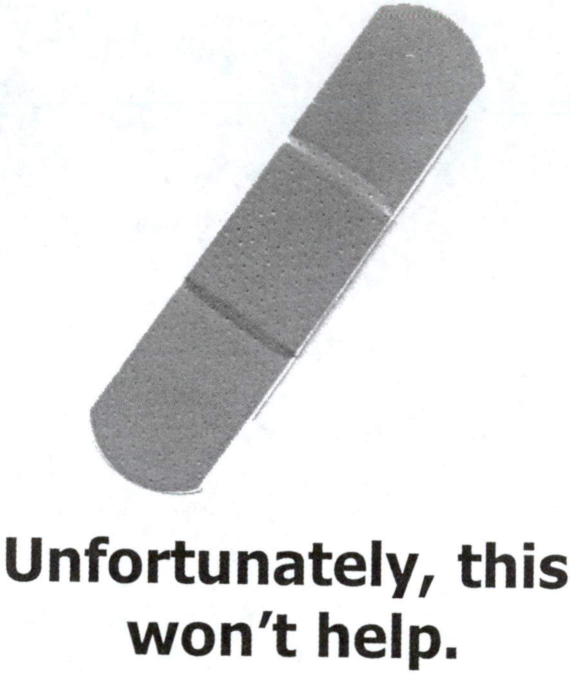

Unfortunately, this won't help.

Figure 7.4   Front cover of brochure for authoring help system.
Used by permission of Jennifer L. Roley.

These won't help either.

Figure 7.5   Page 2 of brochure for authoring help system.
Used by permission of Jennifer L. Roley.

should be clear and provide all necessary information for the reader to take the desired action. It can be a single statement or a paragraph usually found at the end of the brochure.

Tips for Better Brochures

When designing brochures, take advantage of the beginning and the end to accomplish your purposes. Beginning with a strong cover will attract many readers. If they don't choose to pick it up in the first place, your message is lost. Ending with a strong call to action leaves readers with the final urge to act on the message they have just read.

Remember these tips for better brochures:

- Start selling on the cover. Use this opportunity to communicate the most important benefit to your reader.
- Organization of content is important. Think in terms of a beginning, a middle, and an end.
- Strive for a personal tone. Use the word *you* frequently. Use short words, short sentences, (not always complete sentences) and a natural, relaxed, friendly style.
- Stress benefits, not features.
- Be specific.
- Support your claims by using testimonials.
- Keep content lively by using crisp paragraphs, headings, and subheadings.
- Keep content relevant to the creative concept.
- Verify the accuracy of your technical information.
- Don't forget details such as the logo, company name, address, phone number, location, and Web URLs.

Product Sheets

As a subset of brochures, product sheets offer very specific features and benefits of a particular technology or methodology. They are different from brochures because they carry less of a general message and are usually tucked into the folder next to the corporate brochure or as part of an information packet. Product sheets are usually one page, printed on both sides. They offer technical specifications, features, and benefits of the product or service. When marchFIRST, a leading global Internet professional services firm (now known as divine), formed a partnership with NetVendor for the delivery of e-commerce solutions, they created a product sheet to market e-channel solutions (see Fig. 7.6). In the following paragraph taken from the product sheet, notice that the focus of the content is on ben-

Powerful Partners for B2B e-Commerce

Today, A Powerful Partnership Can Deliver Unprecedented Value.

That's why NetVendor™, the recognized leader in providing e-Channel management solutions, and marchFIRST®, one of the fastest growing IT consulting and integration firms in the country, have formed a partnership for the delivery of e-commerce solutions.

NetVendor's e-Channel solutions allow suppliers to support multiple Internet distribution channels to different groups of trading partners – and with marchFIRST providing implementation and legacy integration – customers gain affordable access to a new and global marketplace with unparalleled IT support.

Powerful e-Channel Solutions
NetVendor's sell-side solutions enable you to leverage the Internet to complement your traditional sales channels with online channels. NetVendor's e-Channel solutions link multiple Web channels with your existing sales, marketing, service, and distribution assets, allowing you to simultaneously manage product distribution, product promotion and customer interaction. This combination yields unprecedented capabilities for reaching and serving trading partners through a collaborative B2B e-commerce platform.

Figure 7.6   Product sheet.
marchFIRST is a registered trademark of marchFIRST, Inc. ©2000.

efits and carefully involves the reader with a liberal use of the words *you* and *yours*. (Words conveying the you attitude are in bold type.)

> NetVendor's sell-side solutions enable **you** to leverage the Internet to complement **your** traditional sales channels with online channels. NetVendor's e-Channel solutions link multiple Web channels with **your** existing sales, marketing, service, and distribution assets, allowing **you** to simultaneously manage product distribution, product promotion and customer interaction. This combination yields unprecedented capabilities for reaching and serving trading partners through a collaborative B2B e-commerce platform. NetVendor's comprehensive e-Channel solutions also expand **your** global opportunities through easy access to leading net markets and digital marketplaces. By adding e-Channels to **your** current business practices **you** can tap new and worldwide markets, meet competitive challenges, gain efficiencies and increase customer satisfaction and retention. **Your** company's investment in effective e-Channel strategies and NetVendor's e-business solutions give **you** the advantage **you** need to ensure future success in a competitive marketplace.

Features and benefits are highlighted in the product sheet IBM created to market their NetVista X40i all-in-one product (see Fig. 7.7). The feature begins each paragraph in bold type:

- Space savings in style
- Powerful desktop technology
- Internet-optimized
- Completing the solution

The benefits follow in each paragraph:

- Quick, easy setup
- Lets you store the keyboard beneath the monitor
- Drives tuck away when not in use
- Ability to add accessories with ease
- Easy connection to the e-world
- Instant information exchange
- Allows you to swap storage drives
- Can travel with you to be used on other USB-based PCs
- Fast, easy connection to the online world

The back of NetVista's product sheet offers the reader the technical specifications required for use of their product (see Fig. 7.8). This information provides the sales team the necessary tool to leave behind on the manager's desk.

When you are creating product sheets, remember that the same characteristics of effective brochures apply here: short paragraphs, short line length, ample white space, and the you attitude.

IBM NetVista X40i all-in-one

Highlights

NEW!
Space savings in style
Simplicity is key to the IBM NetVista™ all-in-one X40i. Traditional desktop components offer full functionality in a space-saving design. This sleek all-in-one system features an integrated 15-inch TFT flat panel display—and it's virtually cord-free for quick, easy setup. Plus, the system's unique pedestal design lets you store the keyboard beneath the monitor, and the drives tuck away when not in use.

Powerful desktop technology
Proving that you don't have to sacrifice performance for style, the NetVista all-in-one offers your choice of powerful Intel® Pentium® III or Intel Celeron™ processors; diskette and CD-ROM or DVD-ROM drives; premium built-in speakers, and up to a 15GB[1] hard disk drive. An extremely expandable all-in-one system, the IBM NetVista X40i also has two PCI slots and 5 USB ports so you can add accessories with ease.

NEW!
Internet-optimized
NetVista all-in-one systems are optimized for easy connection to the e-world with eight colorful, programmable keys delivering one-button access to the Internet, selected Web browsers, book-marks and more. And whether you network via built-in 10/100 Ethernet, or

connect remotely through the standard 56K modem[2], optional ADSL[3], or cable, these systems support your choice of connectivity to ensure instant information exchange.

Completing the solution
Many exciting Options by IBM can enhance your computing experience, including the new USB Portable Drive Bay 2000 that allows you to swap storage drives (e.g., CD-RW, Zip drive or a second hard drive) with IBM ThinkPad® notebooks. And, since it implements USB technology, portable storage can travel with you to be used on other USB-based PCs.

The IBM NetVista X40i all-in-one system delivers unprecedented style and simplicity in a space-saving design. Ideal for the home office, you'll find this design doesn't compromise performance for looks, and it's fully optimized for fast, easy connection to the online world.

ⓔ business tools

Figure 7.7   Product sheet front side.

Reproduced by permission of IBM Corp. Copyright 2000. Pricing, offerings, and specifications are for illustrative purposes only and may not be available from IBM.

IBM NetVista X40i technical specifications

	Check detailed specifications at: **ibm.com**/netvista
Model	2179
Mechanical size (WxDxH)	16.26"x10.27"x16.29" (413mmx261mmx414mm)
Integrated monitor	15.0" Active Matrix Thin Film Transistor (TFT) Flat Panel color display
Processor	Intel Pentium III 600MHz[4] or Intel Celeron 533MHz
Memory (std/max)	64MB/512MB SDRAM
Graphics	SiS UltraAGP integrated
Hard disk drives	15 or 10GB S.M.A.R.T.[5] III Ultra ATA/66
Ethernet	Integrated 10/100
CD-ROM/ DVD-ROM drive	24X-10X[6] CD-ROM or 6X[6] max DVD-ROM
Diskette drive	1.44MB
Business audio	Integrated AC 97 with hardware acceleration: Line-in, line-out, MIDI
Slots	(2) low profile PCI slots
Ports	(5) USB on system; (2) USB on Rapid Access III Keyboard
Software[7]	Microsoft Windows 98 Second Edition, Lotus SmartSuite® license[8], IBM Product Recovery and Diagnostics CD, Norton AntiVirus™ (OEM version), Access IBM, PC-Doctor™, ConfigSafe®
Options by IBM	IBM Portable Drive Bay 2000 (19K4480); IBM NetVista USB-Parallel Printer Cable (19K4164); IBM 4X/4X/20X CD-RW Ultrabay 2000 Drive (00N8252); IBM Multi-Port USB Hub (00N8215) Visit **ibm.com**/options for a complete list of compatible options.
Standards supported	FCC Part 15, Class B (Class A when Ethernet in use); UL 1950 Third No.950; ISO 9241 capable; ANSI S12.10

Need more information?

General	1 800 IBM-7255 (U.S.)
Reseller	1 800 IBM-7255 ext. 4750
Canada	1 800 IBM-2255
Buy Direct	1 888 SHOP IBM (U.S.)
	1 800 411 1WEB (Canada)
IBM Fax	1 800 IBM-3395 (U.S.)
	Doc#11135

World Wide Web
ibm.com/netvista

Reminders for Year 2000 Readiness
ibm.com/pc/year2000 (worldwide)

© Copyright IBM Corporation 2000

Printed in the United States of America
4-00
All Rights Reserved.

IBM, the e-business logo, NetVista, ThinkPad and Wake on LAN are trademarks of IBM Corporation in the United States and/or other countries. Microsoft and Windows are trademarks of Microsoft Corporation. Celeron, Intel and Pentium are trademarks of Intel Corporation. Lotus Notes, Lotus SmartSuite and the SmartSuite logo are trademarks of Lotus Development Corporation. Other trademarks are the properties of their respective companies.

IBM reserves the right to alter specifications and other product information without prior notice. This publication could include technical inaccuracies and typographical errors. References herein to IBM products and services do not imply that IBM intends to make them available in other countries. IBM PROVIDES THIS PUBLICATION "AS IS" WITHOUT WARRANTY OF ANY KIND, EITHER EXPRESS OR IMPLIED, INCLUDING THE IMPLIED WARRANTIES OF MERCHANTABILITY OR FITNESS FOR A PARTICULAR PURPOSE. Some jurisdictions do not allow disclaimer of express or implied warranties in certain transactions; therefore this disclaimer may not apply to you.

Made in Scotland, Japan, Mexico, Australia or Brazil or assembled in the U.S. of U.S. and non-U.S. components.

Printed on recycled paper containing 10% recovered post-consumer fiber.

G221-6330-00

---

[1] GB equals one billion bytes when referring to hard disk drive capacity. Accessible capacity may be less depending on operating environments.

[2] These 56K modems are designed to be capable of receiving data at up to 56Kbps with compatible phone line and server equipment and transmitting data at up to 312Kbps. Public networks currently limit download speeds to about 53Kbps. Actual speeds vary and are often less than the maximum.

[3] ADSL runs over existing phone lines. In order to gain access to this service, the user, phone company, and Internet Service Provider must deploy ADSL technology in their own network. Actual speeds depend on many factors and are often less than the maximum possible.

[4] MHz only measures microprocessor internal clock speed, not application performance. Other factors also affect application performance.

[5] Self-Monitoring, Analysis and Reporting Technology

[6] Variable read rate. Actual playback speed will vary, and is often less than the maximum possible.

[7] Some software may differ from its retail version (if available), and may not include user manuals or all program functionality. Warranty, service and support for non-IBM products are provided directly to you by third parties, not IBM. IBM makes no representations or warranties regarding non-IBM products. For non-IBM software applicable third-party software licenses may apply.

[8] Diskettes and hard copy documentation are available at an additional charge. CD may be free of charge depending on country.

Figure 7.8   Product sheet back side.

Reproduced by permission of IBM Corp. Copyright 2000. Pricing, offerings, and specifications are for illustrative purposes only and may not be available from IBM.

Newsletters

If your purpose is to bring in new customers, keep in touch with existing customers, and sell ideas, products, or services, your tactic of choice could be the newsletter. Newsletters are especially effective when informing and educating your audience and establishing expertise and credibility. So, if this is what you are trying to accomplish, then you have chosen wisely. But beware of the classic newsletter pitfall. Can you sustain interesting, compelling articles for more than one issue? Who will be accountable to ensure that topics are forthcoming? If you or your sponsor can't answer these questions, consider other media. Much of what is true for brochures is true for newsletters:

- Identify specific, measurable objectives for your newsletter.
- Determine the message first and then make design decisions.
- Be sensitive to information better communicated in graphics than in text.
- Focus on benefits and not just features.

Understanding Newsletter Jargon

When you are ready to produce a newsletter, it helps if you understand the jargon associated with this print media. That doesn't mean you can't generate an effective newsletter if you don't know the difference between the *gutter* and the *alley*. If you are turning your newsletter over to a graphic designer and he or she asks if you want to break over the alley, you'll be able to answer without wondering what any of this has to do with the alley running beside the building. Figure 7.9 identifies the terminology associated with newsletters.

The Name

Your readers will notice the name of your newsletter first. Don't waste that moment. Choose a name to communicate your uniqueness. Avoid generic names such as *News Brief*, *Update*, and *Outlook*. The reader will know nothing about your product or service by such a name. To determine an appropriate name, go back to your objectives and purpose for the newsletter. Above all, be creative. Take this opportunity to brainstorm. Play with words until you get just the right name. Choose carefully because this decision will drive many other decisions.

The Tagline

You should use the tagline to identify the sponsoring organization because in doing so you identify your audience. Some taglines tell the readers why they should read the newsletter by including a benefit. One newsletter entitled *News Splash* includes a benefit in the following tagline: "Tips for painless pool maintenance for homeowners." The United Parcel Service calls its newsletter *RoundUPS* and uses this tagline: "Published quarterly for customers & friends of United Parcel Service."

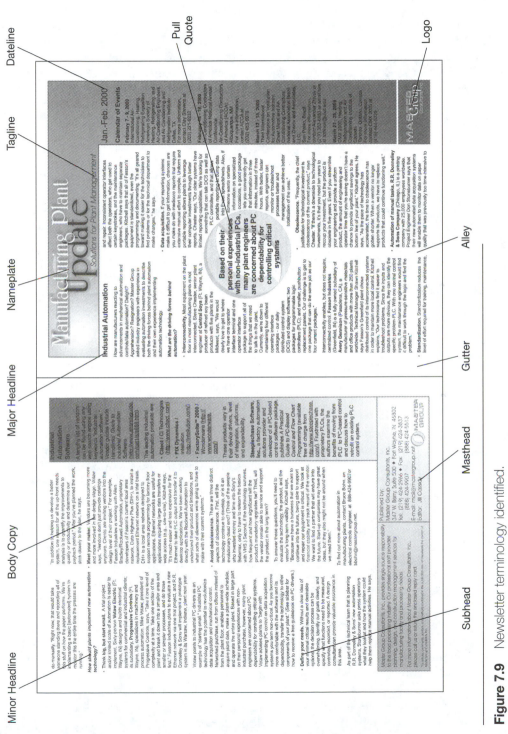

Figure 7.9 Newsletter terminology identified.

Copyright 2000. Master Group Consultants, Inc. Used by permission.

The Content

As in the brochure, you must refrain from jumping right in and designing a newsletter. After you have chosen a name, it is tempting to sit down at the computer and play with different looks. You might try a two-column format or a three-column format. Resist the urge to design your newsletter before you have determined the content. Again, design is important, but primarily to make content accessible. Substance comes before form. In fact, let substance drive your design decisions.

Types of Articles

When you consider all the kinds of information you can put in a newsletter, let this principle guide you: include only the information to help you to achieve your goals in a timely fashion. For example, one technical firm's goal for their internal newsletter was to enhance the feeling of open communications. One of the newsletter's most appreciated features, according to employee feedback, was the photo and biography section for new employees. Another company encouraged readership by sponsoring monthly raffles for the first people to identify certain key words in each issue. The key words resided in content of key importance.

When your newsletter is intended for customers, the following types of articles are useful.

1. *Articles that sell or promote your product.* It's all about features and benefits as you have read earlier in this chapter. To enhance the selling power of your newsletter announce pricing, discounts, or terms. Let your customers sell for you by including testimonials and customer profiles demonstrating how they have used your product effectively.
2. *Articles that provide technical support or insight to your customers.* You can provide technical information to customers in a regular column appearing in each issue. If the information is too technical for all your readers, consider providing information in an insert. Other kinds of support information might be how-to lists, ways to make better use of your products or services, toll-free numbers, and other ways for your readers to get technical support.
3. *Articles that inform your customers about your organization and enhance relationships.* Always keep your readers informed about your company and what's happening there. You can include an executive editorial, staff introductions, and marketing milestones achieved by your organization.

However, if you were writing your newsletter for an internal audience, your content would be different. You might profile a particular department or a specific achievement of a team. Qwest Communication, Inc. in Columbus, Ohio, recently initiated an internal newsletter. Their first issue had the following content:

- Feature article on the front page describing the achievements of the engineering team written by the senior vice president

- A short article describing a successful completion of a project by the Cyber Center PM team
- Announcement that the budget process was beginning
- An article about telecommuting with speed—something many Qwest employees would find interesting
- Congratulations to the employee (with picture) who won the name-the-newsletter competition
- A light-hearted corporate cartoon

On the back of the four-page newsletter, Qwest welcomes new hires and announces internal job changes (see Fig. 7.10).

The Layout and Design

Once you have your content, it is time to consider the design of your newsletter. You should design so the newsletter can be easily converted to PDF files for online use. Research tells us we have only 15 seconds to catch our reader's attention. Design elements help you accomplish that.

The Nameplate

The nameplate is the first thing your readers see and it will solidify their first impression of your organization. You can't have a well-designed newsletter without an effective nameplate, and an effective nameplate will compensate for a newsletter created with a limited budget. The nameplate consists of a stylized version of the name of your newsletter and the tagline. It can also include illustrations, logos, and volume and number information.

Follow these tips for an effective nameplate:

- Set the name in strong typography.
- Make the name the largest element (you should be able to read it from 10 feet away).
- Use bold type for the tagline and place it directly above or below the name.
- Use a bleed if your budget allows.

Masthead

Many people confuse the nameplate with the masthead. The masthead is usually a box containing all the publishing, copyright, and circulation information of the publication. It is also a good place to include names, addresses, and contact information. If datelines are not included in the nameplate, they should be included in the masthead.

Columns

The number of columns you can use in your design varies although most newsletters are two or three columns. Since a line length of 35 to 45 characters is the most comfortable to read, let that guide your decision. Obviously, the longest lines appear in a one-column format; using more than three columns would produce a

The Connection

Program Management Office News   *Vol. 1, Issue 1 • August 2000*

Around the world in 90 days
Engineering goes far in second quarter

by Mike Perusse, Senior Vice-President, Worldwide Network Engineering

I would like to take this opportunity to thank everyone on the Engineering team for our incredible 2Q accomplishments. From normal day-to-day activities to the 271 merger efforts, our organization has proven once again that we are consistently able to exceed expectations and do whatever is required to get the job done. I am proud to be associated with this team that has consistently achieved the highest levels of professionalism and performance!

In particular, I would like to highlight the efforts of those individuals involved in the 271 merger effort. Our team worked relentlessly, both throughout the quarter and especially during the last two weeks of 2Q, to ensure that the merger was completed on time with minimal impact on our customers. Once again, Engineering exceeded expectations and made a seemingly impossible goal achievable in record time!

Next, I would like to thank each of you for your dedication to accomplishing our other 2Q goals — as a result of our superior accomplishments, the corporation has rewarded our SBU (Engineering) with a quarterly bonus percentage of 125%! Below is a brief sample of the many highlights our team produced during the quarter:

Narrowband. Switch ports in the Network were increased by 430,000, including four new 80,640 – port switches in Eureka Junction, Sunnyvale, Salt Lake City, and Eckington, as well as expansions of existing switches throughout the United States. Based on Traffic Engineering's current call mix model for DALs, IMTs, and FGs, 24.18 billion MOUs can be supported in 3Q from this 2Q implementation!

Broadband. The Qwest Backbone Network has grown by 61% in a single quarter! Broadband turned up an additional 15,883,584 DS-3 miles of network. On March 31, 2000, the Qwest Network was a total of 26,119,660 DS-3 miles…as of June 30, the network totaled 42,003,244 DS-3 miles. If we had deployed only one OC-192 channel, Qwest's current network would wrap around the circumference of the Earth nine times!

Product Systems Engineering. The DCR 6.1 software upgrade has been successfully completed! This upgrade provides added capacity for up to a 32-switch network on the DCR platform and replaces UP to NP X.25 communications with an IP hierarchy. Since late February the cost of MOU overflow to OCC has been reduced by an average of more than $700,000 per month. In addition, due to increased efficiency in call routing, there has been a reduction of almost 50,000 ports previously used for network IMT routing. These ports are now available for billable usage, thereby increasing Qwest's revenue potential.

ATM/Frame Engineering. Installed 43 switches and 25 emergency card augments, while reducing the cycle time for emergency card augments to two weeks (100% cycle time reduction). Completed 56% of 3Q switch installations ahead of schedule.

In closing, I would to like to personally thank each of you for your efforts. Qwest's continued success is possible because of the extraordinary efforts of dedicated individuals such as those comprising our Engineering team. As we continue to consolidate US West and Qwest into one company, I would ask that you be patient and continue to support all activities required to make the merger a complete success.

I take great pride in knowing that I work with the best Engineering team in the telecommunications industry and I look forward to even greater accomplishments in our future.

Welcome to the first newsletter for the Program Management Office. This publication is intended to provide news and information on what is going on in our organization and spotlight some interesting people and groups so that we all may know a little more about the outstanding organization that we are all a part of.

I want to take a second to thank everyone in the Program Management Office for the outstanding effort that was made in the 2nd Quarter. I am personally proud to be associated with a group that has the drive and success that this group has so strongly displayed over this last quarter.

Keep up the good work and be sure to have some fun this quarter.

Don Heckman
Program Managment Office

Figure 7.10   Newsletter.
Qwest Worldwide Network Engineering. Used by permission.

line length requiring too much eye movement and, therefore, would reduce the readability of the text.

A two-column format is the most popular format. Making the two columns equal in width provides a comfortable line length. The disadvantage is that the design is not flexible and gives the impression of a page split in half. It also locks you into a balanced design when, in truth, visual appeal is often achieved by imbalance. If a two-column format is chosen, perhaps this disadvantage could be overcome by breaking over the alley with a graphic and tilting it so it achieves the imbalance desired.

An uneven two-column format is an effective design element. Usually the left column is narrower than the right column, leaving the left column for headlines, sidebars, pull quotes, or graphics. To heighten the effectiveness of the uneven columns, allow lots of white space in the left column.

A three-column format is very flexible. It provides flexibility while keeping columns wide enough for efficient reading. Type must be kept to ten points to ensure enough characters per line, and that might be a problem for some audiences. A three-column format is preferable when you are using lots of photos or diagrams. You can use a large photo to dramatically cover two of the three columns, or you can achieve imbalance in many ways by creatively placing more than one photo or graphic on a page. You can also use an uneven, three-column format effectively.

White space is one of the most important design elements of your newsletter. Text intensive copy will drive your readers away. They will never commit to reading the text if you do not create the impression it is a *quick read*. You do that by writing short chunks of information surrounded by white space. Exchange the paragraph indention for a blank line between paragraphs. Use wide margins both at the top and bottom as well as the sides. Use headings and subheads to break up long body copy.

Tips for Better Newsletters

A book of this size cannot include all there is to know about writing effective newsletters. Perhaps what we do provide will get you started. Pay attention to the many newsletters you encounter and ask just what it is you like and don't like? Consider the following design features to remember:

- Use sidebars
- Make charts for numerical data
- Use white space
- Use text wraps around a visual
- Create organized pages
- Use photographs and captions that tell a story

However, the following list contains design features you should avoid:

- Copy in reverse type
- Excessive space between lines
- Ink colors other than black for text
- Placing rules within articles

- A headline not placed above its article
- Using type over halftone screens heavier than 10 percent to 20 percent when screens are in black

Print Advertisements

Print ads are a technical marketing communication staple in trade magazines, business couriers, and exhibition journals. Ads are the tactic of choice when you want to promote your name, brand, or product—especially in conjunction with a multi-touch campaign of direct mail or other media promotions. It takes care and creativity to produce an effective ad. Mary Keller and Carrol Swan emphasize benefits to make your ad more effective. They suggest that you make the benefit obvious but keep it simple.[3]

Fairfax Cone, a man who has been highly successful in advertising, offers his creative philosophy, born out of experience, intuition, and many successful campaigns. These comments can be extremely valuable in providing insight into the whole area of creativity in advertising. First, consider his definition of advertising: "Something you do when you cannot send a salesperson." According to Cone, "Advertising must achieve what a good salesperson achieves—that is, sales. And it must reflect the qualities a good salesperson possesses."[4]

Cone explains his creative philosophy this way:

I believe that every honest advertisement will be successful that meets the requirements of only five rules . . . and that no advertising can succeed that fails to meet any one of them; they are not divisible.

1. The ad must immediately make clear what the basic proposition is. Few if any people have either the time or the inclination to try to solve the puzzle of obscure advertising promises.
2. It is equally important to successful advertising that what is clear shall also be important. The proposition must express a well-defined value.
3. The successful advertisement will express the value of the offering in personal terms. It will be beamed directly at the most logical prospects for the proposition; no one else matters.
4. Good advertising will always express the personality of the advertiser, for a promise is only as good as its maker.
5. A successful advertisement will always demand action. It will ask for the order, so to speak, or it will exact a mental pledge, because its promise is not to be denied.

[Cone concludes]: These rules are illustrated every day in many ways, for they apply equally to advertising in all media. Inevitably, taken together and carefully adhered to, they result in advertising that will command attention, but never be offensive. It will be reasonable, but never dull. It will be original, but never self-conscious. It will be imaginative, but never misleading. Because of these qualities, it will make people act.[5]

An especially effective advertising campaign created by 3Com, meet all the above criteria. They released a series of four ads to the *Wall Street Journal* to market four of their technical products:

- LAN telephony
- Business networks
- Wireless LAN
- Broadband modem

In each of the ads, the simplicity of the graphic attracts attention, and the effective use of multiple choice questions for each ad copy gives them an interactive flavor (see Figs. 7.11 and 7.12 for two sample ads).

Figure 7.11 Print advertisement. Headline copy: Maximum distance of desk from LAN jack: A) 8 ft. B) 10 ft. C) 12 ft. D) What LAN jack? Body copy: Cut the lines and extend your radius. After all, it's the simple connections that let you do the most fantastic things.

Copyright 2000. 3Com Corporation. Used by permission.

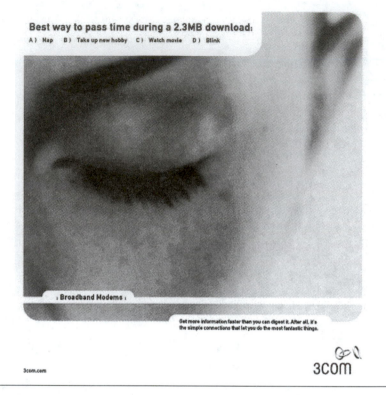

Figure 7.12   Print advertisement. Headline copy: Best way to pass time during a 2.3 MB download: A) Nap. B) Take up new hobby. C) Watch movie. D) Blink. Body copy: Get more information faster than you can digest it. After all, it's the simple connections that let you do the most fantastic things.

Copyright 2000. 3Com Corporation. Used by permission.

Postcards

It might surprise technical marketing communicators to learn a postcard can be an effective marketing tactic. Certainly, alone it will not accomplish a comprehensive result. But as you will read later in Chapter 11, it is a critical element in the classic three-touch tactical approach with direct mail and telemarketing. As a follow-up to a telemarketing call or a direct mail letter, you can use the postcard to point potential customers to other sources of additional information. For example, you could write a brief message on the postcard informing the customers of a Web site URL or a 1-800 number to call. This postcard follow-up provides a terrific reinforcement of other messages.

Postcards are really mini-brochures for much less cost. They are easily read and digested. Since postcards can be designed and created faster, their cost is lower and potential returns are higher. Information is likely to be more current because there is less agonizing over the content and less time required for approvals. Postcards usually seem more *real time* for that reason. Even if you don't attend the free breakfast seminar announced on the card, you're aware of that company's activity in the marketplace.

MYCOM effectively used a postcard to invite customers to attend their CIO Forum (see Fig. 7.13). The back of the postcard contained all the necessary information as well as the copy used to persuade the audience to attend. Sharkbytes, a Web consulting company, also used a postcard to invite people to visit the Web site for the Cincinnati Museum Center—which they had designed. (See Chapter 10 for other references to Sharkbytes and their strong branding tools.) The front of the postcard contained a collage of colorful images from the museum (see Fig. 7.14).

Quick Reference Cards

One of the print tools we haven't covered in this chapter is the quick reference card. Printed cards that quickly explain the basic operating features of software or hardware, or even a service process, are invaluable job aides and training tools. As such, they're not specifically "owned" by technical marketing communicators. In fact, technical writers are typically at the helm for these procedural tools. However, technical marketing communicators should be quick to advocate quick reference cards in their strategic communication plans as a means of speeding adoption of a new product or service. Anything that paves the way to change and acceptance also speeds the related benefits for cost savings or productivity improvements. Quick reference cards are a surprisingly useful means to that end.

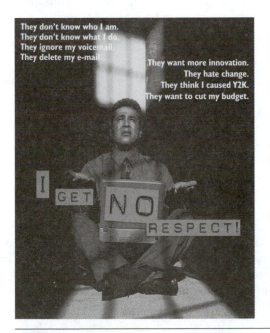

Figure 7.13   Front of postcard.
Copyright 2000. MYCOM. Used by permission.

The impact of an architectural masterpiece on your desktop. Start your visit to Cincinnati Museum Center at www.cincymuseum.org.
It's a killer site that speaks for itself: Visually sophisticated, technically elegant, and totally innovative.

Brought to you by:

sharkbytes

k i l l e r   w e b
www.sharkbytes.com

Figure 7.14   Back of postcard.
Copyright 2000. Sharkbytes. Used by permission.

Closing Reminders

You can certainly find other ways to creatively combine words, graphics, and paper as print media. Don't limit yourself to two dimensions or standard paper sizes. But, as we'll frequently remind you, be sure to match your objectives with your strategy as you choose the appropriate type of media.

Effective writing should evidence the marks of clarity, concision, coherence, and cohesion. Regardless of the type of print media you choose to achieve your purposes, take the time to edit, making sure your copy includes the following:

- Strong subjects placed close to the front of the sentence
- Active verbs (avoid passive voice whenever possible)
- Absence of unnecessary words or phrases
- Short, chunked paragraphs
- Paragraphs focused on one idea

Marketing language is characterized by a you attitude, that is, the writing is always focused on the reader and the benefit your product or service will bring. We have mentioned the you attitude throughout this text because it is one of the most important elements of marketing language regardless of the tactic you choose.

When you are editing your copy for effectiveness, circle the words *I*, *we*, and *our*. If they are not closely followed by a *you* or *your*, you are not writing you attitude copy and you are failing to take advantage of the most important aspect of marketing language.

Summing It Up

If you remember only one thing about print media, it should be the importance of describing benefits. If you remember two things, then remember to write your message in the *you attitude*. It won't matter how much you spend to produce print media, if your readers do not sense how technology can benefit them, you will have wasted your time, effort, and money.

Applying What You've Learned

1. Sit down in front of your PC or place your laptop in front of you and examine it carefully. Make a list of features (characteristics of the product). Beside each feature write the benefit (what's in it for the user?).
2. Make a list of the features of the word-processing package you use most often. Beside each feature write the benefit (what's in it for the user?).
3. Collect three newsletters and three brochures. Examine them carefully. What do they do well? What needs improvement?
4. Find a poorly designed brochure or newsletter and redesign it to be more effective.
5. Find an example of writer-centered body copy in a brochure and rewrite it to reflect the you attitude.
6. If you were responsible to motivate employees to attend a two-hour training session on a new version of software, which print tactics would you use and why?

SMALL GROUP ACTIVITY

Find a poorly designed brochure. Develop three different creative concepts for redesigning this tactic. Make a list of the features and benefits found in the brochure. Sketch out one of the creative concepts to see what the brochure would look like.

Notes

1. William M. Luther, *The Marketing Plan: How to Prepare and Implement It* (New York: American Management Association, 1992), 172–73.
2. Allen M. Cobrin, "If You Write Brochures, Give Yourself a Treat(ment)," *Technical Communication* 36 (1989): 206–09.
3. Mary D. Keller and Carrol J. Swan, *Which Ad Pulled Best*, ed. Philip Ward Burton and Scott Purvis (Lincolnwood, IL: NTC Business Books, 1991), 24–27.
4. Fairfax M. Cone, *With All Its Faults* (Boston: Little Brown, 1969), 58–60.
5. Ibid.

CHAPTER 8

Electronic Media

Overview

"We congratulated ourselves on the move to an online newsletter and uploaded the file."

We were feeling pretty good. One of the technology newsletters we had been printing for our client was going to go online to their Intranet site. We already had a robust editing process for hard copy newsletters. After the client's subject matter experts developed an article with our technical marketing communicators, our editor would review it for grammar and spelling. Then the client would have another chance to make content revisions before initialing approval. We followed a similar process for the online version; however, we passed an electronic file back and forth instead of a printer's proof.

Everything went fine until the final round of revisions. The client had significantly revised one of the articles. When the file came back to our editor, she asked if anything else had changed in the newsletter. No, it had not. So after reviewing that article, she declared the file ready to upload to the Intranet site. We didn't have an electronic sign-off for the client to use, but they agreed it was ready to publish after the changes were made to that last article.

We congratulated ourselves on the move to an online newsletter and uploaded the file. Unfortunately, it wasn't until the next morning we received a call from a very irate client. Somehow, in trading files to edit the last article, we had actually reverted to a previously saved version of the newsletter. The good news: the last article was edited and correct. The bad news: the other articles had typos and content errors from an earlier revision. About two thousand people had the privilege of viewing our mistakes over their morning coffee.

What went wrong? Our editor (and the rest of us were equally culpable) had not gone back to check the rest of the articles in the newsletter. Otherwise, we would have recognized them as an earlier file version with uncorrected errors. The problem is that it wasn't like flipping through a hard copy. The electronic version just wasn't as easy to scan. Would we have made the same mistake if we had been preparing for the prepress of a printed version? Probably not. We would have printed a sample and read through it line by line again. In our online case, it was just a little too easy to press a button and publish the newsletter. We learned our lesson. Online content is no less immune to human error than is printed content.

Sandi

The Nature of Online Media

No technical marketing communication tools garner as much attention today as electronic media. We assume technology people have access to the Internet from work or school. It's a given. CDs are frequently sent through the mail as advertisements because we expect people to have personal computers in their home. Special technology is being developed for handheld computers to receive wireless Web downloads. But the ubiquity of computers in academics and business has led to at least one disarming precedent. Many people, perhaps a majority, believe it is easier to develop content for online settings than it is to write something intended for print distribution. After all, online communication, such as e-mail, is meant to be disposable or have a short shelf life. So why agonize over form or formality? Isn't that the beauty of the Web? Here today, gone tomorrow?

Technical marketing communicators know better than that. The total development approach for online media is no different than any other technical marketing communication tool. Just because it's easy to publish an e-mail message or to post a Web page doesn't guarantee that it's effective communication. We must have a clear objective and strategy applied for a target audience. How can online media help to fulfill that need?

The nature of online media does make it possible to do things that cannot be done using other media. Speed and accessibility are at the top of the list. One person can imagine a communication, create it, and post it for immediate access around the world in just minutes. Animation and sound are easily integrated with textual content to add verve. Distribution and storage options are incredibly cost-effective and convenient. With everything online media has going for it, it's worth devoting a chapter to its nature and use.

Limitations of Physical Media

Go digital. That's the rallying cry as this text is being written. Corporate CEOs demand paperless meetings and online team collaboration. It cuts costs. It's efficient. It's the future. But walk into the office copy room and you'll find reams of paper are stacked to the ceiling. Sure we're distributing files electronically, but we're also hitting the print icon more often than not. Technical marketing communicators are the first to agree that audiences have different learning preferences. Reading from hard copy is still a strong choice among people in our technology markets. Hard copy is portable; you can write notes in the margin, and everyone at the meeting can have a copy to hold. Brochures are a fast, first-pass snapshot of information, and you don't have to find a color printer to print them yourself. Compared to paper collateral, promotional media, such as pens, T-shirts, and mouse pads, strike a different chord with audiences than do electronic communications. But physical media has its limitations.

The paper process can take longer and cost more. It's one thing to hit print for a single e-mail or Web page, but technical marketing communication usually involves more than that. A four-color product sheet or brochure is expensive to print.

We take extra time and care to make sure we edit everything sufficiently before committing ink to glossy paper. Printing lead-time requires days to weeks depending on printer schedules. Physical media has to be stored somewhere before and after it's distributed. Warehouse space isn't cheap. And shipping isn't free.

Even after we receive physical media, a large percentage of direct mail and other promotional materials are indeed discarded without serious audience interaction. Technology seems to leapfrog the latest printed media before its scheduled shelf life has been surpassed. Sometimes we update the brand logo and every previously existing piece of collateral becomes obsolete. We pay for the warehouse inventory, and then pay to securely dispose of it.

Of course, there are certainly effective ways to extend the life of current physical content. Printing on demand lets technical marketing communicators update content online before printing files. That way, the color headers and footers can be printed and stored in bulk. Then, when we receive requests to distribute physical media, we simply print the latest file updates onto the body of the preprinted template.

All physical media, and printing in particular, still have their rightful place in the technical marketing communicator's toolkit. Like any other media, physical media simply should be matched to the technology objective, strategy, and audience opportunity.

Defining Electronic Media

If it's electronic, it involves electricity. Technically, electronic media involves the use and transfer of electrons, as opposed to ink on paper or other physical means. The list includes audio, video, Web, telephony, and electronic file sharing via the Web or otherwise. Electronic doesn't have to mean online or Web. CD-ROMs convey electronic information without being online, as do voicemail and electronic messaging (e-mail). However, almost anything electronic we can create for technical marketing communication can indeed be posted and shared on the Web. On the other hand, we can now do things on the Web that really do not have a place anywhere else in our toolkit (e.g., Webinars and PDA downloads). In the rest of this chapter, we'll take a look at some individual electronic communication technologies and how they can work together. Given the importance of these technologies in today's communication, let's go online.

Marketing with Online Media

"Are you online?"

My daughter asks that question when she wants to use the phone. With one phone line in the house (and no digital subscription service yet) we have to choose whether to use the phone or our personal computer's modem connection. Being online in this case means being connected to the Internet. In general, online means we're connected to other users or sites via a shared network of some kind. We could be online with our company's Intranet or an online service like CompuServ. While we're online, we can send and receive e-mail or files and view Web-based pages with Netscape or Internet Explorer browsers. Once we're offline, we've lost the immediacy of the real-time connection although we may have downloaded pertinent files or applications for offline use.

Is online the right choice? Like all other media options, online information sharing should be only one facet of a comprehensive technical marketing communication approach. We expect to have an online presence, but the role it plays is proportional to how our technology customers or colleagues use it. Just as important is the question of accessibility (see Chapter 1). As in our HR example in Chapter 7, our online communication is wasted if an audience does not or cannot access a particular site or application tools.

Keep in mind our technical marketing communication perspective. Some dot-com companies have no brick and mortar access for customers. As far as customer interaction is concerned, these companies exist only on the Web. Amazon.com and e-bay.com are companies whose Internet commerce transactions are literally their primary source of customer revenue. Yet their promotional marketing communication also takes place in magazines and TV ads. So when we begin to focus on technical marketing communication, and not specific commerce transactions, we really need to understand where customers and colleagues expect to engage our information. Having a Web presence is almost a foregone conclusion, but the weight of its marketing communication role is a subject for careful strategic consideration.

Online Media Audiences

Online audiences have something in common: access to an electronic interface via a Web browser. According to our definition, they have access to the Internet, an Intranet, or an Extranet. Extranets (or virtual private networks, VPNs) provide a secure, password-protected space for customers, partners, or vendors. Extranets may simply be a subsite of the main Web presence or a separate site altogether. In any event, Extranets are meant to control who has access to your information, which is quite the opposite of most public Internet site strategies. Technical marketing communicators usually know whom they're letting in to an Extranet site. Registration log-ins capture pertinent data, or you proactively send out passwords. Extranets tend to be more functionally oriented than many Internet sites. They exist to provide or share specialized information and have the advantage of heightened focus.

Unlike the Internet, institutional or company Intranets have a captive audience. If you don't like the departmental Intranet, you can't exactly click through to somebody else's private site. However, Intranet functionality is directly linked to productivity. Energy expended to access or use information on an intranet site is time lost to other activities.

Other audience assumptions aren't quite as easy to make. Technical marketing communicators need to seek out online profiling information during needs analysis. Is your audience electronically active and literate? Just being technical in some way does not guarantee advanced Web experience. Some online users still have not used advance search engine features or video streaming.

Navigation and browsing tendencies of your audience are also important to know or determine. Can you expect skimmers or readers? Usability studies and click-through reports should add insight as you begin to work with a particular audience. Web users won't sit still to read large chunks of text—of any kind. But what type of content does your audience *want* to see? Sophisticated users may demand your online navigation and content to be more streamlined and intuitive. Less frequent online visitors require more hand holding and direction. And we can't mention technology limitations (bandwidth, computing power) enough. Too many animations or graphics will paralyze anyone with poor access capability.

All of these attributes contribute to the Web experience of your customer or colleagues, known appropriately as their *user* or *guest experience*. Technical marketing communicators and their Web development collaborators are striving for a user experience that compels their guests to return on a regular basis. It may be the value of the content or the functionality of interactive tools that help visitors to answer technology questions. Anything that contributes to an extended user experience or regular returns reflects the site's *stickiness* factor. Putting it all together, we want to build a Web user experience of maximum stickiness as part of our overall technical marketing communication strategy.

Developing Content for Online Media

Technical marketing communicators have had time to experience the Web in the last several years and should recognize the primary rules of engagement for online content.

Keep It Brief and Simple

Content developed for online use has to be crisp and brisk. Long paragraphs, especially on central navigation pages, simply won't do. Even company or department descriptions must be reduced to several sentences. Recognizing the Web's role as only one information sharing media helps to relax the pressure you feel to say everything all at once. In many ways you can think of a Web site interaction as a personal presentation. If you were given only a few seconds to grab your audience's attention (a literal elevator pitch), what would you absolutely, positively, have to say? That's how every Web page needs to be crafted. People usually have no intention of parking themselves at an interesting site and reading for extended periods. They're usually after information they intend to use somewhere else. The way to get them to come back is to help them quickly and get them on their way.

Exploit Online Advantages

The beauty of the Web is its nonlinear nature. Users can follow an information thread totally unique to their interests if you let them. One of the ways to break up longer segments of text is to put them on separate pages and hyperlink them. That way, one user may follow the thread and another may not. The same is true for graphics. Smaller, thumbnail versions of photos or diagrams should have captions that help a guest decide whether to pursue opening or downloading a larger file. We like to list file sizes for things like video clips, so guests know what they are getting into if they decide to download. Use graphics as navigation tools and make them clickable. You can't do that with a hard copy document. The same electronic-only advantage is true for animation, sound, and video as long as user accessibility isn't a barrier. Be sure to include site-specific search capabilities. Guests expect shortcuts and search engines.

Know Your Web Browser

Typically you and your Web developer will consider the audience mix of Internet Explorer (IE) and Netscape as the browsers of choice. Different browsers still manage to affect how we view and navigate Web sites more than we'd like to think. We still have the odd page, drop-down menu, or graphic that simply won't open the way we expect it to on one browser or the other. At the very least, be sure you view and test your content on a cross section of the two brands and their most recent versions before publishing to a production server.

Review Your Content

The main downfall of business at Internet or dot-com speed is that the Web creates an illusion that content is easy to develop since it is easy to publish. Many corporate and organizational technology sites are an English professor's worst nightmare. Some content is simply superfluous and inconsequential; others are riddled with spelling and grammar errors. If your team is going to have in-house contributors to public pages, simply incorporate a robust editing process (preferably with a professional editor). Make sure authors include rework and review cycles into their content publishing timelines. Software that enables you to collaborate your online workflow is an ideal way to make the right people accountable for what shows up on a Web page. Because spell checkers and grammar tools don't account for writing style and content, your review process should.

Online Media Tools and Options

With all that said about user experience and online content, let's look at some of the ways technical marketing communicators can leverage the power of the Web. We've purposely left the details of Web site design and development to other texts. In this text, we are most focused on the technical marketing communicator's use of this electronic media. Still, like every other content sharing vehicle we design and support, Web sites must be well organized, readily navigated, and appropriately up-to-date. Aside from the other functional opportunities we discuss later in the chapter, Web sites should receive equal consideration for a strategic role in your communication plan. We also recommend reading books by experts in Web design such as Jakob Nielson's *Designing Web Usability*.[1]

General Information Access

Technical marketing communicators should exploit the Web for its unique strengths and should not try to make it mimic the physical world. We needn't apologize for including high-level corporate or organizational information on the Web site. However, it needs to be optional as opposed to required home-page reading. Most of us want a little company information before engaging in technology work. News or current PR releases help guests know what has changed since their last visit. Be sure it truly is news. Sharing success stories (case studies) is one of the best shortcuts to visualizing your technology in action. Make them a prominent navigation option on your site.

Use general information links and pages to help share the personality of your organization in ways you would during a personal presentation. If your team supports a particular charitable cause and is truly passionate about it, display that somewhere on the site. Help people come away with the impressions and substance you might impart if they visited your headquarters for the first time. Then, make sure return visitors to the site don't have to wade through the same information all over again.

Online Public Relations

Making use of online public relations sites is one of the few slam-dunks of the online technical marketing communication realm. Because of automated searches, PR releases get picked up like wildfire when a topic happens to be hot. We've been amazed at the visibility return on a few minutes worth of PR content development. Set an organizational goal to generate at least one PR release per week. Reference anything in your technology development pipeline worthy of note, or simply quote one of your technology leaders making an observation about the industry at large. Anything that helps to build recognition for your technologies, organization, personnel, or brand will make future paid promotions more effective. Once you've forwarded a press release to the appropriate online resources, be sure to publish it in your own news section.

Publishing Files to Your Internet Site

Relying on download files to share your information is a double-edged sword. You make something available electronically, but you give up the inherent online advantages of immediacy, searchability, and hyperlinking. Be aware of the recurring risk of unedited content slipping through your review process. Try to avoid file downloads as a mere convenience or shortcut and turn them into a value-add. Personal presentations in slide format are in high demand from technical marketing teams and make sensible file downloads. In-depth technical documentation, when not designed for online use, is better downloaded for printing. PDF versions of print material are usually available via downloads as are nonstreaming audio or video files.

E-Mail Links

Whether you add an e-mail link for technical marketing communication to a navigation bar or individual Web page depends on the traffic volume you expect. Most sites offer a central e-mail administrator address as opposed to a personal contact address. That way, you can automate some responses based on subject line rules. Multiple people in the sales or marketing organization can check the box for inquiries and possible leads. However, some brand-building strategies provide reasons to list personal contact information. If you are trying to garner editorial attention for a brand or product manager, making them directly accessible to the market may be just the ticket. You can always remove the address link after the one-millionth inquiry. Regional sales managers particularly like to have contact information directly linked to marketing communication sites meant to generate leads.

Interactive Guides

Having your Web site *do* something increases its stickiness factor. Technical marketing communicators can actually guide Web guests through decision-making or problem-solving processes that lead to your business solutions. Using hyperlinks and smart databases, interactive questions and answers can converge toward one of many technology solutions. This approach is similar to that taken by wizards in Microsoft software setups. Interactive guides add a degree of active intelligence to your information, making it more valuable to guests. It also acts as your shortcut to qualify potential customer prospects for follow-up. The more someone understands your technology and how it can serve their needs, the less time you have to spend facilitating the identical outcome with sales or customer service representatives.

Many firms use interactive guides to help customers calculate the potential cost of a custom configured technology product or service. These interactive tools work for both consumer and business-to-business clients, speeding the time (and reducing the cost) to close a deal.

Commerce Transactions

The ultimate marketing result is a closed deal. Online commerce transactions are just that. Whether you click a shopping cart or e-mail a purchase order, many technology sites are transaction enabled. Technical marketing communicators should look for opportunities to cross-market additional ideas at the point of sale. Someone ordering a computer is likely to need a printer. A physician ordering x-ray equipment needs lead protective shields. Web technology makes it possible to trigger pop-up promotional screens or dialog boxes to prompt users in this direction. Amazon.com does an effective job of suggesting books similar to the subject matter of your first choice. If you order a technical marketing text, you are likely to receive a future suggestion for additional purchase opportunities. Work with your Web developer to understand your available options for presale, point of sale (shopping cart), and postsale marketing communication follow-up.

Web Portals

Web portals are sites that act as collectors or intersection points for related information and links. For example, a technology portal dedicated to space flight might link to other sites for propulsion, physics, aerospace design, and psychology. If you supported a specific technology within the overall aerospace market, you could possibly garner more attention by participating in a very sticky portal and including yourself as one of the reference links. That way, someone entering the portal for the larger purpose of space flight could learn your technology's role and how they might engage with you. You might otherwise struggle to identify or target that technology prospect.

Portal setups such as Yahoo allow users to personalize their experiences. The good news is that users get a personalized interface that directly reflects their needs and preferences. The bad news is they could simply eliminate your presence from their preferences.

Similar to portals are market aggregators whose express purpose is to link buying and selling groups via their topical site focus. Some aggregation sites charge for vendor participation and create a closed purchase cycle. Sellers are willing to pay to play because somebody else has gone to the trouble of locating and linking their targeted audience(s).

The key message for technical marketing communicators regarding portals and aggregators is that you can't limit your online strategy to a single Web site of your own. In fact, one strategy is to build a bare bones information and contact site of your own but place the majority of your marketing energy in support of your portal and aggregator site selections.

Web Promotions

Web promotions are still unproven ground for many technical marketing communication industries. Web banners are popular as online promotion tools. However, at a recent vendor gathering we attended, technology representatives were offered six different options to market their products and services to a broad audience. Web banners were at the bottom of their preference list. One representative simply compared the cost of the banner time to the other alternatives and said, "Why would I take the chance my target audience would be online at the same times my banner happened to run, or that they would read it? I try not to be bothered by them myself." Jakob Nielson, author of *Designing Web Usability*, even suggests designers avoid making interactive elements *look* like banners because users will purposefully ignore them.[2] Web banners may still have a place in your overall technical marketing communication mix but make sure you obtain detailed tracking metrics of the visitor behavior, both before and after clicking your banner ad.

Other promotions may have more attraction for technology users. Offering a consultation for a one-time, no-cost professional service is a great value for everyone involved. It provides an entry point to a market or client base for you, and a low risk look-see for the prospect. Technical marketing communicators do the same thing by offering white papers or software trials in exchange for market survey information. And if you really want attention, offer a handheld computer. But don't be afraid to be frugal either. We still see great results by seeking customer interaction and feedback in return for a company's logo-emblazoned polo shirt.

Webinars

Real-time events have become much more popular because of the ease of online application sharing. Webinars make it easy for technology prospects and colleagues to view a presentation or demo without leaving their offices. Presenters generally distribute a log-on password to participants in advance, along with an 800-number dial-in. Some regional representatives invite attendees to join them at their local offices, and then cater lunch while watching the online presentation from the home office (see Fig. 8.1).

Without overlooking the technical complexity of some satellite meetings, preparation for real-time events is fairly simple. Slide presentation software can be the shared communications device, as can any other application running on the desktop. When you have multiple presenters, one technical marketing communicator needs to "drive" the application interface while the other speaks. This works even if the presenters are not located at the same site.

You have multiple options to promote a real-time event in advance, including a banner on your Web site or news section. But direct mail post cards with telemarketing follow-up have proven to be successful as well. The best Webinar topics are purely industry or solutions oriented and do not blatantly promote a specific product or service. That's the attraction to the participants. Low risk, low pressure. Then, at their best, Webinars help to break the ice with potential prospects and pave the way for additional follow-up on a solution of their choice. Or they simply help to build brand recognition.

Figure 8.1   Webinar setup.

Training

Training is one of the most valuable online avenues for technical marketing communication. With off-the-shelf (and customized) Web training applications, it's possible to configure and present new technology information to sales and service teams and to measure their adoption rate. Online quizzes are a provocative feedback tool for online students and technology owners alike. We have struggled on numerous occasions to gain the attention of a busy and easily distracted sales force. Then, when new sales lag, finger pointing begins between sales and marketing. "We didn't have sufficient support communication or training," sales suggests, and marketing counters with, "we sent it, and we told you, but you didn't listen."

Now, online interaction is measurable. Sales will have database metrics to say the technology information was read and tested, but insufficient, or marketing will be able to determine the message has not been adequately engaged. It's a healthy opportunity for all teams to strive toward a common goal of enhanced communication and information sharing.

Profiling and Data Mining

Technical marketing communicators love anything that helps them understand their market and customer preferences. Powerful tools are available to record the traffic on your Web site and the navigation sequence visitors follow from page to page.

One Midwest consulting company was elated with their second-generation Web site release. It wasn't just because the number of recorded page views had skyrocketed. Visitors were staying longer. The site's stickiness factor had improved dramatically. Their ability to measure and analyze traffic was helping them to focus their business direction.

The best advice is to capture and record as much data as available to uncover patterns of use. If possible, determine which sites your visitors came from and where they go after leaving. With time, choose a list of your most productive indicators and analyze them regularly, sharing that information with other sales, marketing, and customer support functions within your company. Don't forget to request some form of customer registration in return for valuable information that you provide. A visitor's name and e-mail address are worthwhile; income, budget, and purchase preferences are even better. Just recognize that many of us are losing the patience required to complete lengthy online forms unless the resulting Web functionality earned is tantalizing enough. Depending on the sophistication of your site, this data collection can lead to up-sell, cross-sell, and targeted profile marketing.

Alternative Web Access

Your prospects and colleagues are also using alternative methods to access the Web. Wireless access from cell phones and handheld computer download pushes are available if your information technology department can support them. Be sure to survey your targeted online users to determine if there is a demand for alternative access. It's valuable to respond even if you support something as simple as price updates or breaking industry news. Remember you want to build a traffic pattern of stickiness that is not limited to today's perception of cutting edge technology. Allow your prospect and market preferences to drive your responsiveness and make sure you're not left behind by a more innovative competitor.

CD-ROM Sharing

Not everyone has sufficient bandwidth or the patience to endure long file download times. For them, the answer is CD-ROM. Even browser companies distribute their setup files via CD-ROM. In the past, CD duplication costs limited their viability for quantities less than a thousand (no problem for AOL). We worked with one duplication company who gladly agreed to sell duplicate quantities as small as 100, but their minimum price list still started at the 500 unit level. That's changed over time, and most cities now have competitive duplication rates and companies willing to accept quantities as low as 50 to 100 units for a dollar per CD (jewel cases cost more). That's perfect for medium-size technology sales and service teams or for small, targeted customer distributions.

CDs have also become much easier to create. Most technology departments have (or should have) access to a CD burner. Documents, spreadsheets, and multimedia files can be dragged over to a writeable CD just as easily as to a network share drive. For technology people in the field with slow online access who cringe at the thought of downloading a 5 MB slide presentation or video clip, CDs are a breath of fresh air. In fact, some simply refuse or are unable to stay current with Web downloads. Information technology departments frequently limit e-mail attachments larger than 5 MB depending on network bandwidth. Technical marketing communicators can combat that information-sharing barrier with a biweekly or monthly CD update of key presentation tools. At the going price of a CD (with costs continuing to drop) and postage, it's hard to beat.

CD-ROM business cards are also a great value. These mini-CDs are roughly the shape of a business card and hold up to 30 MB of information. Their front face can be imprinted just as a full size CD, and they leave a great impression with technology prospects and customers. Technologists love these technology toys.

Audio Electronic Media

Sound and the spoken word have a powerful effect on human beings. We've already mentioned the use of music in Chapter 5 on branding. Brands like to associate themselves with music easily recognized and appreciated by a target audience, even when the music itself has nothing to do with the technology involved. In brand situations, music is simply a promotional shortcut to saying, "We already have something in common. Would you like to hear about my technology?" Even computer start-up programs have distinctive brand sounds such as sound clips or musical tones we easily recognize. Have you been talking on the phone and heard the computer boot up in the background? With no additional visual cues, you know a little about their brand preferences for operating systems or software.

The spoken word is equally distinctive. "You've got mail" has instant audio recognition with millions of computer users. Martin Luther King's "I have a dream" speech rings in our memories as much for the substance of his words as for the compelling articulation and emotion of his voice. Similarly, using audio media adds another dimension to our technical marketing communication that visual media cannot duplicate.

Live Audio

Live audio is usually associated with personal presentations (see Chapter 9). Live audio feeds may be in person or via satellite, telephony, or Web. Having a *real* person involved means you can answer questions and spontaneously follow different paths to explain technology, especially if audience participants are confused. Live audio also conveys the sincerity or disposition of the speaker. You can hear the nuance of pleasure and passion in a speaker's voice. That adds a compelling dimension of influence and motivation. Laughter augments a humorous punch line. Dramatic volume can swing the audience from concern to enthusiasm. The human voice also carries affirmation and encouragement for ideas beyond what written words will hold.

In short, nothing is as interactive as a real-time exchange between real people. Technical marketing communicators should encourage live audio as much as possible. It's probably the most cost-effective way to exchange and socialize ideas. For people who are not located at the same site, audio interaction is as inexpensive as the local or long distance lines involved. Web audio is growing in use as well, and IP telephony will converge with data networks in the next several years as bandwidth capacity builds. You will find few technical barriers to limit the use of live audio linkups.

The most important advice for live audio is probably self-evident: Make sure all participants can hear the live audio feed. When multiple locations are calling into a shared conference link, engage an operator to be on hand in case of technical difficulties. The more prominent and important the event, the more you should invest in additional backup and advance preparation. Strange things can happen with telephony links. An unusual buzz or hum can be extremely distracting to the presenter and the other participants. Think ahead and have recovery strategies on hand in case anything goes wrong with your main audio link, even if your recovery plan is to reschedule.

Meetings and presentations involving live audio do require coordination and scheduled time commitments. Time zone differences also complicate matters for live audio. Three-hour time zone differences from coast to coast are enough to challenge some teams. The 9:00 A.M. meeting scheduled at a firm's New York headquarters requires the California staff to be up and on the phone by 6:00 A.M. The challenge becomes greater as you cross oceans and continents. Technical marketing communicators need to be fair and reasonable in scheduling audio engagements with other time zones. Be sure to alternate who suffers the worst of the pre- or post–business hour compromise.

Audio Reproduction (CDs, Cassettes, and File Clips)

Although you can offer multiple audio choices and links for interaction, by definition, recorded media isn't as truly interactive as live audio. Audio recordings still manifest the other benefits of live audio.

You can record or replicate (synthesize) most of the sounds that occur in natural settings within the range of human hearing. Recorded sound is captured or created either digitally or in an analog fashion. Analog tapes, including our old music and sales motivation cassettes, recreate most of the original sound and usually add in some background hiss as well. That's because the magnetic field imprint is an imperfect representation of the original sound, hence the name, *analog*, referring to an *analogous* or similar sound. Although the analog version of an audio recording is an electronic media, it is not truly digital.

Digital sound (and video) actually captures and converts the original sound to ones and zeros. When those same ones and zeros are converted back to an electronic signal for listening, virtually nothing is changed or lost in the conversion. That's why digitally recorded music CDs have become the de facto standard for listening pleasure. For the technical marketing communicator, digital recording is cleaner and easier to reproduce and share than analog sound. Digital files are also smaller. They can be stored on hard drives, Web sites, or CD-ROMs. Unfortunately, digital recording equipment is still a little more expensive than analog tape recorders, but the prices are falling steadily. Analog recording and playback are still fast and inexpensive to create and distribute. You can also convert original tape recordings to digital files, but the quality just isn't as good as sound originally captured in digital format.

Audiotapes and CDs

Whatever the recording capture media, audiotapes and CDs are effective tools for technical marketing communication. One of their biggest advantages is the overall bang for your marketing buck. For a few dollars per CD or cassette tape, you can put an hour of marketing messages into the hands of sales and service teams. That's a lot cheaper than bringing them in from the field for a meeting or conference call. It also puts them in control to listen at their convenience as opposed to yours (remember the time zone challenge). Teams listen in the car or on the plane that might otherwise be dead time. And in this age of virtual offices across multiple regions and countries, technology professionals like listening to another human being once in awhile. Some people-learning preferences also favor hearing information rather than reading it.

Consider these ideas for monthly or quarterly audio distribution:

- Listen to and rehearse scripted elevator pitches and value propositions for new technology products or services.
- Absorb conversational versions of technology success stories from peers and customers.
- Share motivational ideas from key leaders in the organization or industry.
- Provide updates on technical projects, business direction, and competition.
- Remind teams of shared goals, milestones, and progress.

Like other technical marketing presentations, audio collections should make wise use of the listening audience's time. Choose messages that are indeed enhanced by delivery in audio media. Protect listeners from poor presenters or content that is low on substance. Keep the combined listening experience to segments of 15 to 20 minutes each (one side of a cassette or one CD track). Listening times less than 30 minutes are suitable for average commutes and attention spans.

From a process standpoint, audio reproduction is another action best delegated to outside resources. Contract a local audio studio as your central clearinghouse. You can rent local studio time to capture scripted messages by team members or voice talent. Ask hotel or convention audiovisual teams to capture personal presentations on cassette or electronic file at exhibitions and company events. Then send those files to your studio. Many in-house communication teams actually buy software and microphones for digital capture in their own offices. Again, these can then be forwarded to a professional studio for editing. For a few dollars more, studios will also add music backgrounds and segues between audio segments. At your direction, they can clean up files by deleting segments from presentations or speeches not pertinent to your message for technical marketing communication. While professional sound quality is important and encouraged, fight the temptation to make slick audio packaging your end goal. Your real motivation is to deliver the benefits of audio information in a cost-effective, timely fashion. If the overall process becomes too cumbersome or time-consuming, it will quickly be abandoned by all involved. Make sure studios and team participants understand your desire to balance good work with speed and cost.

Technical marketing communicators also need to remind their teams (and each other) that we share information in multiple ways to ensure its assimilation into the collective audience consciousness. The same information distributed via audio media might also appear in written form on the Web or in hard copy newsletters. But the audio versions will deliver the additional punch that is unique to the media.

Audio File Clips

The same audio segments on a cassette or CD can be accessed online as well. Streaming technology and mp3 format make it relatively easy to download and listen to files as audiences complete other office tasks. Or they can be saved for later use in the office, at home, or on the road. Appropriate file sizes for any given organization depend on available bandwidth. Field sales and service organizations with slow dial-up connections are loath to spend hours downloading. Web streaming technology is essential to warrant their engagement.

Again, put the benefits of audio to proper use. If you want a certain passion and enthusiasm infused in a technology pitch or customer service message, demonstrate it on your audio clip. Choose or hire your audio talent wisely. You can ghostwrite hard copy messages for anybody, but voice presentations have to stand on their own merit. Make sure your audio presenters are articulate and energized. For diversity, remember to mix male and female speakers as much as possible. Cultural diversity is often evident in voice patterns, and that should be incorporated into your voice selections as well. Keep individual file lengths (listening times) between 5 and 15 minutes, which is somewhat shorter than a cassette tape or CD segment would be.

Voicemail, Phone Greetings, and Hold Messages

If your company or institution has a voicemail distribution system, it's another effective tool for technical marketing communication updates. One technology manager we worked with issued a weekly voice message to his staff of 20-plus people, including nondirect reports. Their offices were spread out across multiple buildings within the city, and scheduled conference calls were impractical. Instead, each voicemail message lasted four to five minutes and contained highlights of the previous week. Because of the audio format, you could hear this manager's personal charisma come through. He shared feedback heard from his own leadership, and conveyed accolades for significant wins by members of the team. He was clearly proud of the team's accomplishments, and his encouragement was highly motivational. Even vendor contractors were included on the voicemail distribution. Consequently, the team felt they were collectively pulling in the right direction and clearly understood what this manager deemed important. They were never more than one week away from contact with their leader, and the impact was extremely positive.

Voicemail updates are ideal for in-house technology rollouts as well. Technology project teams can leverage distribution lists for an entire office location. The audio updates can describe the status of technology installations, training, and start-up waves. Technology help desks also use voicemail distributions to notify constituencies of scheduled system downtimes. One technology team struggled with the dilemma of how to notify e-mail users that the system was down. They obviously couldn't send an e-mail notification. Instead, they created voicemail distribution lists and developed a process to update users that way. Phone greetings and hold messages are another audio opportunity for technical marketing communication messages. In fact, technical marketing communicators should proactively claim these message opportunities as their own.

One technology company we call has played the same piece of classical music for several years. Aside from the fact that this music doesn't necessarily appeal to the entire audience, it hasn't been updated, and they're missing a golden opportunity to share substantive information about the company.

Telephony messages are valid for consumer, business-to-business, and intra-organizational calls. Technical marketing communicators should review audience needs analysis to understand what types of information are most appropriate for telephony messages. Use the reports from your phone management system to understand average hold times and caller menu options. For example, if caller hold times average less than 10 seconds, a 45-second audio message may never be heard. Of course, if average hold times are too long, you probably have a process problem that needs to be addressed.

Incoming messages should be kept current and updated regularly, just as a Web site news section would be. Because of the message brevity necessary, frequently point to other information sources. "Visit our Web site at www . . . and for online service updates, www . . . or call our national support center at 1-800-. . . . In this way, you can use the hold message to divert traffic to faster, more productive avenues.

Electronic Visual Media

Just as audio media lends itself to the power of spoken nuances, visual media connects with audiences in ways words alone cannot. A diagram of a chemical process is much easier to understand than a textual description would be. What would help you understand the shape of a jet engine blade faster than a rotating three-dimensional (3D) image? Most of the graphics created for print media can be scanned or reapplied for electronic media use in videos, CDs, and on the Web. However, graphics originally designed for print usually look that way. By definition, they have to look their best on a flat surface. Inks and paper types are on the minds of print graphic designers. Pixel density and browser configurations are on the minds of new media designers. That's why today's graphic professionals are likely to pose an initial question to the technical marketing communicator: "Where do you intend to use the graphic?" Their version of the needs analysis influences their color choices, dimensional work, and backgrounds. The technical marketing communicator is free to apply a graphic to both print and electronic media, but a designer's time and cost efficiency will be driven by how well he or she builds in that flexibility from the onset. As with physical media, a graphic should either enhance a message or make it easier to understand. Technology product photos do both. Process diagrams do both.

Ask yourself these questions before including a graphic:

- Am I more attracted to the content because of the graphic? We associate a certain coolness factor with technology graphics. Pushing the edge with unique color shifts or effects does grab a viewer's attention, if the graphics are done well. Like anything else, if we're impressed with the graphic, we tend to project that impression to the content and get off on the right foot.
- Does the graphic speed or shortcut my ability to absorb the content? Any time a graphic helps us to say, "ah, I see . . . now I get it," it's a winner.
- Does the graphic add a dimension or perspective that cannot be represented adequately in words? Most technology process descriptions pale in compari-

son to their image alternative. We would much rather absorb a simple block diagram than read three paragraphs of text.

But beware the potential graphical backlash:

- Does the graphic overshadow the content or message, distracting your viewers or making them work harder to assimilate the target information? In the push to appear current, electronic graphics can go over the edge. Too big. Too busy. Too loud. Make sure graphics don't annoy your target audience.
- Is the graphic superfluous, sending a message that the technical marketing communicator was not engaged in the subject matter? We had to counsel one technology client to remove an image of a globe from the Web site. They were not operating globally and had no global customers. "But we'd like to be global at some point in the future." The globe can wait.
- Is the graphic file too large for your audience? Even with faster machines and lots of bandwidth, large graphic files still pose access barriers to many technology people. It's a shame to have your message blocked by a byte-hogging graphic.

Let's look at three key ways technical marketing communicators use electronic visual media.

Static Graphics

Electronic static visuals are just that, fixed and motionless. Basic clip art is static. Photographs, diagrams, and artwork are static. But today's electronic graphics are increasingly complex and creative. Photographs are layered one over the other; others are grouped in montages. Single images are sometimes enlarged as watermarks for an entire page background. As technical marketing communicators, we are challenged to reflect current Web trends in their technology graphics just to garner attention. People who view your material also surf elsewhere on the Web, and that's how the bar gets raised for your own graphic expectations. Keeping in mind our cautions from the previous section, you will still find lots of room to flex graphical muscle with electronic media.

Graphics have also become an important aspect of electronic navigation. Technical audiences have learned to mouse over and click on graphics in order to follow links to additional information in slide presentations and CDs as well as on Web sites. Photographs and diagrams are easily segmented with multiple linking paths depending on where you click.

Animation

Animations are effective if they add value. For example, an animation that demonstrates the progression of a technical process or methodology is probably worth the design cost and production to include on a Web or CD. A working 3D model of your technology is fantastic if it saves a trip to the plant or lab. The same is true for animations that allow you to swap product features to visualize your purchase options. However, blinking text and flashing images may irritate viewers if they slow the assimilation of substantive information. Mouseovers that reveal additional text or link options are probably the most valuable (and inexpensive) animation formats. Avoid cute animations of logos and icons in our technology realm, especially if they delay access to the target information. If you're unsure of an animation's value, simply add a button or text line option to skip animation, leaving the ultimate value decision right where it belongs: in the hands of your customer.

Video Media

Video graphics are still one of the most underused secret weapons of the technical marketing communicator. Anyone can hire a video production crew to make killer product demos and training presentations. We worked with one client who went beyond video media and actually shot an internal employee technology segment on film. The more expensive film format is usually reserved for broadcast situations. Converted from film to video for distribution and viewing purposes, the result was visually stunning and highly effective. And its main purpose was to introduce a new e-mail application. Video is simply an effective way to share the personal impact of technology leaders or trainers when they can't be everywhere at once.

However, decision makers in business are notoriously wary of the true value delivered by video productions. And with good reason. Expectations for video results are usually grander than the budgets (the occasional filmmaker notwithstanding). The defensive counter to these expensive (but useful) productions tends to be simple settings and talking heads. Shelf life for video, given the usual development and production costs, makes it difficult to justify when compared to other media options.

But today, consumer digital cameras have become inexpensive (available for less than $1,000) and with their editing software have finally made two things possible.

1. In-house teams can capture great visuals without bringing in elaborate lighting fixtures. And anti-motion technology has dramatically reduced the shaky hand look. We've seen handheld and tripod clips under fluorescent and natural lights. They're terrific.
2. Digital files are easily edited online without expensive production facilities. Drag and drop scene editing is a snap.

With the dawn of inexpensive digital equipment, technical marketing communicators should be looking for ways to bring their communication alive with more frequent, timely clips of technology and technology people in action. Why not post a 60-second technology update to the Internet from brand or product managers on a monthly basis? Technology demos? Training procedures? Practice sales pitches or telemarketing scripts? We challenge the technical marketing communication community at large to reinvent the role of video media as an option for compelling communications.

Using Outside Resources

"*I can do that.*"

One final disclaimer for electronic media creation: A lot of well-meaning people in business volunteer to create electronic media marketing tools. Proceed with caution and candor. There's always a diamond in the rough somewhere, but he or she is rarely on your team. If the person is a phenomenal graphic designer or video producer, it's probably already his or her day job. Just because electronic packages are making it easy to create electronic marketing tools doesn't guarantee they're good. Budget for, and use, the appropriate media professionals to help you market your ideas. Still, having said that, when you do have the in-house capability, it's a wonderful luxury.

Summing It Up

Because of the limitations of physical media, technical marketing communicators are going digital. However, before you push the button to publish on the Web, you should consider the unique characteristics of an online audience. You must carefully craft your content to meet the needs of your audience as well as to exploit online advantages. Online marketing can incorporate interactive guides, commerce transactions, Web portals, and Web promotions. But don't forget Webinars, training, and CD sharing. Sound and the spoken word have powerful impact on human beings. Use live audio and audio reproduction to accomplish your marketing purposes. Although electronic visual media can be powerful, use it with care. If used well, electronic media can revolutionize your technical marketing efforts. Because we are involved in *technical* marketing communication, our niche demands effective use of the media.

Applying What You've Learned

1. Think of the different ways in which you personally have online access. When and why do you choose to get certain information from online sources? What would compel you to seek or prefer alternative offline sources?

2. Think of a situation in which your only available information source is online, such as a class or work project. Was the information effectively designed for online use? What would you change to make it more effective online?
3. Find an example of online information that would not be effective in print form. Be prepared to defend your reasons.
4. Find an example of poorly prepared content on the Web. Print the pages and mark it for corrections so it will be effective online.
5. Find an example of PR content online and evaluate its effectiveness.
6. Find an example of a Web portal and evaluate its effectiveness.

SMALL GROUP ACTIVITY

The technology company you work for will release a new handheld computer in three months. Plan your online media-marketing endeavor. Don't forget to start with needs analysis, audience analysis, and strategy. Then choose the electronic tactics your group believes will be most effective. Be prepared to defend your choices. Make a list of issues you should be aware of as you develop these electronic tactics.

Notes

1. Jakob Nielson, *Designing Web Usability* (Indianapolis, Ind.: New Riders Publishing, 2000), 146.
2. Ibid.

CHAPTER 9

Personal Presentations and Events

Overview

"All I have to do is put the slide tray on your projector and I'm ready to go."

I left a manufacturing technology job to accept my first technical marketing specialist role at another company. As part of those new marketing duties, I was asked to give a presentation to a group of technologists who would include my former colleagues from the previous company. Naturally, I wanted to do my best in front of the entire group—but especially in front of the people who knew I was pursuing my new career direction.

Back in my new office, I wrote a strong presentation script detailing the benefits of a particular technology product. I thoughtfully and objectively discussed features, benefits, and unknowns. I planned adequate time for questions and answers, and I felt confident about my delivery. For visual support, I discovered a good set of slides already on file at the new company and selected some of the best for my presentation. Just to make sure I remembered the slide sequence and content, I asked my secretary to go through the carousel to look at each slide and then type a numbered list of brief descriptive statements on a separate sheet of paper. With that in hand, I was able to practice without having to project the slides, which I had already done numerous times.

By the time the presentation rolled around, I felt prepared and confident. We were a little rushed getting into the presentation room, because another group was running late. Our host looked at me and asked, "Will you need any extra time to set up and settle in?" I shook my head and smiled. "All I have to do is put the slide tray on your projector and I'm ready to go." So as everybody found their seats and the lights dimmed, I began to speak, careful to face my audience and not the projection screen. However, after advancing the first slide, I saw some smiles on my former colleagues' faces, smiles that didn't seem to sync with the technology subject matter. After advancing the next slide, one of them discreetly motioned to me with his hand. When I turned to look at the projection screen, I saw the speaker's worst nightmare: the slide image was upside down. A hundred questions ran through my mind as I tried to recover from my surprise and then from my embarrassment. I advanced quickly through a few more slides, finding some were obviously backwards, a few more were upside down, and one in five was correctly positioned. Finally gathering my composure, I asked for the lights, called a brief break, and repositioned the slides before continuing, successfully, with my presentation. How had it happened? My new secretary, who had never been asked by anybody to pull slides and make notes, did not realize there was a correct way to return them to the carousel tray—or she assumed I would do it later. For my part, I had failed to review the slides again before making the presentation, instead relying only on my notes.

During my first marketing presentation, I was fortunate to have learned several important lessons—which I can assure the reader I have never forgotten:

- Regardless of the media, the presenter is responsible to make sure his or her presentation is edited and ready.
- Whenever possible, visit the presentation venue ahead of time to test-run media, just in case there are incompatibles, and to see what your audience is going to see—before they do.
- When a presentation host offers you a few extra minutes in a rushed situation, graciously accept it regardless of your confidence level.

Life goes on and everyone has a humorous story to tell about a personal presentation gone awry. I rarely use slide trays or transparencies anymore, but I have discovered plenty of new analogies for the upside-down visual aid. It's going to happen, and nothing we can tell you will guarantee a perfect presentation future. Of course, with good planning and preparation, you'll avoid many of the potential pitfalls. In this chapter, we consider much more than the conference room one-to-many presentations. In addition, we explore the appropriate uses of personal presentations as well as the best ways to prepare and deliver them. You can find other books and courses devoted to the various aspects of personal presentations, and we encourage you to explore this powerful subject in greater detail.

Tom

When Personal Presentations Are Appropriate

Defining Personal Presentations

Describing an information sharing session as a presentation implies a preset occasion or opportunity. Someone has either asked you for more information about a technology, or you have requested the opportunity to share. It also implies both the involvement of a presenter or presenters and the participation of a willing audience. By definition, personal presentations involve at least one real-time, live human being on the content-delivery side. Real, live people are involved on the presenting and the receiving sides. The content delivery person or people can be in the same room with their audience or electronically linked at separate locations, but they are indeed presenting at the same time the audience is listening or watching. Since our electronic media opportunities include so many virtual reality presentation options it is necessary to clarify that personal presentations aren't always speeches or slide shows; they literally involve anything having to do with people presenting information. The scope involves everything from a customer sales call to an in-house team update. It doesn't have to be big to be a presentation.

More and more, the technical marketing communicator must weigh the need for personal presentations. The speed of doing business and working with technology places a premium on everyone's time. Those of us called on to make presentations want to know it is time well spent. It's too expensive and time-consuming to fly to a different city and share a technology concept that is just as easily accessed from an informative Web site or CD-ROM with video clips. Yet sometimes nothing else will do. E-mail is a wonderfully convenient tool, but eventually a long thread of responses and replies becomes woefully lifeless and empty. We still need to have personal contact. In fact, if time and travel did not present barriers, personal contact would be the arguable communication ideal. People simply relate best to people. However, we don't have that luxury, and we do have the convenience of the Internet for so many of our quick information needs. We must be able to discern when to consider personal presentations. We believe there are at least four good indicators that personal presentations are warranted:

1. **A strong relationship with the audience is important.** Relationships are best built with personal contact. Few of us develop or cultivate our strongest personal relationships without speaking to or seeing the other person. Our technology contacts are no different. Telephone calls help to renew and maintain relationships initiated or established with the help of personal presentation contact. From a different perspective, remember that audiences who welcome personal presentations may consider information contacts such as direct mail or advertising promotions to be impersonal, even rude.

2. **Technological complexities or nuances require explanation.** It's not always easy to introduce or explain technology to a particular audience without the benefit of personal contact. If people are confused while reading your technical literature, they can simply throw it away. If you're across the desk or in front of the auditorium, they can raise their hand. It is essential to combat a potentially high incidence of questions or confusion with the support of personal presence. This solution is especially effective if your audience is less technical or if your technology is difficult to differentiate.

3. **Personal presence and presentation skills are a differentiating asset.** Sometimes personal presentation skills are simply an asset in your toolkit. Some of the most well-known CEOs of technology companies have a natural charisma that audiences appreciate. Using a charismatic presenter to your advantage helps to associate a positive audience response with very nonhuman technol-

ogy. It can bring huge benefits and brand recognition. On a smaller scale, some technology presenters are better than others. Technical marketing communicators should take care to recognize the strengths of potential presenters on their team. They should also coach less charismatic presenters to improve or defer to other presenters.

4. **An audience gathering is already scheduled.** If you already have a venue, it's a great time for personal presentations. Professional society gatherings, technical exhibitions, and company meetings are all geared for personal presentations. Technical marketing communicators need to keep their calendars marked months, even years, in advance in order to target personal presentation opportunities on behalf of their technologies. For preplanned opportunities, the question is not "will there be a venue available at the time I have a technical marketing communication to share?" but rather, "how can I leverage the available venue to make a presentation on behalf of my technology?"

Presenter and Audience Match-Ups

Technical marketing communicators have much homework to do in advance of the actual presentation. In these next sections, you will learn about the thought process and planning you should do before you actually fashion and deliver a presentation.

Personal presentations can involve people in infinite combinations of numbers. The simplest presentation involves one person across from the other. Countless technology presentations take place every day at cubicle desks or coffee shop tables. But that same person presenting to one individual can reach millions of viewers in a televised satellite transmission. Or the tandem team of a salesperson and technical specialist might simply make an office visit to their local technology client. For simplicity, we've developed six categories of personal presentation match-ups (see Fig. 9.1).

One-to-One

One-to-one presentations shed any distractions caused by larger gatherings. On the other hand, they place much more emphasis on the interpersonal dynamics of the two people involved. The two participants can meet virtually anywhere, and it is much simpler to coordinate time and location. The presentation can be in-person or via electronic connection. The one-to-one format also lends itself to informality and intimacy. You don't need to stand at a podium and don a microphone. Fortunately, people are usually less inhibited about asking technical questions in the absence of peers or managers. They may also share insights about their technical program more openly in the context of a personal setting. The presentation format should be less elaborate and more focused on the interpersonal communication that forms the core strength of the setting. You can easily handle and share support tools in the presence of one person.

New office configurations (and cultures) also favor side-by-side seated conversations rather than across the desk. Some one-to-one presenters will want to

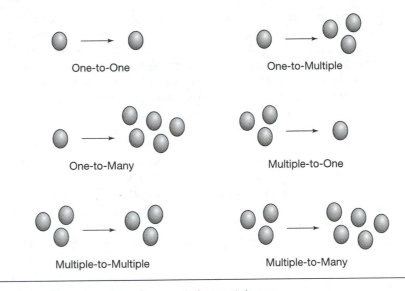

Figure 9.1 Six categories of presentation match-ups.

practice this immediate proximity with a colleague first. The up-close and personal feel can seem awkward or unusual enough to take some people off their game.

Printed media is perfectly acceptable as are laptop computer tools. However, presenters should be careful not to artificially distance themselves from the other participant with too many media distractions.

One-to-Multiple

One-to-multiple presentations simply add several people to the audience side of the table (or electronic connection). In-person presentations require the presenter to make contact with each participant and divide his or her attention more evenly. Presentation dynamics are sometimes complicated by the interpersonal dynamics of the audience members themselves. Strong attendee personalities may inhibit other participants or even challenge the presenter. It's important for the presenter to facilitate one-to-multiple presentations in a way that keeps the technology purpose focused. Presentation materials must be easily seen and handled by all the participants. Even so, electronic projection is not necessarily required for slide presentations if the setting provides a sufficiently positioned computer monitor. Regardless of presentation tools, the presenter should aim for an open and informal, interactive atmosphere.

One-to-Many

In some ways, one-to-many presentations are easier to execute than those in one-to-multiple settings. One-to-many presentations generally take place in large conference rooms or lecture halls. Electronically, they include teleconferences and

Webinars. By nature, the format discourages the degree of interaction possible at other gatherings. That means the presenter is free to focus more on the presentation and less on the audience dynamics. However, the setting also sacrifices some of the intimacy and immediacy of smaller gatherings. If a one-to-many presentation requires handouts or special media, the presenter should incorporate extra help from a colleague or host in order to stay focused on the presentation itself.

Tom spoke at a medium-sized conference (over 200 attendees). He wanted to anchor one of his points with a small handout—and the effect would be best if there was very little delay from the moment he set it up from his presentation script. But waiting until the presentation was over just wouldn't do. It had to be timed appropriately to be worthwhile. The hotel staff cooperated ahead of time to count the appropriate number of handouts per row and stacked them on a tray. Then, with several staff members thus engaged, they rapidly walked the aisle and dropped off the stacks at each row on Tom's cue. Within 90 seconds the effect was exactly as he had hoped, and every attendee had gotten the message.

Multiple-to-One

Many technical marketing presentations take the form of multiple-to-one settings. Imagine a technology team that includes a technical specialist, a project manager, and a technical marketing communicator. Technology teams frequently make presentations to a single individual to garner funding or as a point-of-sales entry to larger organizations. Teams need to project a unified, consistent message. Each person should understand his or her role in a presentation.

On another occasion, Tom worked with a technical marketing team that dutifully brought their national service engineer every time they traveled to visit him. Whether a global sales director or a regional vice president spoke to Tom, the service engineer was also at the table. Like a jazz musician stepping forward to play a solo, any time a truly challenging technical question arose, all eyes turned to the service engineer. He would accurately laser in on the answer, and then return to the rhythm section until the next time. This team was professional and exceptional in their technical acumen. But it wouldn't have been the same if they had constantly needed to say, "We don't know the answer, but we'll get back to you as soon as we call our national sales engineer."

The presenters must be careful not to overwhelm or intimidate a single individual. Each presenter should help the targeted individual understand what his or her role in the technology landscape is and why that is relevant to the presentation at hand.

Multiple-to-Multiple

Multiple-to-multiple presentations usually accompany a meeting between two teams or organizations. Typical presentations match one technology development team to another: a sales team to a customer procurement team; an in-house development team to a user team. At a team-to-team or group-to-group level, often one person aligns with a specific member of the audience either by function or hierarchy. For example, a senior manager may direct his or her presentation primarily to the leadership representative of the other audience team. A sales or marketing person may focus on presentation issues important to procurement, while the presentation team's project manager speaks to the concerns of the operations managers (see Fig. 9.2).

Multiple-to-Many

Multiple-to-many presentation dynamics are similar to one-to-many presentations, but with more presenters. More presenters translates to increased coordination and complexity for the technical marketing communicator.

One large company took elaborate pains to prepare presenters for a two-day technical meeting. All presenters were given a standard slide template file to use, and asked to submit a script draft prior to rehearsal. Following the rehearsal with company executives and the respective edits, the presentations were "frozen" from further change and loaded onto a computer. The company's technical marketing communication team, rather than the hotel's audiovisual group, kept control of the presentation equipment and ran it for the meeting. Each presenter then had a brief dry run at the hotel the day before the meetings began to make sure slides and memories were aligned. Needless to say, with the careful planning and control, surprises and technical malfunctions were definitely kept to a minimum during the actual presentations. There was also a marked lack of spark and spontaneity to the flavor of the meeting. Still, the team's content was clear and solid, which was their primary goal for the meeting.

Messages must be aligned, scripts reviewed for consistency, and media synchronized. The best advice is to include more preplanning time and identify one team member as the main point of contact—namely, the technical marketing communicator.

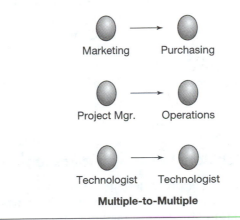

Figure 9.2   Aligning presenter with a specific member of the audience.

Types of Personal Presentations

Regardless of the audience match-up, personal presentations fall into at least six different types. Technical marketing communicators should develop a sense for the most appropriate type of presentation warranted before actually crafting the presentation itself. Goals vary, but presentation types have one or more of our original four personal presentation indicators in common:

- A strong relationship with the audience is important.
- Technological complexities or nuances require explanation.
- Personal presence and presentation skills are a differentiating asset.
- An audience gathering is already scheduled.

Type One: Brand-Building Presentation

The standard technology sales *cold call* is just that: calling on a technology prospect who has not yet warmed up to the idea or value of your program, product, or service. Cold calls aren't far enough along in a sales cycle to benefit from branding groundwork. You're far from ready to submit a quotation or budget request. A technology representative has probably met a prospect at a networking event or through a mutual contact. The contact may have already visited your Web site and browsed that information. Sooner or later, the next step in a technology relationship is to tell more about your company or technology. Brand-building presentations are promotional in nature, with hopes of establishing a relationship foothold for a technology program, service, or product. Brand presentations offer high-level overview information about organizations and their capabilities. It's a sharing process, and frequently occurs at a one-to-one, multiple-to-one, or multiple-to-multiple audience match-up. A major element of a brand-building presentation involves listening to the customer or partner audience to understand his or her needs for the future. Technical marketing communicators provide the collateral material and scripted information such as theme statements and elevator pitch that support a brand presentation (see Chapter 5).

Support Material: Company brochures, product sheets, flip sheets, or slide presentations are all part of the brand-building process. Inexpensive giveaways such as pens or CD business cards are fully acceptable in this situation (see Chapter 10).

Next Steps: Cultivate brand awareness with the prospect to develop a technology relationship.

Type Two: Relationship-Building Presentation

A relationship-building presentation does not require detailed company or technology background information if brand awareness is already established. Relationship building is a way of maintaining contact between technology organizations and their personnel. These presentations provide an opportunity to review ongoing development programs, industry trends, or to review processes in use. Too often technology organizations or clients meet only to transact business or work through a deadline crisis. Instead, two organizations or technology groups who are between projects should use the opportunity to strengthen ongoing work relationships. Technical marketing communicators see these as strategic opportunities to take stock, strengthen communication channels, and clarify the way in which technology organizations work together. It's a great time to share visions for the future.

You will typically find these situations in a multiple-to-multiple presentation scenario although they also occur at the micro level of one-to-one visits. In-house technology teams also benefit from strategically timed relationship building. Bringing pizza in for Friday lunch sets the stage for an informal relationship-building presentation. An executive level session we attended in Silicon Valley recently matched five people from each team in a nine-hour session of reciprocal presentations. Each person took the opportunity to talk about his or her department, technology direction, and hopes for the intercompany relationships. It was fatiguing but extremely productive. A teleconference or Web session would never have conveyed the personal commitment the attendees made as part of the relationship-building presentations.

Support Material: Slide presentations, status reports of ongoing technology programs, survey or anecdotal feedback on shared processes.

Next Steps: Identify specific relationship-building actions for follow-up and establish future meetings.

Type Three: Technology Demonstration

A technology demo is one of the most frequently used personal presentations. Most people want to see technology in action. It transfers an idea or image from a brochure or Web page to reality. It builds credibility. Demos may be elaborate or spartan depending on your audience and budget. Some recently publicized military technology demos used surface-to-air missiles to destroy a target over the Pacific Ocean. It undoubtedly cost more than a Webinar, but nothing else could have gotten the idea across.

While attending a riverboat festival, a wireless telephone company was demonstrating the clarity of new digital technology. Their energetic presentation professionals were armed with brochures, a scripted pitch, and a digital cell phone. Anyone willing to listen to the brief, informative pitch could use the phone to place a call anywhere in the world. It had dramatic impact on the callers and on the surrounding people hearing their end of the phone conversation. That was a job well done by the technical marketing communicators. A successful technology demonstration shows the program, product, or service in action and helps the audience imagine how the same technology could help them or their organization.

Support Material: Follow-up contact information (business cards, Web addresses), technical product sheets, and company brochures for additional brand building.

Next Steps: Seek additional feedback on how presentation audiences could use the technology or contribute to enhancements.

Type Four: Technology Proposal Presentation

If you are trying to increase business or funding, you need a technology proposal. The proposal itself may be a paper document or word processing file. But like relationship building, a proposal is best received and positioned with the support of live people. Technical marketing communicators coach their technology teams to incorporate consistent brand themes all the way from promotions through to proposals. If technical marketing communicators have done their job, then some of the key messages, features, and benefits have made their way to the customer's psyche. It's important to trigger that awareness by affirming thematic concepts with graphics and textual statements during the presentation. We worked with a large southern hospital that was planning to install a new high tech wing for heart catheterizations. Our firm had consistently recommended a modular, resizable design as the cornerstone benefit of our technology solution. Going in to the proposal presentation we were the underdog compared to the large local design firm. As a last reminder of our theme, we gave the evaluation team a small ruler and an eraser. We smiled and said, "We want you to remember that you hold the power to alter the design right there in your hands." After awarding us the project, the team leader said they were most impressed with our flexible design approach. Did the ruler and eraser win the project? No, but it did help to affirm our end-to-end technical marketing communication theme.

Support Material: Proposal; include brochure and product sheet attachments or appendices with the proposal.

Next Steps: Follow-up after presentation to affirm your interest and offer additional information or clarification.

Type Five: Topical Presentation

Typically one-to-many in nature, topical presentations are meant to share technical information aimed at a particular topic. Keynote speakers at professional societies or technical exhibitions deliver topical presentations. Your local chamber of commerce sponsors breakfast and lunch meetings with topical speakers. Technical marketing communicators like to facilitate these opportunities because it positions their speaker as an expert in the field. This position feeds ongoing brand notoriety and credibility. Many technical marketing communication teams assign an agency just to keep some of their key professionals scheduled at high-profile speaking engagements. Other technology professionals are simply in demand enough to choose their own speaking opportunities.

I delivered a topical presentation describing what technology employers look for in candidate interviews. It had nothing to do with the company we were representing per se, but it drew in a number of highly qualified candidates for interviews just the same. Topical presentations may or may not include direct reference to your organization's technology. Just garnering the visibility is a positive outcome. It will seem less like a marketing opportunity and more like industry expertise if your topical presentation remains generic and not self-promotional or product centric.

Support Material: Company brochures and product sheets aren't likely to appear in your material for a topical presentation.

Next Steps: Invite people to contact you for additional conversation and information about your organization.

Type Six: Technical Report or Update

Reports and update presentations are pragmatic in nature. Information and updates simply are what they are. These presentations tend to have fewer frills. But like our other presentation formats, technical marketing communicators should never miss an opportunity to include brand themes or make strategic references to other technologies or projects. Technical report presentations are in the high-risk category for losing audience interest. Do your best to minimize technospeak and lead-up details. Stick to issues and outcomes.

Support Material: Report summaries, organization brochures, and product sheets.

Next Steps: Record action items and follow-up commitments.

Preparing a Presentation

With a sense of the type of presentation needed and the appropriate audience match-up, a technical marketing communicator is much better positioned to craft the presentation itself. But be patient, there are still a few additional things to consider.

Know Your Presentation Persona

Some aspects of personal presentations have nothing to do with technology. The number one rule for presenters is to be yourself. People are most at ease listening and sharing information when they sense *you* are comfortable and at ease—with your technology subject matter as well as your presentation persona. It's natural to be nervous. But people can usually see past that to discern who you are without the butterflies. A big part of your personal presentation style resonates from how you relate to people in general. Are you quiet and thoughtful? Bold and brash? If you're not sure, find a self-evaluation tool on the Web and gauge your natural level of expressiveness and enthusiasm. Tapping into your presentation persona will help you to successfully script and shape your presentations. Play to your strengths and strengthen or avoid your weaknesses.

At one conference we attended, a very charismatic and humorous presenter had the audience laughing and applauding as his presentation closed. Tough act to follow. My heart went out to the next presenter. Then he began to speak in a quiet, even voice as the audience, still energized from the last speaker, fidgeted and settled down. He's too quiet, and they're going to walk out before he's even got his second slide up, we worried. But with that, his eloquent and confident speaking style began to take hold. The speaker quickly established his presence as a knowledgeable and insightful authority. In the end, his quiet, but incredibly informative, presentation had been as riveting as the previous one had been hilarious. Both presenters had used their personal presentation style to their full advantage. Having said that, even though your *personal* style is your *best* presentation style, you may still need to tailor your approach for certain audiences.

For example, some technology-oriented audiences are accustomed to serious, fact-filled presentations—and presenters. Technical marketing communicators will decide if that is the situation as they profile an audience. If possible, technical marketing communicators should even be careful not to match an outrageously extroverted presenter to an extremely introverted technologist or technology team. It just won't do to ask the outrageous extrovert to tone it down just for this meeting. And some of the newer cutting edge technologies are populated by 24 × 7 imagineers of boundless energy and enthusiasm. They're looking for presentations that can keep up with *them.* They might actually get impatient with an understated or overly serious presentation. You won't always have the luxury of matching presenter personas to audience profiles, but you should look for opportunities to present themselves. For all other situations, let the strengths of the presenter be the strengths of the presentation. Trying to make presenters change their inherent style is like trying to make electrons jump out of their natural orbits—you just can't alter quantum mechanics without dramatic side effects.

Plan the Duration of the Presentation

It's easy to let technology presentations run too long. Once we're on a roll, we are always tempted to share one more piece of data and another interesting insight, and then another. And they *are* interesting insights, but they lose their punch after an audience is sufficiently saturated. Complex technical concepts, formulas, or designs will quickly fatigue even the most knowledgeable audiences if they're truly absorbing the content. As a technical marketing communicator, you need to be sensitive to the limits of your audience.

How long is too long? Challenge yourself to be a good steward of other people's time. Wisely prepare for and apply the time they've entrusted to you. A deskside presentation might be effective for 10 to 15 minutes. A large gathering of international colleagues may expect a longer presentation. They may even expect the presentation time to equal the travel time. But we should only present for the time required to share the content, rather than presenting to fill a required amount of time.

A technically-oriented personal presentation should last just long enough for the audience to comprehend technical concepts without disengaging before you can call for action. Topical presentations should rarely exceed 20 to 30 minutes of content before questions and answers, hitting three to five key technology points along the way. This schedule frequently conflicts with the standard one-hour preset agenda of most conferences. However, nothing says you are compelled to artificially fill time at the expense of a successful presentation. Let the presentation content and the audience dictate your time. Technology demonstrations may last longer, as long as 45 minutes to an hour, if they're well orchestrated or interactive. Brand-building and relationship-building presentation segments should also last no more than 30 to 40 minutes although dialog with the audience may last significantly longer.

Electronic meetings seem to have a shorter saturation fuse. We participated in two-hour teleconferences and Webinars that seemed interminably long because of slow network response or lack of audience interaction. Technology participants often combat this dead time by placing their telephones or personal computer microphones on mute. That way they can simultaneously conduct other work at their desk while listening in, a situation that is not conducive to high comprehension. Teleconferences and Webinars should rarely exceed 60 to 90 minutes. If there is additional compelling content, simply schedule additional sessions. However, it's more likely you can distill the essential content to fit the duration of an audience-friendly presentation. To paraphrase the comments of a wise technology presenter, it's better to have them wishing you'd spoken longer, than left earlier.

Choose the Right Location and Setting

If you can choose the location and setting, use that to your strategic advantage. Keep in mind the *location* is different from the *setting* itself. Location refers to their city or yours or a specialty location such as Washington, D.C., or Las Vegas. Perhaps you could consider the site of the next big technical conference whenever possible. You should strategically decide the location for your presentation. One of the larger companies for computing infrastructure has a separate building on its campus just for executive meetings and presentations. It's located at headquarters, so executives can drop in on important client meetings as needed. The center also showcases the company's most state-of-the-art technology. With these star attractions, their larger customers and technology partners consider it a perk to be invited to a meeting at this location.

Presentation *setting*s are at the next level of detail. For example, your office location may have multiple conference rooms and office areas to choose as presentation settings. One-to-one settings are incredibly flexible. Depending on media requirements, you can choose anything from an office cubicle or local coffee shop to the executive boardroom. Each setting conveys a message. The coffee shop might suggest an appropriately friendly and open relationship-building setting. The boardroom could signal the client's level of importance to your organization. A golf resort says this meeting is more about recreation and relationships than technology. Technical marketing communicators want to align the setting and its implications with their overall strategic message and audience profile.

The other important setting variable is comfort: both for your audience and yourself. Don't choose a location where road construction has traffic frozen for the next three months. Don't cram a large audience into a small space or expect them to see electronic media from 30 yards away. Be sensitive to your personal presentation needs as well. Look for sufficient room for media or wall charts. Ensure that you will be able to have eye contact with everybody in the audience without peering around obstructions. Bring in audio equipment if you have to shout to be heard without it. Your audience will receive your technology message better if the setting or its limitations do not distract you or them.

Finally, make sure you can schedule and gain access to the desired venue. Plan in advance and confirm availability before inviting a cast of thousands. It doesn't hurt to have an alternate Plan B in case your boardroom privileges can be revoked for an emergency board meeting.

Drafting the Presentation

Technology by its very nature requires additional focus and energy on the part of the audience. They may simply have to work a little harder to stay on track and comprehend the content. That's not to take anything away from your audience. They're most likely bright, intelligent people who are as capable and immersed in the subject matter as you are. But they're also just as overwhelmed as you are with the speed of change and the difficulty in keeping up with every new idea that comes along. You have to help them. Anything your presentation can do to help them assimilate more easily will only further your agenda for technical marketing communication.

Think of each presentation as the synthesis of six component parts: introduction, agenda, body, call to action, closing, and follow-up (see Fig. 9.3). Each component contributes a distinct communication ingredient to the whole. Imagine a funnel representing your presentation process. At the top of the presentation you are covering broad general ground before you begin the transition to your technology subject matter. As your presentation proceeds, you narrow your focus to specific content items and eventually to a very specific conclusion or call to action. As you exit the narrowest part of the funnel, your goal is to have the audience focused and engaged enough to interact with questions and answers of a specific nature. That's quite a distance from the top where you began with very general information.

This format is just as appropriate for one-to-one cubicle presentations as it is for teleconferences or Web-enabled technology demonstrations. In fact, technical marketing communicators sometimes fail to plan sufficiently for their smaller settings, thinking they can just wing it. But a presentation session that rambles or gets off message may seem sloppy or poorly planned. Audiences become uneasy and

Introduction
Agenda
Body Content
Call to Action
Closing
Q&A

Figure 9.3 Six components of a presentation.

even confused if they don't know where you're going with the presentation. Audiences may even associate a poorly organized or delivered presentation with the technology itself. Conversely, the format works to your advantage as well. A well-organized and executed presentation enhances the impression of the technology subject matter itself.

Consider adopting the discipline and rigor of a consistent presentation format. It doesn't mean every presentation is the same. The content for each section is what conveys your creativity and innovation. You can always add or delete a section when the situation calls for it.

Introduction, Goals, and Housekeeping

Before diving into your subject matter, take a little time to introduce yourself and interact with the audience of one or many. Smile warmly. Scan people's nametags and address a few of them by their first name if possible. Some of the following ideas can help you get started:

- State your name and occupation.
- Tell the audience your hometown.
- Tell the audience your alma mater.
- Share a recent industry anecdote of interest.
- Relate some latest humor about your technology.

Being conversational helps to put everybody at ease. It also builds familiarity with the presenter as you transition to the technology subject matter. Remember you're asking the audience to consider you credible and trustworthy enough to speak on behalf of the technology at hand. It pays to take a little time to earn or cultivate that sense of trust. Teleconference and Web-enabled presentations have less in-person visual contact, but they also benefit from introductions.

If you're presenting as a guest at someone else's location, be sure to complement your hosts and their facility. Thank everyone for taking the time to attend and participate. Next, speak to any environmental or housekeeping issues. Announce the location of the restrooms. If you'd prefer pagers or cell phones to be off, make that request in a reasonable manner. Ask if anyone is uncomfortable with the temperature or lights. A presenter we know with a hearing disability usually asks audiences to signal him with a touch or a hand wave if he doesn't respond to their question or comment. It doesn't hurt to ask if anybody else in the audience has special needs to consider. Accommodating them, within reason, will help them participate more willingly.

Finally, deliver any instructions the audience will need to remember before they are dismissed at the end of the presentation. For example, remind them to sign the attendance form being circulated, complete (or e-mail) your feedback survey sheet, or pick up your information packet.

After you have made introductions and addressed housekeeping issues, close the first segment by affirming your goal(s) for the presentation. Once again, you should affirm your goals whether you have one person in the audience or one thousand. Your presentation goal should be clear and concise but not overly elaborate. For example, consider the following goals:

- Demonstrate a new feature of this technology.
- Explain the cost savings to be realized by funding this new technology.
- Gain your approval to move forward with this technology proposal.

For smaller gatherings, especially for relationship building, ask if this goal will make your audience's time commitment worthwhile. You might ask if your goal sounds reasonable or if they have other goals they would like you to address. Stating and affirming your goal ensures that no one in the audience is left wondering why they are there. Busy technology people get pulled into meetings only to later lament they would not have stayed if they had known the point of the meeting. Given the opportunity, savvy technology people will also build on your goal statement. They might suggest your goal is fine, but they may have other ground they want you to cover. Presenters should welcome an opportunity to fully engage a member of the audience as they modify a presentation goal to his or her satisfaction.

We encourage you to state a goal even if your presentation is simply a topical one. You can start by announcing your topic, followed with your goal for the presentation. For example, the simplest topical goal is that your audience will understand how they could use the technology in their own organization. Remember to recap your goal at the end of the presentation and ask if you were successful in achieving it. If not, you'll still have time to revisit any points that need to be clarified.

Agenda

Don't forget an agenda. It's a road map for your presentation, and technology people like those kinds of details. Once you've put everyone at ease during the introduction, and your goals are clear, explain how you intend to allocate your time together. Presentations don't usually list a timed agenda as a meeting would. Instead, explain the basic content flow of your presentation so that attendees can mentally keep track of your progress. Try to keep your agenda conversational and personal. For example, a new technology presentation agenda might look like this:

- Introduction and goals
- What does this technology do?
- How will this technology help you?
- How can you learn more?
- Questions and answers

Note that this technology is clearly positioned to help the audience. They also know right from the start that they'll be told how to get more information, so it's not a concern. If they're too self-conscious to interrupt the presentation with questions, they can do that at the end. Even with Q&A scheduled, presenters appear more accessible if they encourage audiences to interact at any time. This type of interaction isn't practical for large audiences, but it is essential for smaller relationship building presentation audiences.

As you did with the presentation goals, ask if they have anything to add to the agenda. The majority of the time an agenda won't be second-guessed. However, posing the question builds an interactive atmosphere and once again affirms you are accessible. As soon as everyone is aligned and in agreement, it's time to present your information.

Body (Message Content)

The message is the heart of your presentation. With the introductions and agenda in order, all attention can be placed on the technology content itself. Limit the main body of your technology presentation to three to five key points or segments, regardless of their length or content. People simply can't absorb and retain more chunks of information than that. Focusing on a short list of key items also demonstrates your own ability to discern and select the most salient information on their behalf. If you have more to tell, engage the audience by offering opportunities for follow-up. Keep your information sequential. Provide what they need to know in order to understand the first point and then the next. Abstract concepts don't play well in presentations unless your goal is to stimulate abstract thought processes.

The presentation content should also mesh with your overall strategic information approach for the technology. Be sure to weave in brand themes and reinforce ideas presented in other tactics or media related to this effort. Of course, wherever possible make use of visuals and multimedia to augment text and the spoken word (see Chapter 8).

Call to Action or Challenge

Tell your audience what you want them to do next: Wait? Learn? Call? Try? They'll appreciate it if you articulate a specific call to action on their behalf. Tell them with conviction and enthusiasm. If you really want them to take a next step, tell them so in a way that conveys your passion for the subject matter. Now is not the time to equivocate. A call to action is often the reason your company funded your time and travel in the first place. You may just want to issue a challenge so the topic of your presentation doesn't fade from an attendee's mind as soon as you've finished. Use your call to action to remind attendees of anything they need to do on your behalf. For example, remind them to sign the attendee form, pick up the information packet, or complete the feedback survey. You should affirm any instructions issued as part of your introduction and housekeeping.

At one corporate marketing presentation, Tom had developed a brief "elevator pitch" for the technology team. His call to action charged the audience to memorize the elevator pitch and be prepared to answer with it the very next time someone asked, "What does your company do?" Immediately following the presentation, Tom entered an elevator with another gentleman on his way back to his room. To Tom's amused surprise, the man smiled and asked, "Who are you with?" Tom told him, and the man's next question, as you'd expect, was, "What does your company do?" Tom was ready for him.

Close

Before inviting questions, make a final assessment of your presentation and your time together. Thank your hosts again if appropriate. Some presenters reserve their closing comments until after the question and answer session, but that can backfire. If any of the audience members begin to leave (or log off) during the Q&A, it may make your closing seem rushed or protracted.

Question and Answer

If you've sufficiently prepared for your presentation, the question and answer session should actually be quite enjoyable. It's an opportunity to engage your audience on a more personal level and to hear firsthand what is important to them. Remember to restate questions so everyone in the audience (or on conference call lines) can hear them and understand your answer in context. Be patient at the start of a Q&A and try to coax the first question to break the ice. Affirm each questioner: "Good question," and thank them after you've answered. When you've reached your scheduled time limit or when there are no further questions, thank all the attendees and declare the presentation complete.

It's extremely important to keep your composure during questions and answers. We have witnessed wonderful presentations marred because presenters lost their patience with an insistent or recalcitrant audience member. You make your final personal impression during the questions and answers, and it should be a positive one. Reserve some of your best energy and concentration for this purpose. Don't let your guard down just because you have delivered the message content.

Choosing Presentation Delivery Tools

Choose presentation tools to enhance your message content. One of the most effective technology presentations we've ever seen involved an engineering manager and an overhead projector. With full confidence and command of his subject matter, he cycled through five overhead transparencies. Each bore his crisp, neatly *handwritten* notes and several hand-drawn diagrams. His brief and knowledgeable update presentation of engineering project work was impressive and easy to follow. His communication support tools were perfect for the situation.

Slide software has since become a universal presentation tool, but don't bore your audience with too many screens full of bulleted text. Insert a nontext graphic or chart wherever possible. Slip in a cartoon to break things up with a little humor. It's also easy to insert video clips or arrange to have a video cart and monitor.

Reach outside the technology zone to make a particular point. One presenter we enjoyed was trying to emphasize the importance of teamwork for an upcoming technology rollout. After stating his case, he asked everyone to watch the video monitor. His audience laughed in unison at a contemporary movie clip where the overacting bad guy threatened his thugs that they'd be sorry if they dared to double-cross him. He made a serious point, and the team probably referred to that clip more than once during the project. On another occasion, a presenter used the metaphor of fishing to train the technology sales team about prospecting for clients. He brought in fishing poles, nets, and a wide array of lures to help make the point. Very nontechnical, but very memorable.

It's also easy to patch in other presenters to provide additional perspective, either by satellite or more conventional means. At one recent presentation of a technology proposal, we were asked to demonstrate progress with a particular vendor partner. At a predetermined time, we simply had the vendor representative call in to the conference room's speakerphone from their home office and make a brief statement before taking questions. After ten minutes, we disconnected and continued with the presentation. This conference call was much more productive than reading some quotes, and more sensible than flying someone in for a ten-minute conversation.

It's also possible to let other members of the audience dial in to participate. With Web sharing tools, they can follow along on the same slide presentation and interact with the rest of the participants. Presenters should remember to address the attendees who are joining a presentation from other locations. Refer to them at different intervals to make them feel welcome and included. Flipcharts are also good presentation companions to collect important questions or insights for later follow-up. Some teams call this chart a "parking lot" to park ideas for follow-up later. If good handwriting isn't one of your presentation gifts, ask a colleague or audience member to act as scribe. For a show-and-tell effect, pass around an object related to your subject matter just to physically engage the audience as well. This object can be a document, chart, or technology sample. But remember to describe it for virtual attendees who can't see it.

Keep your production support tools simple. Elaborate productions don't have to seem elaborate. In the end, presentation tools are meant to support the message, not the other way around.

Timing Isn't Everything, but It Helps

Personal presentations are just one of the tactical options available to technical marketing communicators. Scheduling personal presentation dates and times will depend on the sequence and timing of other tactics in a technical marketing communication plan. You may find they work best before or after another specific tactic. But you're not always in the scheduling driver's seat. You don't always have the luxury of choosing your presentation date and time. Sometimes other people or circumstances determine that. If you're the keynote speaker on the first day of a technology conference, then you have no choices. It's probably not wise to reschedule a presentation *requested* by the president of your company. But when you do have some flexibility, take a few of these suggestions into consideration. They're not absolute, but our personal experience backs them up.

- **Try to avoid presentation slots immediately preceding or following the lunch hour.** Audiences with prelunch low blood sugar get cranky and distracted. Well-fed postlunch audiences start to nod off about 45 to 60 minutes after eating. It's true; just check your watch next time. Actually, the same is true for pre- and postdinner audiences as well. If you've drawn one of these time slots, go out of your way to include interaction with the audience. It's more difficult for them to disengage if you pose questions or call on them for examples. Also, don't make people wait for their meal if you want to leave a good impression. We've heard presenters earn boisterous applause at the onset of their presentation by declaring, "Even though my segment is starting late, I still intend to get you out of here at the scheduled lunch time."

- **Be sensitive to the diversity of holidays or special industry dates that might limit audience participation.** One technology team we know traveled by air to make a proposal presentation at the urgent request of their host team. Unfortunately, the respective presentation schedulers from each group were traveling the week before and didn't do a thorough job of confirming everyone's calendar. On arriving, the presentation team learned that half of the host's scheduled attendees had canceled since it was both Columbus Day (an optional holiday) and Yom Kippur. A little extra communication would have saved everyone significant time and expense. Similarly, if everyone in your technology field is at the same national conference for a week, schedule your presentation in the host city or don't schedule them at all during that time.

- **Understand cultural and process-related scheduling distractions.** For example, some technology sales organizations can be extremely difficult to schedule for presentations. Monday is bad because they are getting set up for the week's account calls. Friday is bad because it's their day to catch up on administrative work. Tuesday through Wednesday is booked with sales calls, and on it goes. In all fairness, technology salespeople have to remain busy by definition, or they don't get paid. So some teams compromise by blocking out early mornings or late afternoons for important presentations. Others meticulously schedule days full of presentations at quarterly gatherings and require technical marketing communicators to work to those dates.

- **Consider natural schedule conflicts.** Assume that most people appreciate an hour or so to get into the office, recover from traffic, listen to their messages, and check e-mail. At the end of the day, assume most people like some time to do the same before leaving at a reasonable hour. Scheduling a presentation you hope will grab everyone's undivided attention during these time slots isn't productive.

There's really no perfect answer for the absolute best time to schedule your presentation. Poll your audience representatives to determine times and dates when their members will be most receptive. From our experience, the *sweet spots* for best audience focus and least interruption seem to be from 9:00 to 11:00 A.M. (missing the postcommute and prelunch distractions) and from 2:00 to 4:00 P.M. (missing postlunch and precommute distractions). Find what works best for you and your technology audiences. Time and experience will tell.

Promoting an Event: Audience Prework and Expectation Setting

It's great if you can have access to your audience in advance of a presentation. As with other forms of communication, technical marketing communicators like to prepare the way for the message and have it reinforced by the presentation itself.

For small group presentations, and especially for in-house teams, you may want attendees to think about technology concepts and their implications in advance of the presentation. Send them files or messages with exactly that in mind. "Please review the attached product overview file (or Web page) before our scheduled presentation. We welcome and encourage your feedback during our question and answer segment of the presentation." You can't base an entire presentation on the requested feedback because you have no guarantee they'll review the material. But it signals a collaborative flavor and may prompt some additional insights.

Some teams refer to advance information review as *prework*. For a presentation on technical marketing communication, we sent a short list of instructions to registered attendees that included, "Make a list of your five favorite communication tools and explain why you prefer them." That challenged most people to think of three communication tools besides e-mail and voicemail. It also moved some of the attendees to say, "I never think of these communication options as *tools*." It piqued their interest enough to attend and *listen* in a more proactive manner. That preserved precious time and attention span for the presentation itself.

Technology conferences will request and publish summaries of presentations in their advance materials (see Fig. 9.4). These publications help attendees choose presentations that most interest them. That means the title of your presentation should be informative and perhaps a little provocative to garner attention. Consider your presentation title to be a mini-billboard for these situations. For example, "Ten reasons this technology will change life as we know it," or "Technology they wouldn't tell you about in school," aren't as dry as others might be. Make brand tie-in where possible, and keep your audience tastes (not yours) at the forefront of your creativity.

Is Anybody Listening to Me?

"I sent e-mail, left voicemail and even pinned a note to the cafeteria bulletin board—but I still haven't gotten any hits on my new corporate Intranet page. Isn't anybody listening?"

Join Sandra Harner at the Intranet Designers Symposium in Dallas February 12 to learn the "Ten truths of Technology Teasers." *Telling* people where to find *your* information isn't enough. They need compelling reasons to recognize and engage your solution to *their* information needs. Like any other marketing communications endeavor, you'll need a more strategic approach—and Sandi will tell you how.

Figure 9.4   Summary of presentations in advance materials.

Above all, make sure people know about your presentation, why they should attend, and how to participate. For small groups, you may contact people on an individual basis via phone or e-mail. Planners for large seminars and training events probably do the advance work for you, and they simply require your presentation overview. For strictly promotional presentations, such as executive coffees or networking events, technical marketing communicators may want to proactively advertise and engage public relations channels. Direct mail, telemarketing, Web banners, and publication advertisements are all appropriate for important presentation events.

Delivering the Presentation

As we suggested earlier, be sure to inquire about or check out your presentation surroundings and media ahead of time whenever possible. Your presentation setting is much more than the layout of the chairs or tables although that's very important. Think about it from two perspectives: yours and the audiences. For situations in which you have no control over the setting, identify the key logistical points:

- Can the audience see your media?
- Can the audience see and hear you?
- Can you see and hear the audience?

These are fundamentals that must absolutely be attended to. People become fatigued and less interested if they have to struggle to hear or see. It's worth taking the time to ensure that satellite video feeds, microphones, and projectors work. If you are dialing in to analog Web lines or LAN connections, make sure data transfer rates are acceptable. Determine the best possible overhead lighting combination so people can see their notes and presentation media as well. If you are not locked to a lectern, think carefully about where you can wander in the presentation area without blocking cameras, your audience, or presentation media. Check wireless transmitters for dead spots in the room. For media on carts such as video monitors, understand where power cords will run (avoid tripping) and check volume levels.

If you have a hand in planning the layout of a room or hall, be even more attentive to audience needs. See to their comfort by giving them adequate space between chairs. Learn where the temperature controls are and how they work. A hot room puts your audience to sleep, and a cold room annoys the people in short sleeves and skirts. Anything you can do to eliminate audience distraction helps your audience to listen to your technology message.

Don't be afraid to improvise in order to enhance the presentation setting. Sooner or later every technical marketing communicator ends up in a conference room with a media projector and no projection screen. That's fine if you're projecting on to a flat, white wall, but it's terribly distracting if it's a textured or carpeted wall. Grab some masking tape and a few flipchart pages to make your own screen.

On more than one occasion, when faced with a textured wall and a small conference room audience, we've simply hauled in the most available computer monitor and connected it to the laptop computer in the conference room. Even the laptop screen itself is sometimes better than a projected image on a poorly surfaced wall.

The same rules that apply to the audience apply to the presenter. Your technology message will be more consistent and connected if you are not distracted by logistical problems during the presentation. Put yourself at ease by knowing the layout, temperature and lighting controls, and the contact person if you experience facility or audiovisual problems. If these details tend to distract you, bring along an assistant or enlist a colleague to run interference for you.

Presentation Follow-Up

Don't miss any opportunities to follow-up after the presentation. You should get a list of attendees and their contact information. Many conferences are beginning to use bar-coded nametags for this purpose and will offer presenters a printed list of attendees. You can also set up your handheld computer to beam electronic business cards. But when all else fails, send around a sheet of paper and a pen. Have a stack of your business cards readily available as well as any printed material or premiums you wish to distribute. Offer your e-mail address and encourage people to contact you. Many well-intentioned people will not contact you unless invited to do so, assuming you are already too busy to respond to their inquiry. Once you have acquired attendee information, you should enter it into a master database and add it to ongoing technology updates. We encourage technical marketing communicators to adopt a policy that gives audiences the option to remove their names from future distributions.

If challenging questions or comments are made during a presentation, promise attendees a response. Offer to post the information on a Web site or in a newsletter by a certain date, record it on your outgoing voice message, e-mail it to the attendee list, or deliver it via some other option. In any event, be accountable and follow through as promised.

Of equal follow-up importance is the need to solicit continuous improvement feedback from your audience. Technical marketing communicators should develop a repeatable feedback format for their presenters and establish a baseline of comparison to gauge improvement. Surveys should be simple and easy to complete, with about five questions and room to add general comments. Typical survey questions and statements can be ranked on a scale of 1 to 5 ranging from poor, needs improvement, neutral, above average to excellent or some other scale consistent with your organization's customer service program (see Fig. 9.5).

You can distribute surveys before or after the presentation. If you offer them ahead of time (placed at each chair or distributed with presentation materials), attendees can make notes as they listen. Distributing them at the end provides an extra opportunity for you to emphasize their importance. The logistics are up to you. Either way, make sure attendees understand you value their input and the extra

Today's Presentation

Audience Feedback Form

Your feedback will help us to continually improve our presentations and customer service. Please rate each question according to your experience today. Thank you!

5—Strongly Agree   4—Agree   3—Neither Agree/Disagree   2—Disagree   1—Strongly Disagree

1. The presentation *facility* enhanced my experience. _____

2. The presentation *content* advanced my knowledge of the subject matter. _____

3. The presentation *materials* were informative and compelling. _____

4. The *presenter* effectively *conveyed* the content. _____

5. I would attend another presentation in this series. _____

Please add your other comments and suggestions below:

Figure 9.5   Typical survey instrument to evaluate presentation.

bit of time it takes for them to complete and return the forms. Have them return the forms to an assistant or a third party to remove any bias or discomfort in handing feedback directly to the presenter.

Presentations and Event Coordination

Personal presentations can stand alone or accompany and support a larger event. The overall approach we've described thus far is flexible enough to scale for any number of attendees or presenters. In this closing section, we've added a few additional insights specific to various presentation opportunities.

Single-Person Presentations

Single-person presentations follow the format we've described throughout this chapter. The presenter needs to be in sync with any brand building or companion efforts being led by the technical marketing communicator. Other than that, he or she has free reign to combine content and media to deliver the message.

Multiple-Person Presentations

Multiple-person presentation teams require additional prework coordination. Co-presenters need to understand who is individually responsible to develop and deliver the different content elements. Presenters need to share a common party line of information and be supportive of each other. One person on the team, preferably the technical marketing communicator, needs to make sure that the presentation content doesn't conflict or overlap. Ideally, the team should meet or conference call to review the agenda flow and affirm individual responsibilities (see Table 9.1). Once in front of the audience, you should not try to work out your differences of opinion on technology nuances. Some teams even develop information

TABLE 9.1	Conference Call Facilitator's Agenda
Agenda Item	**Facilitator's Role**
Call setup and establish link	Log in ahead of time to ensure that the conference call link is working. If the facilitator has a separate dial-in number or code, be sure that other attendees are not experiencing any technical difficulties joining the call.
Greetings and housekeeping	At the scheduled time greet attendees and introduce yourself as facilitator. Explain any pertinent housekeeping rules. Remind people to place their phones on mute if they have background noise or other simultaneous conversations taking place. Explain whether questions should be saved to the end or whether they can be interjected at any time.
Establish time expectations and agenda	Clearly state your time expectations for the call. This helps to focus the participants as well as the speakers. Briefly describe the scheduled topics and related speakers.
Introduce and transition each speaker	With expectations established, introduce the first topic and speaker. From there, the facilitator should keep an eye to the time and be prepared to help the speaker field questions or technical surprises.
Facilitate questions and answers	Once the topics have been presented, invite questions and facilitate answers from the speakers. Keep to the promised time schedule.
Thank yous and final call to action	As you wrap up the call, reiterate the steps that were taken as promised; you stuck to the agenda described, heard from the scheduled speakers, and had an opportunity to ask questions. "Your next step should be . . . "

hard-stops to indicate how much or how little information they'll share on particular subject matter. "We'll say this, but we won't offer this." Of course, presentation teams should develop a common visual theme to their presentations, especially if they are built around a brand concept.

Satellite Meetings and Seminars

Many seminar events are simply a string of presentations. For example, if the seminar topic is technical marketing communication, one presenter might be assigned to discuss marketing concepts, another communication, and still another strategy and tactics. The seminar presentation leader has the added responsibility of coordinating logistics for each individual presenter and building in continuity among them. Different from a team presentation, seminar coordination requires each presenter to understand clearly the scope of information he or she will cover so as not to encroach on someone else's topic. All presenters need an audience profile and set of goals for the seminar. Seminar coordinators should also list dos and don'ts for duration, slide formats, media availability, Q&A, and use of promotional materials.

Exhibits and Shows

Organizations and companies are frequently called on to staff exhibit booths for conventions, trade shows, and technology expositions. All too often, the people staffing the booth are left to fend for themselves without personal presentation guidelines. Technical marketing communicators are accountable to package a mini-presentation format for exhibit booth staff. The mini-presentation should guide the booth staff to briefly interview visitors to determine their needs and interests (and capture personal contact information). It should then segue to a presentation of the prepared information (using appropriate media or content tools) and a call to action or follow-up for additional information. The presentation format should be timed to accommodate the traffic flow estimated for that particular exhibit attendance.

Exhibit opportunities are too expensive to just wing it. Technical marketing communicators can really make a difference in the results of these opportunities. Remember to promote your attendance via other communication tools, including your Web site, newsletters, and telephone hold messages. (See Chapter 10 for additional trade show insights.)

Conference Calls

Conference call presentations have become wonderfully easy to coordinate. Attendees can have dial-in access, and even mobile participants can literally call in from the road. As easy as they are to arrange, conference call presentations require extra attention to remain crisp and effective. Because calls are expensive, participants should respect the timing established in the agenda. Be sure to advise callers how long you intend to present and how much time you have allocated for questions. As with other presentations, declare your objectives and provide an avenue for feedback. Incorporate telephony call-in features to your benefit as well. For example, with some systems, presenters can choose to mute caller audio until the presentation is completed and thus limit interruptions. If an audio-only format severely restricts your presentation effectiveness, you can add media in the following ways:

- Presend a slide presentation file to attendees. They can open the file at their workstation or laptop and follow along as you advance through your presentation (not recommended for mobile participants unless they pull over).
- Post Web pages of your presentation content and provide the URL to participants. Either way, visuals will dramatically extend the effectiveness of your conference call presentation.

Webinars

Hosting a Webinar presentation is similar to a teleconference with slide files, but it has added functionality. With a Webinar presentation, attendees are given password access to a host site that has a presentation or application set up for them to view. While the attendees can view the secure Web site, the presenter is in the driver's seat to advance slides or click a mouse through a technology application.

The audience sees the same thing the presenter sees. Well, not necessarily. We were presenting a fairly graphic-laden value proposition to people who were online at various regional locations. They had logged on to the Web at a variety of connection speeds, and some image downloads were simply not keeping up. A third of the way through our pitch someone finally spoke up on our conference call connection to say the download speed caused them to be two slides behind the script. We thanked them and began asking every other slide or so to make sure people saw what we were talking about. We've since made it a practice to ask Webinar audiences to speak up as soon as the sound doesn't seem to match the picture!

However, the response time and graphic quality will vary depending on the system bandwidth and hardware of the attendee. Some Webinar technologies have added features such as polling (viewers can see real-time results) and whiteboards that allow attendees to draw and share their own diagrams with the others. Unless everyone is using the same system access, software, and hardware, the most common way to share audio is to have attendees dial in to a shared conference line. Again, the Webinar differs from a typical teleconference because the presenter is able to interact with the presentation media in real time as the attendees watch from their own Web connection.

Summing It Up

Personal presentations involve real, live people on both the presenting and the receiving sides. These can occur in six different ways: one-to-one, one-to-multiple, one-to-many, multiple-to-one, multiple-to-multiple, and multiple-to-many. Personal presentations can be one of six types: brand building, relationship building, technology demonstration, technology proposal, or topical. To have a successful personal presentation you must choose the right location and setting and plan how long it will last. It is extremely important to plan your presentation carefully, being sure to include an introduction, agenda, body content, call to action, closing, and Q&A. Planning, delivery, and follow-up are crucial to extracting maximum value and achieving maximum success from your personal presentations.

Applying What You've Learned

1. Make a list of situations in which personal presentations would be the tactic of choice. Choose five of those situations and determine which combination of match-up would be best for each of these presentations.
2. Sketch out the content for a brand building presentation for your company or school.
3. Prepare a topical presentation on a subject approved by your instructor. Deliver the presentation to your classmates.

SMALL GROUP ACTIVITY

You've been asked to deliver a topical presentation about rebooting a personal computer after a blue screen lockup. Your audience is a ninth grade computer class in Fairbanks, Alaska, and you are not authorized to travel there from your campus in Maine. Describe your preparations for the presentation, logistics, content funnel, presentation tools, and follow-up ideas.

CHAPTER 10

Trade Show Exhibitions and Giveaways

Overview

> "Sure, my calendar's free . . . We should be able to pull this off."

"I've been thinking about sending some of our sales reps to a trade show. We've never done it before. But I was talking to Jim last week, and he said that the company he used to work for went all the time. How does your schedule look for January 26 to 29? There's a great show in San Diego."

It was the senior vice president for marketing on the phone. San Diego in January sounds nice. You flip the pages of your calendar to January: the 26th through the 29th are blank. You could go, but you realize that's just five weeks away. Can you get ready for a trade show in just five weeks? You've never done this before, but something tells you it's bigger than just buying a plane ticket and flying to San Diego. But this *is* the senior vice president.

"Sure, my calendar's free. I'll take Mark with me. We should be able to pull this off," you answer.

And pull it off we did. The problem is that we spent much of the next five weeks getting ready for the trade show, and when it was all over, no one was convinced that it was worth all the effort. No one ever again listed trade shows as a possible tactic to broaden the media mix. I overheard the senior vice president tell someone later that they spent a lot of money to ship two guys and a display to San Diego and they didn't sell a single thing.

It's really unfortunate that technical marketing communicators make the mistake of assuming that a trade show won't result in effective marketing when they haven't given it a real chance. In this chapter, you will learn how to avoid the mistakes this company made when they decided to attend a trade show. Trade shows are not unlike any of the other tactics you have read about so far in this text. It starts with a strategy and results in a plan.

Sandi

Strategy First—or Why Are We Doing This?

Karen Klein gives us insight into the *why* question. She writes, "In this age of the Internet, when virtually any business transaction can be handled from your own personal computer, the trade show seems like a quaint and clunky relic. Why would you trek off to some distant city with staff and gear in tow, erect the grownup equivalent of a lemonade stand, and spend three long days on your feet in a noisy convention hall, smiling, schmoozing, shaking hands, and selling until you're ready to drop? Why would you shell out a small fortune for airfare, mediocre meals, and sterile hotel rooms, not to mention the costs of exhibits, good PR, and follow-up, and take precious time away from your business and family? Why, in short, should you bother with a trade show at all?"[1] Her answer is quite simple: "Because you have to."

The following briefly summarizes her explanation for the necessity of trade show exhibits:

- They enable you to develop trust and rapport with your customers.
- They give you access to a captive audience that's primed to buy.
- About 123 million people will attend a trade show this year.
- Despite the outlay of time and money, a trade show is still a very economical way to build your business.
- It enables you to see immediately what your customers think of your product or service.[2]

So if technical marketing communicators are even considering this tactic to include in our media mix, we must start with the strategy question *why*. Consider the following objectives that could be accomplished by having a presence at a trade show:

- Reinforcing an overall, comprehensive campaign
- Generating sales leads
- Achieving immediate sales
- Launching a new product or service
- Penetrating a new market
- Meeting existing customers and building customer brand loyalty
- Changing or enhancing company image
- Carrying out market testing and research
- Generating press coverage and building media relations
- Recruiting new agents or distributors
- Obtaining competitive intelligence[3]

You may be able to think of other reasons. But the important matter is that you discover why you want to participate in a trade show.

Consider this: A sales vice president in a technical company had absolutely no patience for trade shows and cringed at the huge chunks of marketing dollars he felt were extorted for that purpose. "There's only one reason I'm at these shows," he'd grumble, "and that's because my competitors are." Still, a measurable reason, just the same.

As you have read in the previous chapters, the objectives you set should be clear and measurable. What companies expect to gain from a trade show varies from one company to another and even from show to show.

In a survey reported by Ali Poorani in "Trade-Show Management: Budgeting and Planning for a Successful Event," trade show exhibitors were asked about setting objectives: "Sixty percent of the respondents indicated that they set clear objectives and over forty-eight percent reported that they quantify those objectives. Since many companies do not quantify their objectives, the return on investment becomes hard to define or to quantify. Obviously, it is difficult to measure trade-show productivity and cost-effectiveness without knowing whether the objectives for participating in the first place have been achieved."[4]

Are some objectives better than others? The survey reported the following statistics: "The top three reasons for companies in this survey to exhibit in trade shows were (1) generating sales leads (89%), (2) increasing the firm's visibility (81%), and (3) meeting with existing customers (52%). Thirty-seven percent indicated that closing sales at the trade show was an objective of exhibiting in trade shows and twenty-seven percent mentioned to create or change company image as one of the objectives."[5]

From the data collected in the survey, the following observations were noted: "Notwithstanding those respondents who desire to close sales on the show floor, many trade-show managers believe that an emphasis on show selling somewhat detracts from other objectives as well as future sales. This statement is true because many show visitors may be at the show simply to collect information and are not actually involved in purchasing decisions. Booth personnel therefore need to be trained and familiar with the industry and, if trying to sell, must learn to ask qualifying questions to determine the actual authority held by the potential customer."[6]

If you determine that a trade show display will help you to accomplish your marketing objectives, then you should begin to prepare. Unlike our opening scenario, you need three to six months to plan adequately because the real secret of success at trade shows lies in the extent of planning and preparation that occurs before the show.

Your plan should include the following:

- Authorize a budget
- Select and train exhibit staff members
- Create a show plan

Authorizing a Budget

Of course, you have to think of the cost. Can you justify the budget for having a presence at a trade show exhibit? Many elaborate exhibits actually have multiple levels and thousands of square feet of space. For these, price tags of greater than one million dollars are not unusual. Most companies like to say, "Well, even if we close one deal or save one client, the show will have paid for itself." One dot-com company got even more specific at their regional technical exposition. Their team agreed that success would be measured by achieving five postshow meetings with qualified potential clients, by preserving shaky relationships with two key customers, and by at least one tentative handshake on a new deal. The goals were not outlandish and they served to motivate and interest the team.

The following list, though not inclusive, suggests some things to add into your budget.

- Creation or purchase of display materials
- Display space, storage, and utilities
- Materials to promote the trade show
- Training for the sales staff
- Print materials for distribution
- Premiums or other giveaways
- Shipping display and materials
- Travel, lodging, and meals for sales staff

Be sure to get firm quotes on everything possible and to make careful estimates on everything else. Don't be caught by surprise when the bills come.

Selecting and Training Exhibit Staff Members

Selecting the right staff should involve more than simply choosing people because their calendars are open. Just as you choose the best trade show to attend, you also choose the staff based on experience and knowledge of the company, its products, and services. Personality and attitude are also important. You should choose people who find it easy to meet new people, who are articulate, and who are positive about the company, its products, and services. Those exhibit staffers who are chosen simply by availability and location do not usually prove to be motivated or successful.

Klein reports that "trade show attendees who leave dissatisfied complain that salespeople did not meet their needs, weren't available to help them, or seemed untrustworthy. Brenda Tildon, a regional exhibit trade-show manager for Bell Atlantic, once attended a trade exhibition with a purchase order for $25,000 in her briefcase. At a vendor's booth, she stood around waiting to get noticed, then got a fast brush-off. When asked a question about the product, a business card was all but thrown at her with the comment, 'Give this to your boss.' Instead, Tildon made a U-turn right into a competitor's booth and gave them the order."[7]

To train the people staffing the exhibit is a crucial decision. Do not overlook the importance of this ingredient because the success of your exhibit depends on it. A well-trained staff can ignite buyer interest, enhance the corporate image, and provide expert assistance to those who visit the booth. In the opening scenario, training was not an option. Time did not permit it, and we have to assume that lack of training played a large part in the failure of the exhibit to produce what the senior vice president had hoped it would.

Decide which topics should be covered during the training. The following is a list of suggested topics that you should consider for training sessions:

- Objective setting
- Integrating the exhibit or brand theme into staff activities
- Engaging techniques
- Prospecting by profiling
- Nonverbal communication
- Interpersonal skills
- Listening
- Communicating the message
- Closing a commitment
- Using a lead card
- Using giveaways
- Attitude and etiquette

When you have determined which topics should be covered in the training, decide who will do the training. Perhaps you have people in-house who can easily handle this task. If so, that's a bonus. But don't sacrifice good trade show results by relying on less-than-adequate trainers. If you don't have in-house trainers who can deliver excellent training, contract with a professional trainer to do the job. Remember, once you have trained a staff, you can use those resources repeatedly.

One year we hired a trainer to help our entire exhibit team overcome any latent reticence to engage prospects. He had us practice walking up to each other, reading nametags, and shaking hands. "No sitting down, no food or drinks in the booth, and no clustering off to the side with your fellow employees." It took over 20 people to staff our 150 × 50 foot booth, and not everyone was a seasoned sales professional. But with that extra bit of preshow confidence building, we had one of the busiest and most productive booths at the show.

Creating a Show Plan

The real secret of success at trade shows lies in the extent of planning and preparation for the show. Consider doing two kinds of planning: preshow planning and booth planning. In preshow planning you must figure out how you are going to attract visitors to the booth. These usually involve compelling visuals, creative incentives, and effective communication with passersby to inspire them to step up to the booth.

Preshow Plan

The previously mentioned survey showed that 66 percent or 131 respondents created a preshow plan. Forty-eight percent said they plan 3 months or less in advance; 30 percent plan 4 to 6 months in advance; 21 percent plan 7 to 12 months in advance; and only 1 percent plan 13 months or more in advance.[8]

Preshow planning can range from simply mentioning the upcoming show in your ads to sending personal invitations. The mailing list for these invitations can come from your own customer lists or you can purchase a list of participants from the host of the conference. You should also consider direct mailers and personal phone calls to motivate attendees to visit your booth. Be sure to include the cost of preshow materials in your budget.

Booth Plan

The booth plan consists of deciding who will staff it, what they will wear (matching company shirts?), and what the booth will look like. You can rent or purchase trade show booths custom-made to meet your needs. It is usually best to let experts design the booth or collaborate with you. Exhibit companies can be found on the Internet or in the Business-to-Business Yellow Pages. It is probably worth the expense to have a booth custom-made since it is a resource that can be used over again. Keep in mind as you make design decisions to choose a booth that is flexible. For example, using Velcro to attach pictures and other material to the backdrop allows you to change the display easily. A 10×30 foot booth should have 10×10 or 20×20 foot setup variations.

Remember, the booth is an excellent place to perfect the branding process and build purchasing preference where hundreds of buyers can see and remember your brand. Before attendees have even reached the show floor, you've had a number of opportunities to make them aware of your brand—brochures, catalogs, preshow mailings, advertisements, and previous sales calls. But, now that they're at the show, you have the chance to build their awareness of your brand through your trade show presence and interaction.

Many different booth accessories can be imprinted with your company logo, slogan, or whatever best fits the consistent message you're imparting about your brand. These accessories include the following:

- Banners to hang above your booth or on its walls
- Mats to place on the floor of your booth
- Product displays
- Promotional inflatables to attract attention to the booth
- Director's chairs for your guests to sit in while discussing business
- Ceramic mugs or plastic tumblers for guests to drink from

All of these products can be imprinted with your company or product logo for maximum brand exposure.

When choosing any of the booth displays or accessories, always keep in mind the image of your brand. Make sure that your logos and other brand images always appear consistently—using the same letter fonts, colors, and shapes. The booth backdrop, drapes, rugs, and other elements should complement your logo. If possible, you may want to consider color coordinating all of these elements to match your logo color, as a subtle, yet effective, reminder of your brand.

Sharkbytes, a high tech company, created a trade show exhibit that effectively communicated their brand. People were drawn to the booth by its stark simplicity (see Fig. 10.1). This was a visual personification of their shark-related tagline: Powerful . . . Streamlined . . . Strategic. Prospective clients were invited to the exhibit by a press release that went the extra mile—using an expensive die-cut strongly associated with their brand (Fig. 10.2). Visitors at the booth went away with business cards that were an equally strong brand reminder (Fig. 10.3). Later in the year, their qualified clientele received a Christmas card—again strongly tied to brand (Fig. 10.4).

At one show a company had a technical exhibit installed in a large modular building. They knew one entire side of the structure would be facing an aisle in the exhibit hall and somebody in the office observed, "That space sure would make a nice billboard." So with the zeal to go above and beyond the call of duty, they painted the entire modular building white and hired a local artisan to paste on a 12-foot high, 30-foot wide vinyl logo. They felt pretty smug—until they saw it in place at the exhibit hall. For reasons hard to describe unless you saw it, the much-greater-than-life-size logo and name were just a little too overwhelming in the context of the rest of the exhibits. They painstakingly peeled off the vinyl letters in time for the show and began planning for the next year's exhibit.

Figure 10.1   This technical exhibit draws attention to the computer technology.
Copyright 2001. Sharkbytes. Used by permission.

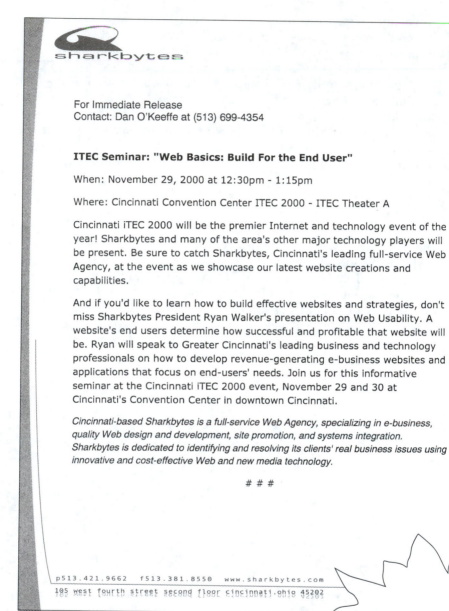

sharkbytes

For Immediate Release
Contact: Dan O'Keeffe at (513) 699-4354

ITEC Seminar: "Web Basics: Build For the End User"

When: November 29, 2000 at 12:30pm - 1:15pm

Where: Cincinnati Convention Center ITEC 2000 - ITEC Theater A

Cincinnati iTEC 2000 will be the premier Internet and technology event of the year! Sharkbytes and many of the area's other major technology players will be present. Be sure to catch Sharkbytes, Cincinnati's leading full-service Web Agency, at the event as we showcase our latest website creations and capabilities.

And if you'd like to learn how to build effective websites and strategies, don't miss Sharkbytes President Ryan Walker's presentation on Web Usability. A website's end users determine how successful and profitable that website will be. Ryan will speak to Greater Cincinnati's leading business and technology professionals on how to develop revenue-generating e-business websites and applications that focus on end-users' needs. Join us for this informative seminar at the Cincinnati iTEC 2000 event, November 29 and 30 at Cincinnati's Convention Center in downtown Cincinnati.

Cincinnati-based Sharkbytes is a full-service Web Agency, specializing in e-business, quality Web design and development, site promotion, and systems integration. Sharkbytes is dedicated to identifying and resolving its clients' real business issues using innovative and cost-effective Web and new media technology.

# # #

p513.421.9662   f513.381.8550   www.sharkbytes.com
105 west fourth street second floor cincinnati.ohio 45202

Figure 10.2   Sharkbytes' press release with strong brand reminder.
Copyright 2001. Sharkbytes. Used by permission.

For the most return on investment, choose booth components and accessories that will build your brand image by making clients aware of what your company stands for, and what products and services it's selling. Make the most of this opportunity to have an impact on your clients' purchasing decisions by presenting your brand in a way that is attractive, meaningful, and, most of all, memorable (see Fig. 10.5).

Figure 10.3 Sharkbytes' business card.

Copyright 2001. Sharkbytes. Used by permission.

Figure 10.4 Christmas card from Sharkbytes.

Copyright 2001. Sharkbytes. Used by permission.

Figure 10.5   Technical exhibit.
Used by permission. Advantech.

The largest booth you can afford is the right one for you. It is best to secure a location near a major entrance, the food stands, restrooms, or any other place that concentrates people. On the end of an aisle is also good for the same reason.

Measuring Success

It's not over when you dismantle your exhibit, pack up, and board the plane for home. Now the really hard work begins. Follow-up on all your sales leads—as soon as possible—while customers still have a face in mind to put with the direct mails, phone calls, and ads. And as in all good business ventures, you should take time to evaluate. This evaluation gives pause to analyze what you have learned from the trade show experience and adjust what you're doing accordingly. Be sure to budget for postshow debriefing meetings.

How can you determine if your trade show experience was successful? One important criterion in measuring success is to determine if the effort was cost-effective.

In "Trade-Show Management," Poorani suggests that "measuring the cost-effectiveness of trade shows is difficult due to the time lag between the show itself and actual sales. Moreover, many existing customers may visit a booth and later place an order. How can one identify whether such future sales were the result of the exhibitor's participation in the show? It is therefore unwise to rely on sales figures alone."[9]

Gillian Cartwright writes, "In 1991 the Exhibition Industry Federation questioned 345 exhibitors across 12 industry sectors on the effectiveness of exhibitions as a sales medium. The average number of sales contacts made by respondents was 222—or over 50 contacts per day. It would require a significant investment in a sales force to achieve the same level of business, and would take a lot longer."[10]

Sometimes goal setting at trade shows can backfire. One year our technical marketing team agreed to hold a lead contest. The rules were simple. The person turning in the most business cards at the end of the week won a large cash prize. Can you guess what went wrong? The marketing team received hundreds of business cards, but precious few from serious, qualified customers. They had the right idea—but the wrong incentive.

In the absence of a successful tracking system, how do you evaluate the cost-effectiveness of a trade show display? Again we can learn from Cartwright, who suggests measuring a show's success on the basis of any one or combination of the following criteria:

- Calculate the value of sales achieved
- Count the number of qualified leads
- Establish the cost per useful contact
- Count the number of new contacts made
- Survey levels of brand awareness before and/or after the show
- Measure and evaluate media coverage generated
- Consider any other benefits that may have accrued[11]

A Final Word About Trade Shows

You are the only one who can accurately determine if a trade show exhibit should be an important part of your media mix. Weigh the issues carefully. Make good decisions and plan well in advance of the event. What if you decide not to go? In high tech sectors, trade shows are a preferred venue for brand building. "When you're buying something expensive, there are times you've just got to kick the tires. You've got to be there for those customers—further proof, apparently, that ninety percent of success in life is just a matter of showing up."[12]

Premiums or Giveaways

It is true that premiums or giveaways are closely linked to trade shows, but you can find other occasions to use them effectively. Sales representatives can leave them on a customer's, or potential customer's, desk after a face-to-face call. They serve effectively as reminders of your product or service. A *premium* is any product with a marketing message on it that you give away. Classic premiums include T-shirts with your company name or logo on them, coffee mugs, pens, wall calendars, baseball caps, stress balls, raffles for golf clubs, and literally the list goes on and on.

By using a premium, just as with all marketing endeavors, your goal is to build recognition and ideally to change someone's behavior. Achieving this goal might not be easy with a cheap premium—a plastic pen or mug. As always, start with your objectives. Yes, you must even identify what you want to accomplish with your premium. And you end by imagining ways that premium items can help you accomplish your goals.

Imagine that your marketing goal is to have your current customers contact your sales representatives to learn about the soon-to-be released software upgrade. You have decided to have your company's slogan imprinted on pens that you will distribute in the next mailing of advertisements for the upgrade. Will the potential customer open the advertisement, see the pen, read the slogan, and eagerly place the call to learn about the upgrade? Probably not. But it is possible that if you choose a premium that not only sends a message of high value—both in the selected premium and the quality of your product—but also provides some useful function, it is far more likely that the customer will place the call.

Imagine instead that your advertisement reaches the desks of your potential customers in a small padded envelope. Curiosity will cause them to open the envelope. They will find an advertisement carefully crafted to communicate the features and benefits of the new soon-to-be released upgrade of a popular help authoring tool. Inside the padded envelope is a small gift or gadget, such as a desk clock with your company's logo and phone number clearly visible. The clock catches their interest, and it becomes a permanent and often used accessory on their desks. Each time they look at the clock, they are reminded of your upgrade that will soon be available. Chances are more likely that your company will get the call when the upgrade is available.

In the early days of high field magnets for magnetic resonance imaging, the various magnet vendors came up with ingenious premiums based on, you guessed it, magnetic principles. There were pens that would float under a little stand on your desk. There were magnetic business cards to stick on file cabinets, and even powerful miniature magnets made up to look like the real thing. They were pretty nifty—until the design engineers who received them discovered now and again that their computer diskettes and credit cards were mysteriously erased. On to the next creative marketing idea.

When you use premiums at your trade shows, you can attract a crowd of people who want one of your gifts. It is conceivable that the right giveaway can actually attract a line of interested people. And while they are waiting in line to receive their gift, you can take that opportunity to explain your services and collect leads. When visitors are in other locations at the convention and see people walking around with cool gifts, they will actually seek you out. It is not uncommon for visitors to stop people and ask them where they got a specific item. They usually aren't going to stop and ask about a plastic pen, but a clock will certainly cause most people to inquire.

A quality premium given at a trade show will also leave behind a good feeling about your company. While any gift is appreciated, a special one can create a connection between what you do and your prospect's needs.

When choosing the right premium, be creative. Try to choose a gift that will not only incite your prospects' curiosity but also tie in with your business. We have said some disparaging things about plastic pens. Don't miss the special opportunity this inexpensive premium can offer. Of course, the recipient of your company pen will know full well that you have not spent a lot of money on the giveaway; the one advantage of the pen is its high "pass-along" value. Once given to a prospect, the pen will be used at work, could be lent to a colleague, or left behind in the office. As a result, your company name will travel and inspire brand recognition.

What you spend on promotional items is largely dependent on your budget and the tastes and perceptions of your customers. Also, note that it is acceptable to buy two different sets of giveaways to distinguish between good leads and serious prospects.

And don't forget to consider a drawing. Providing business cards for the chance to win a handheld computer or golf club are frequent successes at technology shows.

Marketing for Dummies suggests using this quality strategy: "Most marketers think about the message (the copy and/or artwork) that they put on the premium. But this focus can lead you to forget that the premium itself communicates a strong message. The premium is a gift from you to your customer. Therefore, the premium tells your customers a great deal about you and what you think of them. A cheap, tacky gift may look good when you run the numbers, but it won't look good to the customer who receives it. Yet most premiums are of low or medium quality. Few are as good as, or better than, what we'd buy for ourselves."[13]

Summing It Up

Before you commit to a trade show exhibition, determine whether it fits with your overall technical marketing strategy. If the answer is yes, you have a lot of work to do before you purchase your plane tickets. You have to plan a budget, select and train your exhibit staff members, and create a show plan. Premiums or giveaways are closely linked to trade shows, but you can find other occasions to use them effectively. It is true: the quality of the giveaway reflects on the quality of the service or product you supply. So cheaper is rarely better. Choose wisely to be sure that any giveaway will actually achieve the intended purpose.

Applying What You've Learned

1. Search the Internet to find a list of companies that sell promotional products. Make a list of their Web sites.
2. Search the Internet to find trade shows. Make a list of the different kinds of professions represented.
3. You are a technical marketing communicator who works for a high tech company in Boston who has never had a presence at a trade show exhibition. Your manager has asked you to look into the possibilities of taking a display to a trade show in the Silicon Valley. Determine the objectives that you hope to accomplish by attending this trade show.

4. Create a reasonable budget for your company to participate in the trade show in the Silicon Valley. Be sure to cover **all** costs of participating, including travel and lodging for participants. Use the Internet to find airline tickets and hotel prices.

SMALL GROUP ACTIVITY

Your university has been invited to participate in a job fair. Your department has been approved to have a special exhibit for the technical marketing communication major. Create a plan for selecting and training exhibit staff members. In addition, create a show plan. Determine what you will take to the job fair, including literature and giveaways.

Notes

1. Karen E. Klein, "Trade Secrets," *Business Week's Frontier,* August 16, 1999.
2. Ibid.
3. Ali A. Poorani, "Trade-Show Management: Budgeting and Planning for a Successful Event," published in *Cornell Hotel and Restaurant Administration Quarterly*, August 1996, Vol. 37, No. 4.
4. Ibid.
5. Ibid.
6. Ibid.
7. Karen E. Klein, "Trade Secrets."
8. Ali A. Poorani, "Trade-Show Management."
9. Ali A. Poorani. "Trade-Show Management."
10. Gillian Cartwright, *Making the Most of Trade Exhibitions* (Oxford: Butterworth-Heinemann, Ltd., 1995), 17.
11. Ibid. 169–71.
12. Ali A. Poorani, "Trade-Show Management."
13. Alexander Hiam, *Marketing for Dummies* (Foster City, Calif.: IDG Books Worldwide, 1997), 191.

CHAPTER 11

Aligning Tactics with Strategies

The Technical Marketing Communication Plan

Overview

> "At the heart of our communication work is a plan."

I have a colleague who works with an e-business product company that is extremely high tech and up-to-date with personal digital assistants, e-mail, cell phones, and intranet sites. Still, he was having trouble getting company associates interested in a new Web portal technology concept. His content message was seemingly ignored online and at a series of personal presentations. Although he published a newsletter article, the staff was simply too preoccupied with other client work to assimilate the message about another intraorganizational technology change. Finally, he thought about his target audience one more time and looked for a unique but likely avenue to tap into their attention span.

His solution: One of the highest traffic technology areas in their co-located office complex was the coffee break area. Virtually all of the hard-working staff ventured there at various times throughout the day. To get there, associates had to turn at a fabric covered building-support column in the aisle. My colleague began tacking a series of provocative one-line questions about the new technology to this column. He alternated them at different heights and angles on the column, changing them frequently throughout the week.

His extremely low tech, retro approach quickly created a buzz of conversation and speculation about what the next posting would say. At first, it was simply the tactic that got their attention. It also generated genuine inquiries into the new technology itself. None of the more sophisticated communication had accomplished that. And that was the point of his unlikely tactical approach.

The moral of this story is that you cannot plan everything ahead of time. Sometimes you have to find the column in the aisle by the coffee station of your market and tack paper messages to it. As technical marketing communicators, we've got to think on our feet and adjust to the dynamics of our market environment. But that's the exception, not the rule. At the heart of our communication work is a plan (see Fig. 11.1).

Tom

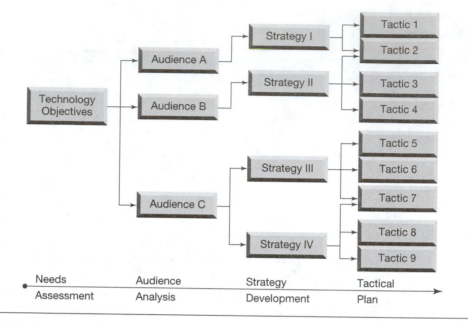

Figure 11.1   Communication plan.

Figure 11.2   Choosing and aligning tactics with strategies is the fourth stage in the communication cycle.

What You Have Accomplished and What's Next

So far in this text we've developed the foundational elements of technical marketing communication. We know how to conduct a needs analysis in order to clarify program objectives. With our goals defined, we dig deeper into our target audience profiles to analyze their individual communication preferences and nuances. Once the technical objectives and audience analysis are in hand, it's possible to strategize the most effective ways to communicate. Why should we communicate certain information to one group and not another? Why choose one combination of media over another? Why is the sequence of communication different across the various audiences? Fleshing out the cause and effect of our targeted communication relationships fulfills our strategy development.

Recall our summary from Chapter 4: When you ask *what*, the answer is the overall objective for your technical marketing communication. To be successful, what must have occurred? When you speak of the final outcome itself, you refer to the *result* of sound strategy, not the strategy itself. When you ask *who*, the answer is the combination of targeted audiences or markets to be addressed. Each may warrant a unique *strategic* approach. When you ask *how, where*, and *when*, the answers are tactical considerations you must make *based on* strategy. But when you ask *why*, the answer should describe your strategy. Strategy answers *why*; tactics tell us *how*.

The how-tools we have available for our tactical approach are the various media and technology options discussed in earlier chapters. How do we fulfill a strategy? By applying the most effective combination of tactics A, B, and C. Depending on the project or program, tactics could mean a combination of e-mail, documentation, and personal presentations or a heavily promoted (and financed) rollout of magazine ads, direct mail, and special event sponsorships. You must choose each of these tactics for their specific and appropriate contribution to strategic fulfillment of the objectives (see Fig. 11.2).

Expensive tactics can't make up for bad strategy any more than brilliant cinematography can cover a poor movie plot. But combined with solid strategy based on clear objectives, a tactical plan is the road map to execution and accomplishment of technical marketing communication objectives.

How Are You Going to Do That?

Our text has come full circle to tactical execution. We've admonished technical marketing communicators to chafe at clients who urge that "we need a Web site" or "we need a newsletter" as tactical solutions without regard to objectives and strategy. Similarly, we should not decide in a vacuum to attend a trade show or sponsor a local mini-marathon apart from all other tactical options. But once we have developed the targeted audience strategy and have made the objectives clear, the technical marketing communicator is fully accountable to propose and execute an effective tactical plan. Ironically, you may eventually decide to develop that Web site and attend the trade show. But for every tactical recommendation, we should first answer a key question: *How does this tactic fulfill a targeted audience strategy in a way that accomplishes the overall technology objective?*

Tactical Communication Choices

Your plan needs to draw from an adequate (and growing) toolkit of tactical communication choices at your disposal. Keep your audiences interested and engaged with the different ways you package and deliver content. In Table 11.1, we have summarized a list of tactical choices from the various media we've discussed thus far. This is only a partial list because we're always thinking of new ways to communicate. Challenge yourself and your team to mix and match tactics without falling into a predictable pattern. It's often the unique approach (the message tacked to a column by the coffee area) that gets the attention of your audience. But once you've used the tactic, it's no longer unique—for that audience. On to the next creative idea!

Combined Tactical Solutions

A single tactical communication rarely succeeds alone. Tactical solutions are the combined sum of multiple tactics. Assemble tactical solutions with budgets, timing, and available resources in mind. If your budget is barely big enough to design a good graphic, it's silly to dream of ad placements in *CIO* magazine. Complex multimedia animation attracts attention, but if you need something for tomorrow's presentation, it's unrealistic.

Combined tactical solutions for business-to-business marketing communication should involve at least three to five *touches* or customer contacts. Many consumer marketing campaigns strive for six to eight touches. Just think of consumer automobile sales. If your local car dealer has a minivan sale, you are likely to receive a mass mailing letter and a rebate coupon. You'll see a TV commercial during the morning and evening news and hear a radio ad during the commute to work. For added visibility, you will see large, colored balloons on 100-foot tethers above the dealership itself. Of course, print advertisements will appear in multiple editions of the local newspapers and suburban posts. All of these tactics satisfy the objective of increased sales, and you should create and place them in accordance to strategies for minivan audiences. These audiences, who are usually family oriented, probably wouldn't respond to tactical communication placed in singles' bars.

The same principles are true if you are marketing technology products. The digital camera industry has discovered a new market for their product: grandparents. Since grandparents are sharing information by e-mail and on the Web, they have discovered the digital camera and its ability to share pictures of their grandchildren. So this audience is likely to receive a mass mailing letter (contacts obtained through AARP), a rebate coupon, and an advertisement in *Maturity Magazine* stressing how easy it is to use the digital camera. Again, these tactics fulfill the objective of increased sales.

Business-to-business and intraorganizational tactics have to feature multiple touch points as well. For example, consider demand generation activities involv-

TABLE 11.1	Tactical Choices for Various Media
Tactical Choice	**Best Used For**
E-mail	Short, concise messages to targeted audiences including promotional distribution. Use e-mail to point to other media (Web sites) and to schedule events (presentations and training). Avoid using e-mail to distribute documents, and never as your sole communications channel.
Document	Lengthy technical papers, proposals, policies, and procedures. Use documents (online or print) for content that will be accessed more than once, and as reference material.
Voicemail	Team and project updates. Use voicemail to add personal sincerity to information content.
Quick reference card	Instructions and procedures. Speeds adoption and start-up by capturing the most essential information.
Web site (or page)	Regularly updated content, data, and reference information. Perfect for large, dispersed geographic audiences.
Web application	Adding functionality to Web sites. Anything that helps Web visitors to learn more about your technology, to order it, or update it is useful. Many interactive applications help to enhance Web site stickiness.
Slide presentation	Personal presentations, online Web meetings, and kiosks. One of the most frequently used communication tools.
Conference call	Personal presentations, team updates, and gathering feedback. Best used when there are no visuals involved or in conjunction with a Webinar format.
Webinar	Personal presentations, team updates, and gathering feedback, with the added feature of shared real-time visuals.
Video	Prerecorded live action and multimedia content. Video clips on Web sites and CDs are great ways to inject the "live" feel to your technology work.
Personal presentation	Sales call, one-to-one meeting, one-to-many meeting, seminar, professional society, chamber of commerce, local business events, and trade show presentations.
Focus group (or other guided discussion)	Gathering input and feedback with the help of an unbiased facilitator.
Training document	Instructions, processes, and procedures.
Information binder or packet (folder)	Packaging multiple but related items such as brochures, product sheets, documents, and CD-ROMs.
CD-ROM	Distributing large collections of files, or multimedia presentations requiring lots of storage. Many multimedia files run faster from a CD than they do from a Web site, depending on the user hardware and access bandwidth.
Survey	Collecting feedback. This can take the form of print, online, or personal call.

(continued)

TABLE 11.1	(Continued)
Tactical Choice	**Best Used For**
Telemarketing call	Making contact with prospective clients, gathering information, announcing products or events, and setting up opportunities for further contact (e.g., sales calls).
Personal letter	Reaching a specific individual identified on a list or database. Best used in combination with other tactics including telemarketing calls and advertising promotions.
Postcard mailer	Fast, inexpensive information sharing. Best used for product and event announcements in combination with other tactics.
Poster	Exhibits, common areas, and team presentations.
Banner	Exhibits, common areas, and team presentations.
Advertisement(s)	Promotional efforts placed in various media, including Web banners and magazines.
Press release	Proactively notifying the press about company, personnel, program, or product information. Media outlets are very agreeable about picking up this type of information and distributing via their media channels, especially on the Web.
Editorial article	Publication in trade media, usually written by a third party with reference to your organization, staff, or technology. Best with testimonial quotes.
Sponsored seminar	Gathering targeted audiences to promote your technology products or concepts. Companies and organizations often bring in third party speakers to discuss a general topic that may be served or supported by your product, process, or program.
Exhibit booth	Establishing presence at a trade show or conference. Exhibit booths are the magnets to attract prospective clients or colleagues to learn about your technology. Visitors can be greeted with personal presentations, collateral material, or multimedia presentations.
Brochure (print or online)	General information and follow-up details about a company, service, product, or process. Brochures are best used in combination with other tactics. Brochures are meant to promote follow-up contact.
Product sheet (print or online)	Detailed information about a product, service, or program. Product sheets should be more detailed than a brochure, and often include technology specifications, features, and benefits. They should also include a contact phone number and Web site URL.
Newsletter (print or online)	Providing regular information updates about an organization or program to targeted audiences. Best used when kept current and populated with valuable information. In many ways, Web sites are the newsletter of our time, providing timely information to targeted audiences.

TABLE 11.1	(Continued)
Tactical Choice	**Best Used For**
Specialty item(s)	Special promotions and branding opportunities. Clocks, pens, and sport bottles with your logo imprint are effective in the right circumstances. It's important to demonstrate a logical link to the choice of gift, the situation, and the related subject matter or brand. The item's cost and quality directly impact its perceived value.
Event sponsorship	Brand recognition when you are necessarily making a presentation or demonstrating your technology. Technology organizations sponsor community events (museums, charities) and industry activities (conferences).
Spokesperson	Connecting a personality to your technology, service, or organization. This is helpful when a technology itself is difficult to relate to or appreciate. It's often easier to promote a charismatic individual to speak on a technology's behalf.
Case study	Demonstrating the success of your technology in actual practice (also called success stories). Helps prospects and clients to visualize how they might benefit from the same technology.

ing direct mail and telemarketing. The purpose of the typical business-to-business telemarketing call is to identify and contact the appropriate technical person for additional sales follow-up. Technical marketing communicators agree that only 5 percent of telemarketing calls yield actual customer sales by themselves. And yet millions of dollars are spent on telemarketing in conjunction with complementary effort. It's the total tactical solution that pays dividends.

A simple, tactical solution combines direct mail *and* telemarketing in an attempt to generate multiple customer touch points. First, the technical marketing team selects a target market to call. For example, you decide to target the chief information officers (CIOs) of companies with annual sales greater than $100 million within a 50-mile radius of a metropolitan area. You can either purchase a mailing list from the local chamber of commerce or a trade magazine in their market, or pay a telemarketing firm to develop a list for you. You could also find many list services on the Web. Once you have the list in hand, should you start calling right away? Well, not yet. To position yourself for multiple touches, it's best to send a brief letter and some background information (see Chapter 7). Ideally, this personal letter notifies your target audience to expect a call within the next brief period of time related to your technology initiative. Then, after making your telemarketing calls, you should send each contacted party a follow-up postcard or letter indicating other ways to get additional information such as a Web site URL or an 800-number. This approach is a basic three-touch tactical solution for direct mail and telemarketing.

Three-Touch Tactical Solution

1. Personal letter in advance of a telemarketing call
2. Telemarketing call and prospect qualification
3. Postcard, letter, or e-mail follow-up to confirm call

Less than half of the target audience will probably read your letter, take your call, or glance at your postcard. However, the chance of reaching somebody who is in the market for your product, service, or program is much greater than if you had relied on a single tactic. The CIOs in question might scan and toss your letter. Chances are approximately 60 percent that the CIO will listen to a voicemail message from the telemarketing firm. However, when the postcard follow-up arrives, you have a much better chance that he or she will make a mental connection to your message. If the CIO is in the market for your technology product, service, or program, your team will probably get a call from him.

The combined tactical solution approach also builds brand recognition for the future. Even if the CIOs who receive your information aren't interested this time, they'll have had contact with your technology or brand. You'll also be able to improve and update your overall client database based on the contacts you have made during the telemarketing calls. You can find countless ways to build tactical variations of this basic three-step approach. Technical marketing communicators learn what's best for their market audiences, just as fishermen learn which bait works on a certain lake or at a certain time of year. Having happened on a successful approach, many technical marketing teams are able to reapply that tactical solution to other markets or products.

Examine Table 11.2 carefully for other common tactical solutions. These are only a few sample ideas, and you can imagine many, many more. We have no perfect formulas. Make your best effort, record the results, and learn for the future.

Phases of Tactical Communication

Even with the right tactical solution set, technology audiences aren't capable of, or interested in, receiving all of your communication at once. They need to assimilate new ideas and prepare for change over an appropriate period of time. The time span is different for dot-com organizations as compared to genetic research or military defense technology programs. One organization or client culture might require much more advanced notice of change than another. Some technical visionaries look years into the future to build awareness. Other Web cultures assume constant and immediate change. Regardless of the exact units of time, most technology products, services, and programs are best represented by four tactical communication phases:

1. Introduction and awareness
2. Expectation development and direction
3. Communication fulfillment and support
4. Follow-up and improvement

TABLE 11.2	Common Tactical Solutions
Tactical Solution	**Best Used For**
E-mail Voicemail Slide presentation Poster Postcard Training Web site Specialty item	**Technology rollout**—This is a robust combination of tactical tools to reach in-house teams for technology rollouts, introductions, or updates. This combats the common tendency to simply "send an e-mail," and leads to multiple touches. A specialty item awarded after internal customers pass a Web-training test provides follow-through incentive. Nothing more expensive than a polo shirt or desktop toy is necessary.
Press release Editorial article Advertisement series Web banner series Sponsored event Webinar series Video on demand Multimedia CD-ROM on demand Trade show attendance and exhibit booth Professional event presentations	**Build brand recognition**—Most sales teams will tell you that they simply want to stay in front of the customer as much as possible. They want to make sure that a client has heard of their company and technology *before* the client needs them. This combination of tactics might take place over the course of several months. Each item plays on the other to build brand recognition, and each tactic should include information pointing to the other tactics. You can scale the cost of this solution by the frequency with which each tactic is applied, or by limiting the combination of tactics.
Press release Editorial series Web site information Multimedia CD-ROM for registered Web requestors and telemarketing follow-up Web banner advertising Telemarketing Brochure follow-up (also online) Sales team contact Sponsored seminar series	**New technology, product, or service**—This solution includes tactics similar to brand building, but the content is focused on a particular technology product, program, or service. Your Web site information should be online in time for press release and editorial articles to publish the links. The Web site should offer ways to order the multimedia CD-ROM. Web banner advertising on other sites can drive traffic to yours. All of this should benefit the technical sales and support teams who are making personal presentations arranged by your telemarketing campaign. Sponsored seminars should fall in the middle of your campaign when a critical mass of awareness has begun to build among your target audience.
Personal letter Telemarketing call Postcard mailer Webinar or sponsored seminar Survey Sales team follow-up	**Local demand generation**—This is a more elaborate version of the 1-2-3 approach explained in the text. You lead with a letter, follow with calls, and confirm with postcard mailers. It's ideal if you can point people to the next event or activity such as an online Webinar or local seminar. A general survey about your technology is sometimes a door opener to engage clients and prospects. This solution emphasizes demand generation, trying to establish prospective contacts for sales follow-up.

(continued)

TABLE 11.2	(Continued)
Tactical Solution	**Best Used For**
Focus group Specialty item incentive Survey Usability testing Spokesperson or testimonial	**Technology project research/prework**—This solution set is meant to gather information and feedback for a technology project team. Contacting existing clients is a way to make them feel valued, and for you to receive relevant field input. You may or may not have to provide incentives to motivate people to participate. If you uncover a particularly enthusiastic and positive participant, he or she may even make an ideal spokesperson for your project.
Intranet Web site Newsletter Personal presentations Video E-mail Voicemail	**Team or organizational updates**—Today's technology teams pool people from different functional groups within the organization and from multiple locations. The technology is complex enough, but maintaining good communication with each other can be just as challenging. Many organizations assign a technical communication person to apply marketing tactics just to keep team members and their constituent departments aligned throughout a project. Tactical solutions like this one appeal to teams more than monthly meeting notes.

These phases of communication run parallel with the actual technology development and deployment. While technologists are focused on testing and completion, technical marketing communicators are helping to prepare, educate, and train the appropriate audiences. Each of these communication phases should have its own combination of tactical solutions.

Phase One: Introduction and Awareness

Whether working with a product, service, or program, audiences want to be introduced to the technology. This phase could occur weeks or months in advance of product availability. Technical marketing communicators build awareness and prepare audiences for change. Decision makers begin to learn of programs being introduced to the budgetary cycle and their purpose. Technology teams continue to plan and prioritize resource allocations. Sales and training teams look for new competitive advantages coming in the future. Ultimately, the technology customer is reminded that new features and benefits are on the way.

Phase One provides a particularly good motivation for technical marketing communicators to build relationships with technology editors in their respective trade journals and publications. These are places to share new ideas and directions. Newsletters (online news pages and print distribution) are also good tools to use when you introduce new technology directions while building awareness. You especially want to feed ongoing ideas to sales teams for general conversation with clients, even if you have no official brochure or presentation involved. Personal presentations and team updates should add high-level information about works in progress.

The main goal of this phase is to make sure no one is surprised later. You are specifically avoiding the *no one told me it was coming* syndrome so common in technology development, especially for intraorganizational technology. Too many technology users in corporations and academe shake their heads after the latest technology update or introduction and say, "I wish they had asked for our input."

You should remind people frequently that new technologies, and the resultant changes, are on the way. Even though you have few descriptive details available during this phase, you should not wait until you have all your project or program's information. You must earn the respect and trust of your audiences over a period of time so they count on you for a peek over the technology horizon. They'll be grateful for the advanced insight and forgiving if you need to update and clarify your message in the next phase of information sharing.

Content Messages for Phase One

You're trying to gain mind-share during this phase without demanding detail focus from your audiences. Editorial and presentation references will be general and high level in nature. Reassure intraorganizational people in the budgetary approval cycle that this direction is the right one for their areas of responsibility. You can duplicate some of the same content in different tactical packages. Text block inserts to duplicate in various communications are common during Phase One.

- New technology is on the way (general time frames, not specifics).
- New features bring new benefits.
- Training will be required.
- Budget and staff resources may be affected.
- Watch for more information.
- Think about how this may affect the way you work with technology.

Types of Tactics

Choose tactics that appeal to high-level information. It's too early to release a detailed report or specifications to an audience that isn't prepared for your technology. You also need to gather information and feedback from targeted technology audiences to update your communication strategy.

- Webzines and newsletters
- Editorial articles
- Technology team updates
- Personal presentations (meetings, conferences, exhibits)
- Teleconferences
- Intraorganizational communication channels
- Focus groups and guided discussions; threaded Web discussions and chats

Phase Two: Expectation Development and Direction

Once you've introduced a technology concept and built some preliminary awareness, it's much easier to develop healthy expectations and set specific directions for the next course of action. People shouldn't be surprised by your directional communication. They should have heightened expectations and be curious to learn the next level of detail concerning the technology. You can publish tactical timelines, plan and announce training and sales seminars, and give firm dates to expect marketing tools and online information access to sales and technology support teams. Your personal presentations should now add specific information about the technology and what exactly it will accomplish for the end user. You should clearly communicate features and benefits. Although you have not yet published brochures and documentation, you have gained enough information from the technology subject matter experts to begin content development.

Technical marketing communicators push to set communication deadlines that clearly depict when they'll have the balance of technical information for training and documentation. This requires technologists to be accountable for their activities and commitments.

Many technology rollouts bypass Phase One introductions and jump right into expectation and direction setting. Slow starts and adoption delays then frustrate marketing and sales teams because they are now forced to build awareness among their audiences after the fact. If people are stopping to ask, "what is this technology all about?" you've waited too long to raise awareness. Phase Two works only if Phase One was executed well.

Content Messages for Phase Two

Phase Two content messages build on the awareness you have raised during Phase One communication. You're now setting clearer expectations for milestone dates and execution.

- Provide details on why it's worthwhile to learn, sell, train for, acquire, and use the technology (value propositions).
- Announce and publish dates when technology will be available.
- Publish training and informative seminar dates. Begin scheduling attendees.
- Be specific about change requirements. Give detailed outlines of equipment swaps, software upgrades, and new process implementations.
- Continue the flow of technology information and repeat feature/benefit messages.

Types of Tactics

Tactical choices should make it easy for your target audiences to access information. Make sure you employ an adequate media mix appropriate to your audiences. Tactics should also help to keep audiences accountable. Do they need to register for information? Is training a prerequisite to participation? Will legacy (superseded) technology become unavailable or unsupported?

- Advertising (trade magazines, Web banners, print and broadcast media)
- Targeted audience mailings, brochures, e-mail, and Web site pushes to registered users
- Public relation releases
- Personal presentations (provide technical and sales support team scripts)
- Administrative scheduling (training, seminars, trade shows, Webinars, service dates)

Phase Three: Communication Fulfillment and Support

Phase Three is the culmination of your tactical efforts. It is often called the rollout phase. You are now ready to publish informative Web sites rich in content and functionality, to conduct online and instructor-led training for internal teams and then for technology customers, and to distribute detailed brochures and multimedia sales tools. In addition, you should mine telemarketing efforts for leads. Finally, this is the time you should conduct seminars. At each step, technical marketing communicators are delivering the goods—on time and on budget.

As a technical marketing communicator, you are accountable for your content to be clearly understood and actionable. If you establish realistic expectations in Phase Two, each person in the technical marketing communication chain will be ready to receive and share information according to the directions set. Teams and clients will adopt and adjust to the technology as it becomes available.

Content Messages for Phase Three

You're much more focused on education, training, and adoption during this phase—from sales teams and in-house trainers all the way to clients and end users.

- How to train, how to sell, how to acquire, how to use
- Success stories and testimonials of early adopters
- How to get support help

Types of Tactics
- CD-ROM
- Webinar
- Web site
- Collateral (brochures, product sheets, specialty items)
- Training documentation and job aids (quick reference guides)
- Sales support

Phase Four: Follow-Up and Improvement

Technical marketing communicators learn something from every endeavor. Surveys and guided discussions help to debrief from a technology deployment and to prepare for the future. They answer the following questions:

- Which tactical choices were most successful?
- How did audiences respond to directions?
- Were people sufficiently aware in advance?

This phase also helps to recover any major outages for key audiences during a technology rollout. If people are not adapting well to a new technology, communicators may need to fine-tune Web sites and CD-ROM content or send out emergency quantities of troubleshooting quick reference cards.

Content Messages for Phase Four

- How did we do?
- What have we learned?
- How can we improve?
- What needs immediate attention?

Types of Tactics

- Survey (Web, print, and telemarketing)
- Guided discussions, threaded Web discussions
- Team conference calls
- E-mail
- Help desk follow-up
- Service and support team focus groups

Tactical Lead Times and Sequencing

Every tactical effort has a lead time involved. *Lead time* is the time it takes to plan and develop the tactic right up until it is executed or distributed. In Table 11.3, the length of each arrow spans the amount of time required to develop a tactic prior to its deployment or distribution at the arrowhead. For example, an e-mail is relatively easy to compose, approve, and distribute. You can push the send button in a second, but the message probably requires some content gathering and team approvals before sending it to a key audience. Posters and postcards require more design effort and additional time for printing. A specialty item like a T-shirt is easy to select from a catalog but might require two to three weeks for delivery. Training materials and sales documentation take the most time to develop and are the most resource intensive.

Note how you must start some of the tactics in Table 11.3 during a previous phase in order to roll them out in the targeted phase. Don't hesitate to educate your technology counterparts on the length of time you need to prepare communication prior to execution. Otherwise they won't hesitate to ask for communication at the last minute. Explain the six basic time elements of a tactical communi-

TABLE 11.3	**Tactical Lead-Time**										
	Weeks Preceding an In-House Technology Rollout										
	Phase One			Phase Two			Phase Three			Phase Four	
Tactical Solution	1	2	3	4	5	6	7	8	R	+1	+2
Newsletter article	→	→									
E-mail updates	→			→	→						
Voicemail updates	→			→		→	→				
Slide presentation						→	→	→			
Lobby poster							→	→			
Postcard mailing			→	→	→						
Training Web site			→	→	→	→	→	→			
Specialty item					→	→	→	→			
Post-rollout survey									→	→	

cation development cycle (see Fig. 11.3). Each of your tactics is actually a project in and of itself, requiring detailed follow-up and execution (see Table 11.4).

Each of these communication steps varies for each project. We advocate thorough user testing of tactical pieces such as quick reference cards to make sure users understand them and that the content is indeed accurate. If you find serious errors in the content, you may need to recycle through the media and approval steps again. Likewise, production times vary by media. For hard copy media, you must plan for one to two weeks unless you expect to pay rush charges. You must plan for adequate lead times to duplicate and distribute electronic media such as CD-ROMs.

TABLE 11.4	**Tactics Require Detailed Follow-Up and Execution**				
	Quick Reference Card for New Technology				
Tactical Elements	Week 1	Week 2	Week 3	Week 4	Delivery
Information gathering	→				
Content development	→	→	→		
Media packaging (graphics)		→	→		
Editing and approvals			→	→	
Testing				▲	
Production (final version)				→	→
Distribution					▲

| Information Gathering | Content Development | Media Packaging | Edit Approval | Production | Distribution |

Figure 11.3   Six basic time elements of a tactical communication development cycle.

On the other hand, beware of the enticement of Web immediacy. Avoid the temptation to press-and-publish unless approvals and testing have taken place. Tools for online work processes effectively incorporate electronic signature approvals.

Publishing a schedule that visually depicts lead times helps to illustrate your requirements. Any of the commercially available software applications for project management work fine, or you can create simple visuals with word processing tables. Stick to the basic elements of communication lead times.

Tactical Plan for a New In-House Technology Rollout

Your manufacturing company has decided to adopt a new Web-based presentation tool across the entire enterprise of one thousand employees. We'll call the package *Enterprisation*. Your company has four satellite plants of two hundred employees each. About half the people have desktop computers, and the other half have shared access to pooled computers mostly at manufacturing sites. People make frequent trips to headquarters, and travel costs have been getting too high for training and other departmental meetings. The information technology (IT) team has identified *Enterprisation* as a best in-class application solution for online information sharing. Company associates can log on to a secure Web site and simultaneously view the same presentation slides or training documents in real time while conducting audio over a telephone connection.

Enterprisation has some additional, but limited functionality, allowing interaction among the participants during a Web share. Company associates can type questions in real time and even draw on the shared Web screen. However, other people in the company have used more expensive and full-featured products available on the market. The chief information officer (CIO) has heard their grumbling about wanting the advanced features, but she realizes *Enterprisation* is the best solution based on the available budget allocations. The company president has delivered a clear mandate. He wants *Enterprisation* operational in three months, with everybody in the company trained and able to use it. Funding for communication is no object as long as it is covered by the expected travel savings.

The CIO isn't too worried about adapting the technology and scaling it to the enterprise, but she has no idea how to get everyone else in the company interested and involved in such a short time. Fortunately, the president has assigned a technical marketing communicator to the job, and you are the one he has chosen.

State Your Objectives

After a meeting with the CIO and president, you're able to articulate the overall technology objective. You decide to document your plan and make it easy for everyone on the team to follow your progress. Your first step is completed (see Fig. 11.4).

Analyze Your Audience

During your needs analysis, you identify six key audiences who will influence or be influenced by the introduction of *Enterprisation*. For our purposes in this text, we've displayed only two of their key profile columns (see Table 11.5). Refer to Chapter 3 for additional audience profile details.

Develop Audience-Specific Strategies

Each of the targeted audiences requires a strategic communication approach. You review the audience profiles to determine cause and effect relationships to effectively engage them in ways that support the objective. Note that the strategies don't answer the question, "how will you do that?" That answer is deferred to tactical solutions. Once the tactical solutions are identified and you ask "why were these tactics chosen?" the answer should be, "they fulfill these target audience strategies" (see Table 11.6).

Choose Your Tactics

You have only 12 weeks to develop and execute the entire project, so you need to be careful about lead times. However, a reasonable amount of budget money is available if the estimates for travel savings prove to be accurate. With that in

---

Technology Objective

Have Enterprisation *installed and engaged by employees across the company within 12 weeks.*

Success Criteria

1. *Enterprisation* will be accessible to all employees within 12 weeks.
2. Employees will be trained and active in the use of *Enterprisation* within 12 weeks.
3. Travel to headquarters for meetings and training will decrease and be demonstrated in the company's next-quarter expense update.
4. A survey sent to employees one month after the start-up will report that employees clearly understand how to use the *Enterprisation* tool, and that they have adopted it for their own use. An initial baseline survey will gather feedback about the current state of travel to headquarters for training and meetings.

Figure 11.4 Overall technology objective for *Enterprisation.*

TABLE 11.5	Audience Profile for *Enterprisation*	

Audience Analysis

Audience	Influence	Key Audience Issues
Executive Team (CEO, President, CFO, CIO, COO)	Influence business vision and direction	• Enhance productivity, profitability • Reduce business costs • *Meet president's objective*
Department managers (Finance, Purchasing, Manufacturing, Quality, HR, Operations)	Influence their respective functional staffs, department peer managers, and executive team	• Minimize disruption to ongoing business processes • Do the training and rollout once; get it right the first time
Technology Development Team (*Enterprisation* team)	Influence technical outcome and training process	• Make the technology work • Scale the technology to enterprise • Support the communications and training effort without slowing technology team progress
Technology Support Team (Installation, help desk, and repair)	Influence customer (end user) satisfaction and support; participate in rollout processes and detail	• Learn the new technology • Obtain installation and troubleshooting tools • Prepare the help desk staff
Training Staff	Influence the training process and rate of adoption	• Learn the new technology • Need access to technical subject matter experts • Develop the training tools and materials • Coordinate training process
End Users (All employees are end users of this technology)	Influence the rollout process if asked; influence future rollouts with their feedback if asked. Rate of training and adoption influences success of executive team in accomplishing president's objective	• Minimize change to current processes • Minimize time in training • Avoid technology false starts or disruptions

mind, you are strongly considering the use of outside resources to develop content and media.

This is an intraorganizational rollout, so you have no need to involve commercial advertising or public relations tactics. However, you must definitely consider promotional elements for your audience strategies. Your strategic approach

TABLE 11.6	Target Audience Strategies
Audience	**Communication Strategy**
Executive Team	**Key Issues** • Enhance productivity, profitability. • Meet president's objective. • Reduce business costs. **Communications Strategies** • Provide frequent updates to report whether the project is on track to achieve the president's goal. • Continuously calculate and communicate rollout costs to demonstrate that expenditures are appropriate and to defuse any preemptive cuts on communication efforts. • Demonstrate executive leadership endorsement of *Enterprisation* to department managers and end users in order to promote compliance. • Develop and review a recovery or exit communication plan with the executive team just to be prepared in case the deadline is missed.
Department Managers (Finance, Purchasing, Manufacturing, Quality, HR, Operations)	**Key Issues** • Minimize disruption to ongoing business processes. • Do the training and rollout once; get it right the first time. **Communications Strategies** • Notify managers in advance of all communication planned for their employees. • Work directly with department managers to signal cooperation. • Build enthusiasm for *Enterprisation* among managers in order to positively influence their staffs.
Technology Development Team (*Enterprisation* team)	**Key Issues** • Make the technology work. • Scale the technology to the enterprise solution. • Support the communication and training effort without slowing technology team progress. **Communication Strategies** • Create a communication conduit for the technology team to feed technology and project information on a real-time basis to communication and training teams. • Find a way to make the technology effort more personable to the company in order to defuse any we-them alienation over the change in travel processes—especially for the regional office staffs.
Technology Support Team (Installation, help desk, and repair)	**Key Issues** • Learn the new technology. • Obtain installation and troubleshooting tools. • Prepare the help desk staff. **Communication Strategies** • Ensure that the support team is knowledgeable and confident of the product use before engaging them with end users.

(continued)

TABLE 11.6	(Continued)
Audience	**Communications Strategy**
	• Help the support team to anticipate likely rollout issues in advance in order to avoid confusion or dissension during the actual rollout. • Take extra care to motivate and build an element of fun for the support team staff in order to create a positive atmosphere around the effort.
Training Staff	**Key Issues** • Learn the new technology. • Need access to technical subject matter experts. • Develop the training tools and materials. • Coordinate training process. **Communication Strategies** • Work with the training team to create effective interactive training tools that can be deployed at each location simultaneously without one trainer having to visit each office. • Develop some training shortcuts to help meet the deadline, combined with clear follow-up actions to complete the process. • Ensure that the training staff has full access to the technology information as fast as it becomes available.
End Users* (All employees)	**Key Issues** • Minimize change to current processes. • Minimize time in training. **Communication Strategies** • Overcome the grumbling about *Enterprisation* not having all the bells and whistles of competing Web applications by emphasizing the ease and speed of training, combined with ease of technical support—which means less downtime and disruption. • Build in an element of humor to overcome any negative perceptions about cutting back travel to headquarters.

*End users also include team members.

calls for enthusiasm, some humor, and simultaneous rollouts across the multiple office locations. You and the other company associates each have access to a variety of communication tools (see Table 11.7). Given these options, your team has the flexibility to work with quite a few tactical deliverables that you can outline against your communication phases. You may not decide to use all of them, but it's good to know they're available.

For now, your communication choices include the following:

• Web pages
• Print pieces (such as flyers or postcards)
• Quick reference cards
• Personal presentations

TABLE 11.7	Variety of Communication Tools Available
• Voicemail • E-mail • Company mail truck deliveries to each site three times per week • Individual access to the company Intranet site • Meeting rooms at each site	• Desktop computers with CD-ROM players • Slide presentation software • Conference call capability • VCR player at each site • Common areas at the employee entrances

- Conference calls
- E-mail and voicemail
- CD-ROM information and training
- Specialty items

The team is also hoping to think of some clever, humorous tactics to help build enthusiasm.

Four Phases of Communication

With the deadline defined in advance, communication Phases One through Three can span a maximum of only 12 weeks. You'll worry about Phase Four after meeting the president's deadline.

After interviewing the CIO and the technology team, you've learned that they'll need at least four weeks to work out some of the software customization issues with the *Enterprisation* vendor. They need another four weeks to scale the architecture and order the additional hardware. Then they'll be in a sprint to get everything installed and tested in time for the final release in Week 12.

Since the technology team is dividing the project schedule into three equal sections, the technical communication team's approach will be fairly similar. However, as the technical marketing communicator, we're going to pull an extra week of time to the front end. We'll use that time to get up to speed on the technology and assemble our plan. We're keeping the third phase a little shorter since we'll need the additional preparation time for training and developing support tools. That leaves four weeks for Phase Two. That's where we'll really work the strategy to build enthusiasm for the companywide Phase Three start-up. (See Table 11.8 for our beginning tactical execution layout.)

Now let's discuss the overall approach of the technical marketing communication team.

Phase One: Introduction and Awareness—
Weeks 1 to 5

As the technical marketing communicator, you know lots of things will be going on all at once. The technology team has a clear mandate to adapt the vendor software to their computer network. In so doing they have to make sure it scales properly, that is, works just as well for one thousand people at multiple sites as it does

TABLE 11.8	Beginning Tactical Execution Layout											
Enterprisation Technology Rollout Communications												
Weeks	1	2	3	4	5	6	7	8	9	10	11	12
Technology	Customization					Architecture			Install and Test			
Phases of communication	Phase One Introduction and Awareness					Phase Two Expectation Development and Direction			Phase Three Fulfillment and Support			
Tactic 1												
Tactic 2												

in a single location. The training team is anxious to develop their training materials, and the technology support team has a customer service reputation to live up to. Part of that customer service prework will be to anticipate start-up challenges and develop troubleshooting solutions.

Meanwhile, the department managers are already demanding to know how one thousand people are going to be trained without disrupting their on-going business targets. Knowing the president's sense of urgency, the executive team has aggressively offered to step in and provide motivation if schedules start to slip. For now, the soon-to-be end users of *Enterprisation* haven't heard enough about upcoming changes to get too riled up.

You know that during Phase One you have five weeks to introduce the technology and raise awareness about the rollout for everyone—the various team members as well as the end users. With no time to lose, you must make decisions about technical marketing communication:

Phase One Deliverables

1. You immediately get on the executive team's calendar for week 1 of the project in order to present your rollout plan. You'll then make the same presentation to the department managers, with any executive-recommended changes or modifications.
   - *Deliverables:* Personal presentation and technical marketing communication plan.
2. To make sure no one is uneasy about communication, you set up a voicemail distribution list for everyone participating on the project and begin leaving weekly summary messages every Friday morning.
   - *Deliverable:* Technical marketing communication voicemail updating rollout plan and progress to all team members.
3. The vendor's *Enterprisation* Web application name must disappear from the project. It's too vendor-centric, and the company could always upgrade to some other Web-sharing software in the future. You decide to gather some of the team members together to pick an *internal* brand name and theme state-

ment for the project. That way your communication program will be consistent regardless of whose software engine you use. Identifying the brand is also a good team building exercise and will capture their impressions of features and benefits of the technology.

- *Deliverables:* Internal brand name, theme statement, features, and benefits.

4. Just to make sure you understand any barriers or differences among end users at the different locations, you schedule a conference call to conduct a guided discussion with attendees from each location and department. You'll report the findings to the technology, training, and support teams in case it affects packaging or delivery of the technology.

- *Deliverables:* Conference call prework and report.

5. Following the team brand naming session and the end user conference call, you will make your first high-level draft of features and benefits for the program. You'll reuse and apply these thematic messages in presentations and communications as you begin to build the brand. The graphic artist you've retained for the project will also review these themes with you in order to design the brand visuals for presentations, print, and online materials. Because of the time frames involved, you expect to pay rush charges and premiums for printing.

- *Deliverables:* Content draft for features and benefits and brand visuals.

6. Sharing information in a timely way among the various teams is paramount, and they agree a joint project Intranet site will be the best way to view real-time updates. However, they are also concerned with having to take time to draft and post the content. This is a perfect task to outsource to a freelance technical marketing communicator, and they agree to provide the necessary security access to the Intranet site. Each team will have a section on the site, and the freelancer will gather and post information updates twice each day. Viewing access will be teams only, not end users.

- *Deliverables:* Retain a technical marketing communication freelancer and coordinate Intranet information site with graphic artist and technology team.

7. By the third week, you'll want the president to make an introductory announcement to the company at large. You intend to script a brief voicemail broadcast, a corporate e-mail message, and to publish a summary in the "What's New?" section of the company Intranet. The message content will introduce the technology as an internal brand, convey the president's enthusiasm, and emphasize one or two key features and their benefits. You will provide a promise date for the next communication with an action-direction to "watch for the next update." Department managers will receive advance copies of the text and an explanation of when their employees will receive the information.

- *Deliverables:* Draft, coordinate, and publish the voicemail script and broadcast, a corporate e-mail message, and a summary in the "What's New?" section for the company Intranet.

8. To incorporate an element of friendly competition, you plan to reward the office location having the fastest rate of training and adoption of the new technology. Since everyone is tasked with saving on travel costs, the president

agrees to reallocate some of the savings to employee airfare for a four-day weekend at his condominium. You'll work out these details and a name drawing at the winning location with his executive assistant.

- *Deliverables:* Reward weekend package and coordination.

9. At your prodding, the technology team will conduct an early pilot presentation in Week 4. You arrange for the president to participate, along with each of the department managers, the training team, and the support team. You will videotape the session for training and promoting the new technology.

   - *Deliverables:* Coordination and presentation of Web application pilot and video capture.

10. As the introduction and awareness phase comes to a close, you will release a five-minute videotape with clips from the pilot presentation. The clip will include testimonials from the various department managers emphasizing statements by the training and sales managers who have to help sell the cutback in travel costs. You plan to show the tape at weekly staff meetings and post the clips on the company Intranet. A one-page teaser communication will be distributed with the video at the staff meetings. The teaser piece reinforces the message of the high-level features and benefits and advises people to watch for details of preparation, training, and the travel contest. You announce that an Intranet Web site will be available in Week 6 (Phase Two). This site will leverage the brand and list training and start-up details.

    - *Deliverables:* Video editing and copying, content development for teaser sheet, Intranet site for end users.

11. Together with the training team and department managers, you identify two people at each site to act as lead trainers and coordinators. They will participate in their local training waves, answer high-level questions, and then redirect technical troubleshooting to the technology support team.

    - *Deliverables:* Identify local training coordinators, contact them, and schedule them for the first pilot class.

12. Behind the scenes, the training team has begun to develop the trainer materials, presentations, and documentation. You introduce them to the graphic artist who will help them to apply the team's new brand look. The freelancer will update the information on the Intranet site. You have also consulted with the training team to devise a quick reference card as a job aid. The technology team agrees that a quick reference card can convey the majority of key content for users. You have scheduled the graphic artist to begin layout of training announcements and communication to distribute during Phase Two.

    - *Deliverables:* Content development and packaging of training materials and quick reference cards.

Phase Two: Expectation Development and Direction—Weeks 6 to 8

You now have three weeks to make sure everyone has not only heard about the *Enterprisation* rollout (under your new brand name) but knows what needs to be done and what is expected. You will actually prepare a good portion of the Phase

Two deliverables during Phase One. The lead times required to gather information, draft content, package it, and produce the deliverables can't wait until Week 6.

You must now set four key expectations and directions with audience-sensitive voice and style:

1. Expect the new technology they have heard about to roll out during Week 12 and bring about change related to travel, training, and information sharing. Features and benefits first described in Phase One will come to pass as promised.
2. Everyone is expected to participate, as affirmed by the president, the executive team, and the department managers.
3. Training, training material, and technical support will be readily available. Real-time information updates are available on an Intranet Web site. Questions and concerns can be communicated to the technical marketing communicator at any time before and after the rollout via e-mail, voicemail, or intranet.
4. Individuals must prepare in advance to log on to a Web site and download a software configuration tool.

Phase Two Deliverables

1. Now that the president has endorsed the project with his first voicemail and video participation, you strategically assign the sales manager, training manager, and CIO to deliver the next series of companywide voicemail messages. This will demonstrate solidarity across functional groups and defuse any animosity over who *owns* the technology change. The sales manager is scripted to leave a message in Week 6 announcing the branded Intranet information site. This URL is also published in an e-mail and posted on a lobby poster at each office location. The site content emphasizes our four key expectations (see above) and provides strong positive reinforcement of the features and benefits as well as testimonials from the pilot test. It also has a digital counter set up for each office location to count how many people have successfully completed training and participated in the first sample Web presentation. This will fuel the friendly competition over the travel drawing award.
   - *Deliverables:* Scripted voicemail for sales manager and Intranet site posting.
2. Not all manufacturing employees have 1:1 access to desktop computers. Therefore, you must consult the department managers to identify any scheduling challenges related to shared technology. You must scrutinize names, mail locations, and shift times to ensure training can proceed without affecting production or personal time.
   - *Deliverables:* Research and create a database slice for accessibility-challenged end users.
3. Early in Week 6, you test the training format and the draft of the quick reference card on a small group of end users. Incorporate any final improvements and changes before printing the materials and preparing for the train-the-trainer session. Include representatives from the technology and support

teams to ensure nothing has significantly changed with the Web application itself.

- *Deliverables:* Coordination of testing session, editing, and final production.

4. During Weeks 7 and 8, the training coordinators from each site are brought up to speed on the technology and prepared with question and answer tools.

- *Deliverables:* Conduct train-the-trainer sessions for each site.

5. During Week 7, you distribute a printed information card to every technology user in the company. The card carries the brand theme and provides a step-by-step procedure to download a Web configuration tool before training. This desktop configuration step is essential to the technology rollout. For added incentive, each card will be preprinted with a four-digit number. Users are directed to call the support team desk to register their number. Five of those numbers from each office location will be preselected to win modest gift certificates to local dining establishments. This begins to engage the technical support team and helps to gauge participation and interest among the end users. The Web URL is printed on the card, along with information explaining how users can contact you. Post winning names on the company Intranet news site and the branded technology site.

- *Deliverables:* Printed card distribution to all employees and award certificate coordination.

6. To close Week 8 and Phase Two, the training manager distributes a voicemail confirming three waves of training over the next three weeks. A final, friendly challenge is issued to each location to win the travel award drawing. You distribute detailed training schedules to the department managers to share at staff meetings. You post the same information on the Intranet site and distribute it via e-mail. You also post an early copy of the training presentation on the Intranet site. You place posters displaying schedules in the lobbies where employees enter each office location. Again, direct employees to contact you with questions and concerns.

- *Deliverables:* Scripted voicemail message for training manager and advance copy of training presentation posted on Web site.

Phase Three: Communications Fulfillment and Support—Weeks 9 to 12

Phase Three activities will deliver on the expectations set in prior communications. Two additional strategic initiatives will proceed as well. Now that training content development is completed, these communication resources will be reassigned to create a CD-ROM version of the promotional information, video clips, training content, and quick reference tool. A master copy of the CD will be pressed and ready for additional distribution for two reasons:

1. The executive team requested a backup strategy in the event that the Web application technology deadline should slip. If it becomes awkward to reschedule the entire business for group training, you can distribute CDs as an alternative training method. CDs will advance the training effort even if you experience a temporary problem getting the actual Web application to work.

2. Despite the presidential mandate, some people will inevitably miss the training, and new employees will join in the weeks to come. The CD tool will be easy to distribute and update. Depending on the company's network bandwidth, you can locate these same tools on the Web site as well.

Phase Three Deliverables

1. Lobby posters at each office location will remind employees that training is scheduled for their location.
   - *Deliverables:* Poster production and delivery.
2. Training materials and quick reference cards will be distributed to employees at each group training session. The training session will feature a live online Web presentation in a conference room or training room setting. Employees will watch their local training coordinators log on and participate in the shared Web session. They will follow along in their training materials or with the quick reference card.
   - *Deliverables:* Training room coordination and training materials distribution.
3. At the close of each session, attendees will be given an assignment for Week 12 to log in and attend their follow-up Web meeting for their office location. Their recorded attendance at this final live Web session will confirm they have mastered the basic participation skills. You can use this count to determine which office location is onboard first.
   - *Deliverables:* Instruction sheet for follow-up Web meeting and a plan for the local coordinators to conduct the actual follow-up meeting. Employee participation counts will be posted real-time on the Intranet site.
4. The final online Web presentation should recap the project itself and articulate remaining actions required of the end users, if any. You will share contact information for questions and technical support along with any related processes or procedures. An element of humor can be inserted to poke good-natured fun at any barriers to the technology change such as travel restrictions or the impersonal nature of long-distance communications. Presentation coordinators should anticipate and prepare for questions and answers.
   - *Deliverables:* Script and agenda for the local office training coordinators.
5. Distribute a final voice message from the CIO during Week 12 to congratulate the technology team, training team, and support teams. She will again reinforce the features and benefits of the technology and make a forward-looking prediction of future updates to the technology. This will be a good opportunity for her to make a good-natured competitive comment on behalf of the training progress of her office location.
   - *Deliverables:* Script and voicemail distribution for the CIO.

Phase Four: Follow-Up and Improvement— Weeks 1 to 2 After Rollout

First, the president will thank everyone for participating, and he will choose names out of a hat for the local office winners. You want to collect feedback from everyone as soon as possible after the rollout deadline. The technical support team's help desk is perfectly positioned to send surveys or record feedback from callers. Your technical marketing communication freelancer should also be retained to proactively contact a cross section of team members, managers, and users. Most importantly, you need to confirm the president's objective was met as defined by your original success criteria. Any outages from a technology, training, or communication standpoint must be immediately addressed. You make an appointment with the president or another executive team member to report your findings and to make recommendations for future technology rollouts. One of your recommendations was clear from the start: "Avoid 12-week technical marketing communication rollouts that have no advance planning cycles." In this case, the president agreed to accept costs related to temporary staffing and production charges, but the schedule prohibited the allowance of any recovery time for technology complications. Invite all team members to a final debriefing session to close loose ends and share insights for future technology projects.

- *Deliverables:* Survey forms and process, data review, team debriefing meeting, feedback report, and recommendations for executive team.

Tactical Timeline

The previous narrative helps to articulate our technical marketing communication thought process and to identify specific deliverables. Mixed in with these deliverables are additional content development and coordination efforts. Remember that each individual tactic warrants an individual plan all its own with milestones and responsible parties.

Table 11.9 visually depicts our high-level tactical plan by audience and week. Technical marketing communicators are not personally executing every tactic, but we are accountable to assign responsibilities and ensure that milestones are achieved.

Final Notes from the Example

Until now, we've only planned and anticipated our technology communication rollout. We haven't actually created the brand or contacted the department managers yet. It's not clear whether the technology can actually be scaled and implemented within 12 weeks. There's no guarantee we can actually accommodate the various production and office schedules in order to get everyone trained.

Despite the unknowns, we have a plan. If someone were to ask us what our goal is, we can answer that. If they want to know our strategies, we've got them—for *six* audiences. How are we going to do it? We have a week-by-week detailed list of tactics. Of course, we'll be challenged to think on our feet and make modifications to our plan as we go, but we have a clear structure and approach from which to act. Most importantly, we aren't waiting for the technology to be up and running before communicating with our various audiences. End users cannot legitimately say, "No one told us it was coming."

The budget rollup for each tactical effort can be estimated according to time and material requirements (see next section). Presenting the plan and budget esti-

TABLE 11.9	**High-Level Tactical Plan by Audience and Week**

Enterprisation Technology Rollout Communications

Weeks	1	2	3	4	5	6	7	8	9	10	11	12
Technology	Customization				Architecture				Install and Test			
Communication Phase	Phase One					Phase Two			Phase Three			
For All Project Team Members												
Weekly voicemail Brand name and theme ideas		▲										→
Features and benefits ideas		▲										
Intranet team site												→
Executive												
Marketing plan presentation			▲									
President's voicemail			▲									
What's New article								→				
E-mail introduction			▲									
Weekend reward												▲
Final report												
Department Managers												
Review plan												→
Team updates												→
Team intranet												→
End user lists					▲							
Staff meeting coordination	▲											
Technology Team												
Web pilot						→						
Pilot video					→							
Team review						→						
Support Team												
Team updates												→
Team intranet												→
Pilot training						→						
Survey												→

(continued)

TABLE 11.9   (Continued)

Enterprisation Technology Rollout Communications

Weeks	1	2	3	4	5	6	7	8	9	10	11	12
Technology	Customization				Architecture				Install and Test			
Communication Phase	Phase One					Phase Two			Phase Three			
Training Team												
Team updates			─	─	─	─	─	─	─	─	─	►
Team intranet			─	─	─	─	─	─	─	─	─	►
Content coordination				─	─	─	─	►				
Trainer materials			─	─	─	─	─	►				
Train trainers						─	─	►				
End Users												
Conference call audience needs		▲										
President's voicemail			▲									
What's New article			▲									
E-mail introduction			▲									
Video overview				─	─	►						
Teaser challenge					─	►						
Sales manager voicemail						▲						
Intranet site and contest				─	─	─	─	─	─	─	─	►
Deskcard and giveaway					─	►						
Training manager voicemail								▲				
Training materials						─	─	─	►			
Quick reference card							─	►				
Final Web meeting									─	─	─	►
General project												
Retain TMC freelancer		▲										
Retain graphics firm/artist		▲										
Brand visuals			─	─	─	─	─	─	─	►		
Intranet site			─	─	─	─	─	─	─	─	─	►
User test					─	►						
Print/distribute			─	─	─	─	─	─	─	─	►	
Training rooms						─	─	─	─	─	►	
CIO voicemail											▲	
Weekend awards						─	─	─	─	─	─	►

mates to the executive team in the first or second week of the rollout allows for an immediate reality check with their expectations. They can balk or question the need for an individual tactic, but the technical marketing communication team can then point to an at-risk audience strategy that might threaten the president's objective. From a different perspective, a solid communication plan lends confidence and credibility to the entire technology effort, defusing the rumors and uncertainty that accompany change.

The Rollout in Action

Let's imagine some other details for the rollout in action from the perspective of each of the four phases of communication.

Introduction and Awareness

The executive team approves the plan. You gather the technology, training, and support teams together at a local ice cream parlor and brainstorm brand names for the project. At first, no one is that enthusiastic about replacing the vendor's *Enterprisation* name since it cleverly refers to an enterprise-presentation-application. However, the team begins to loosen up and homes in on the president's desire to limit travel. After a round of brainstorming, a technologist suggests they've made things too complicated. "It's simple," he says, "I'm here and you're there, but we're sharing information as if we had no distance barrier." With some additional massaging, the name becomes *Hear-N-There*, with the N standing for *no barriers*. The brand name for the program will be able to represent any communication efforts related to online Web sharing, whether the *Enterprisation* product is involved or not. This paves the way for a longer brand life.

Mindful of potential negative reaction to travel restrictions, the teams challenge you to think of a rollout theme that hits the travel issue head-on. They enjoy the slightly edgy slogan that states, "I'd rather be traveling to Headquarters." It's meant to parody "I'd rather be fishing" bumper stickers. The creative juices flow, and the team applauds an idea to collect employee wish lists of what they would rather be doing than flying to headquarters. Of course, they come up with the idea to award the most creative alternative, and the best (most humorous) ideas will adorn the Intranet site, posters, and printed materials. The team even muses over scripting a travel wish for the president to use in one of his communications.

Shifting to more serious matters, the main *Hear-N-There* technology features are described at the meeting, and the team articulates both company and end user benefits. They emphasize that the technical benefits reach far beyond travel savings. Sharing live presentations on the Intranet will speed the way the company makes decisions and conducts business. Regardless of travel savings, the technology shift is essential to their future success. One of the key *internal* marketing communication messages will center on this need to advance information sharing technology and the speed it brings to business processes.

The team's Intranet site goes up quickly, and the technical marketing communication freelancer becomes well known to all team members as she collects daily information. The executive team, department managers, technology team, training team, technology support team, and the technical marketing communicators all have separate sections on the page.

The president's voicemail introduction to the company at large and the pilot session with *Hear-N-There* comes off without a hitch. The video edits take longer than expected, but you still manage to get them sent out with the printed piece (teaser) for the staff meetings in Week 5. The response is an amused, but favorable, reaction to the brand theme, and a genuine curiosity emerges for the new technology.

Not everything is rosy, though. In fact, the technology team is having major difficulty acquiring some of the server hardware they need to scale the architecture. The biggest risk is that *Hear-N-There* will operate, but much too slowly because of network congestion. One of the executive team members reads this update on the Intranet and reminds everyone that the original schedule deadline remains. Although they are having difficulty integrating the technology, the user interface is unlikely to change significantly, so the training team continues preparation.

Expectation Development and Direction

The all-employee Intranet site is released in Week 6, along with the travel contest announcements. The president has generously agreed to fund three separate employee trips to his oceanfront condominium for the winning office location. As evidence that a spirit of competition has begun, the technical marketing communicator is receiving requests to release training materials early. The requests are denied.

The technology help desk reports a flurry of calls from employees registering the random number from the Web configuration printed deskcard mailed in Week 6. They are anxious to win the dinner awards promised for early callers. This turns out to be a communication *miss* because users can register their number without having actually downloaded the required Web configuration files to their desktop. You advise the help desk to remind callers of this important step and issue an additional reminder to department managers for their subsequent staff meetings. Despite the miss, the brand recognition is rapidly building.

In a separate activity, employees have inundated the technical marketing communicators with "I'd rather be traveling to . . ." alternative submissions. Many are humorous; some are insightful and heartwarming. The activity has had a surprise team-building effect across the various office locations, independent of the technology rollout itself.

Train-the-trainer classes take place for the on-site coordinators chosen at each office location. The trainees complain they don't have enough step-by-step information listed on the quick reference cards since that is the primary tool the end users will likely use. After a heated team meeting and funding approval from the executive team, you send the quick reference card back for a redesign with additional pages and rush printing—at significant additional expense.

Communication Fulfillment and Support

The training classes take place although the technology problems have yet to be resolved. The rollout teams, with the department managers' approval, have collectively placed the bet that things will be resolved in time for the Web meetings in

Week 12. Despite the best efforts to schedule everyone for classes, a significant percentage of employees simply cannot attend at the scheduled times. Fortunately, your back-up CD training tool will be completed ahead of time and distributed to the employees who need them. The executive team gratefully acknowledges this recovery move as erasing the previous communication snafus.

Ultimately, the large majority of employees successfully attend the Week 12 *Hear-N-There* online Web meeting. The technology is implemented in the nick of time, thanks to round-the-clock weekend work. The president declares the entire effort a resounding success. He also reinforces in his scripted remarks that this is not about changing the way employees travel—but the way they share information. In his closing remarks of congratulations to the participants, he scores personal points for declaring what he would rather be doing than traveling to headquarters.

Follow-Up and Improvement

In the subsequent feedback sessions and surveys, the entire rollout team is gratified to learn that employees felt well informed and prepared for the change. The technology team, led by the CIO, reports to company executives that a strategically-oriented technical marketing communication approach made all the difference. The executive team agrees, and thanks you.

The Cost of Successful Tactical Plans

The tactical plan is the road map used to fulfill strategies that accomplish the technology objective. Despite the methodological word *plan*, this development also requires some freewheeling creative elements. Technical marketing communicators are free to creatively choose and combine any media communication vehicles that their hearts desire, within reason. *Reason* usually has three components, namely, timing, budgets, and resources.

Timing

In the ideal situation, technical marketing communicators help to drive timing and budgets for technology programs that include their own communication work. When a program or project is developed correctly, the technical marketing communication team is asked to estimate marketing communication costs and lead times on behalf of the overall technology development plan (see Fig. 11.5).

It's when time and communication budgets aren't accounted for up front that technical marketing communicators get forced into a corner. "How much time do we have left? What's left in the budget?" Both answers can be quickly discovered during a needs analysis. But in the ideal situation, the recommendation of technical marketing communicators will actually drive the *original* budget requests and timing recommendations for the proposed technology program. The corresponding technical marketing communication recommendation sounds more like, "For

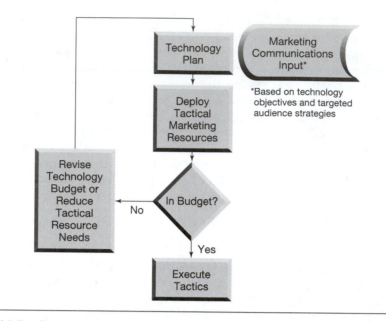

Figure 11.5   Process of estimating marketing communication costs.

your technology program to be successful, we'll need 12 weeks to assemble our marketing communication program, two technical marketing communicators to get it done, one graphic artist, and $10,000 in media development."

Budgets

The cost estimate calculations for technical marketing communication are as straightforward as any other budgeted technology component. Technical marketing communication solutions require time and materials to develop. Graphics require design time. Videos require production crews. Content development requires research, composition, and approval time. CD-ROMs have to be pressed and shipped. The relative skill levels of the people doing the work also affect the budget. If a company or organization is privileged to have multimedia designers and the requisite software packages in-house, budgetary costs are calculated as time and overhead charges (hours × dollars).

Example: High-Level Tactical Cost Estimate for Budgetary Planning Purposes

This example (see Table 11.10) assumes that objectives and strategies have been developed. You must obtain quotes from outside resources to handle media solutions your in-house staff cannot manage. You may even choose to budget for special project-driven tools such as graphics software or a digital camera. There's always the chicken and the egg question: "How can I determine the marketing communication costs if the technology hasn't even been developed yet?" It's not always easy, but technical marketing communicators have to take some calculated risks

TABLE 11.10	High-Level Tactical Cost Estimate			
Tactic	**Resources**	**Time (hours × $)**	**Materials**	**Total**
Direct mail card	Content Writer	10 hours × $70 = $700	Set up, print and ship 5000 copies = $5000	$7100
	Graphic Design	10 hours × $90 = $900		
	Project Management	5 hours × $100 = $500		
CD-ROM training	Content Writer	80 hours × $75 = $6000	Press, package and ship 5000 copies = $5000	$18,800
	Graphic Design	40 hours × $90 = $3600		
	Technical Support	20 hours × $110 = $2200		
	Project Manager	20 hours × $100 = $2000		
Digital camera	Administrative Assistant Research/Ordering	4 hours × $35 = $140	Camera purchase: $750	$890
	Tactical Project Totals	$16,040	$10,750	**$26,790**

too. Since we urge technology teams to include us in the planning, we need to shoulder some of the budgetary responsibility as well. If you have prior experience or data that exemplifies successful tactical approaches for your targeted audiences, it's a starting point to build your latest budget.

Many technical marketing communicators approach tactical budgets by estimating the expected incremental revenue or productivity gains to be made. For example, a telemarketing campaign is meant to contact 5000 sales prospects. Past experience with your target audience tells you 5 percent of those called (250) usually request follow-up by your technical sales team, and about 10 percent of those contacts lead to sales. If you can calculate the revenue and profit margin of those 25 possible sales, it gives an indication of the value of your telemarketing campaign. The same exercise can be done for any other tactical efforts.

Example: Estimating Tactical Value for Budget Estimates

Not every marketing communication outcome has to be measured by return on investment. Intangible results can also lead to future revenue opportunities (see Table 11.11). These are based on enhanced brand awareness or increased company goodwill. Still, a budget requires you to think more rigorously through the bottom line value of your efforts.

TABLE 11.11	Estimating Tactical Value for Budget Estimates			
Tactic	Target Audience	Projected Yield	Net Revenue/ Gain	Considerations
Telemarketing campaign	5000	250 new contacts	25 new technology sales and increased brand awareness	Compare call costs to incremental sales revenue
Web banner advertising	250,000 visitors to targeted Web portal	25,000 click-through requests for additional information	Increased traffic to corporate Web site and additional profiling metrics	Estimate value of market information collected from new site registrants
In-house technology training for an improved process	500 employees	90% awareness of new technology; better internal communication	20% productivity gain over old process	Beyond gains, consider value of enhanced morale when employees feel included in change
Technology seminar sponsorship	100 local business leaders	25 attendees	3 technology consulting engagements	Consider long-term growth potential and referrals from new consulting engagements

Tactical Support

You can accomplish tactical work in the following three ways.

1. **Do it in-house**. This strategy means that you use people and tools from the same organization that is developing or applying the technology involved. If you have experienced technical marketing communicators onboard and the project requires minimal media production, this may be a viable option. As we said in Chapter 1, technical marketing communicators have a wide breadth of expertise including content development, interview skills, and general technology acumen. They also enlist the participation of subject matter experts, administrative resources, and technology specialists.

2. **Outsource it**. If an organization or company is staffed for technology and little else, they may be best served by hiring technical marketing communicators and media professionals from the outside to develop the list of tactical deliverables. Technology teams refer to this outside hiring practice as *outsourcing* or *staff augmentation*. If the need for resources is temporary (e.g., for the project duration), the added cost of outsourcing may be more cost-effective than hiring somebody as a permanent employee. Either freelancers or agencies can provide the resources, but someone still has to assume the project coordination leadership (see Fig. 11.6).

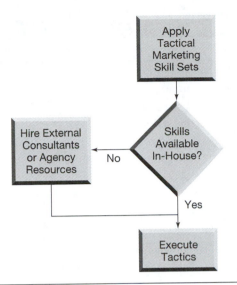

Figure 11.6 Process of determining need for external resources.

3. **Combine in-house and contracted resources**. The most likely tactical scenarios combine in-house technical marketing communication staff with select outsourced (contracted) media skills. We have seen many projects suffer because well-meaning staff members tried the do-it-yourself approach for pivotal media elements. Graphic designers go to art school and spend years developing their talent for a reason. The same can be said for video producers and voice talent. Someone that is not adequately trained or experienced in media degrades the impact of your finished tactical solutions. They are also less productive to the company or organization in their usual (nonmedia) role as well. Technical marketing communicators take the lead to assemble the right resources for the right tactical job.

Table 11.12 depicts a likely technology organization's communications resource mix. It's not unusual to outsource graphic design and production work (printing, video duplication, direct mail coordination) while retaining content development and project management responsibilities. There are infinite combinations possible.

Summing It Up

This chapter is all about asking how a specific tactic fulfills a targeted audience strategy in a way that accomplishes the overall technology objective. One tactic will rarely accomplish that purpose. Most people recommend at least a three-touch tactical solution. You make your choices based on your communication

TABLE 11.12	Possible Resource Mix		
Tactical Skills	In-House	Outsource	△ Cost to Outsource
Technical marketing communications planning	X		
Project management	X		
Technical content composition	X		
Online graphics		X	
Print graphics		X	
Video production		X	
Media placement	X		
Web design		X	
Web commerce interface	X		
Database development	X		
Telemarketing		X	

phase: introduction and awareness, expectation development and direction, communication fulfillment and support, or follow-up and improvement. This chapter reflects the message of the previous chapters as you see a case study of a technical marketing communication plan in action.

Applying What You've Learned

1. Find a print tactic. Determine the possible objective it could fulfill. List the cause and effect relationship of this tactic to the strategy you imagined.
2. Find a Web site. Determine the possible objective it could fulfill. List the cause and effect relationship of this tactic to the strategy you imagined.
3. Determine which tactics best meet the objectives you have already stated (see Exercise 3 in Chapter 2) to market the university's technical marketing communication major. Complete the marketing plan for the university's technical marketing communication major by combining the needs analysis, audience analysis (from Chapter 3), strategy (from Chapter 4), and the tactics from this chapter.

SMALL GROUP ACTIVITY

A university has hired you to develop a strategic marketing communication plan for the rollout of a new e-mail system. The plan should include needs analysis, audience analysis, strategy, and tactics. Develop the plan to encompass the four phases making a list of deliverables for each phase.

CHAPTER 12

Looking Back in Order to Look Forward

Overview

How do you know if your technical marketing tactics are delivering their strategic content?

In our Preface, we envisioned enjoyable conversation and dialog with you across the many concepts shared thus far in our text. If you have stayed with us to this last chapter, you have been challenged to think differently about technical marketing communication. We have defined the terms *technology, marketing,* and *communication* in an attempt to help you to see the processes through a fresh lens.

- *Technology*: Any scientific, methodological, specialized work related to the development, sales, service, distribution, application, and integration of technology.
- *Marketing*: The strategically oriented business of understanding markets, aligning products and services with target markets, and coordination of efforts to attract, capture, and fulfill sales to those markets.
- *Communication*: The development, application, and distribution of content across various media to convey information that is clearly understood by a particular audience.

After providing the discrete definitions of terms, we put them together for you to create an exciting definition of our discipline. In fact, if you remember only one thing from reading this text, we hope you remember that successful technical marketing communication is clearly *understood* by a targeted audience, *valued* for its content, and clear in its *actionable* directions. For in that one statement, we have distilled our message to you. We would like to add these thoughts:

- Before you can begin the process, you must first understand what you want to accomplish (needs analysis and goal setting).
- The idea of a targeted audience conveys the necessity of actually knowing your audience—not just identification, but analysis and classification.
- In order for the audience to value the content, you must link the content to causal strategies. You must ask the *why* question before you ask the *how* question.

- We have given you a plethora of tactics to choose from—print, electronic, and other media. Regardless of the tactics you choose, you must make sure your readers know exactly what you want them to do after they have come in contact with each tactic. In other words, you have given them clear, unmistakable directions for the desired action.
- Finally, we have helped you to see the need for a multimedia mix and given you specific advice on how that might come together.

Before we close we need to ask one final question: How do you know if your technical marketing tactics indeed are delivering their strategic intent? When you have finished Phase Three, communication fulfillment and support (see Chapter 11) in any marketing endeavor, you should take a look back and see what you can learn from those events. In this chapter, you will learn the necessity of looking back in order to evaluate (see Fig. 12.1).

Sandi and Tom

What You Need to Know

As with all project plans, technical marketing communicators strive to build in metrics for gauging their success. According to our definition, technical marketing communication is judged successful if it is understood, valued, and clear in its ac-

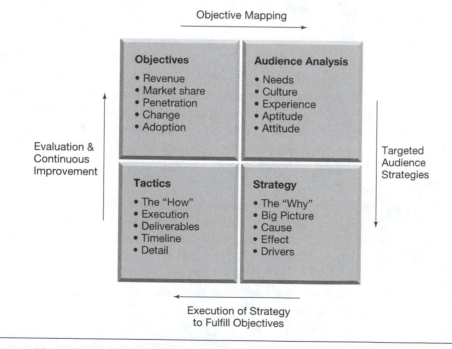

Figure 12.1   Evaluation is the final stage in the communication cycle.

tionable directions on track to achieving the technology objective. The important question then becomes: How can you *determine* if your message was understood, valued, and clear in its actionable directions?

Evaluating How Well the Message Was Understood

In the academic arena, when instructors want to know if content is understood, they have standard ways of getting that information. They hold discussion groups in class and carefully listen to determine at what level individuals *understand* the content. By asking the right questions and leading the discussion down the correct path, instructors can get a good idea of how their students have understood the content. Instructors also administer tests to determine how well their students have understood.

When your readers have encountered your technical marketing message, you want them to walk away saying, "Now I understand." That will only happen if your message is appropriate and clear. And you can determine whether they have truly undertstood by using guided discussions, surveys, and tests, and even more importantly by observing their actions (adopt, change, do, wait, etc.).

Evaluating Whether or Not the Message Was Valued

Now that they understand, are they glad you told them? That's the essence of *valued*. Obviously this step takes you deeper into engagement with your audience. They may understand your message but not necessarily make an emotional commitment. It takes persuasion to bring someone to your side of the table—to see things the way you see them, to recognize that they need something and you have what they need. As a technical marketing communicator, your task is not just to tell the facts and provide information, but to motivate and compel—to sell. Persuading a reluctant prospect to agree with you is one of sales' most invigorating challenges. Words, images, and sounds must create a mood, an excitement, and a desire for the product or service that you are trying to promote.

How can you measure if your readers are glad you told them? Their speed to react and adopt is a key indicator of the value implied by your strategic content. If your audiences' enthusiasm to share your message is not evident, then you need to determine whether they understood the message. Although your audiences' emotions are involved, the result can be objectively evaluated. You need feedback concerning how they felt after they received your message, and a well-designed survey or a well-planned focus group are among the tools to accomplish that objective.

Evaluating the Action Taken

Once your readers understand and value your message, you want them to respond with "What do you want me to do?" And any successful marketing endeavor always clearly communicates specifically what you want your reader to do. It's much easier to measure discrete action taken than it is to measure an emotional outcome. If your goal was to effect change, then determine if change has occurred. If your goal was to sell products or services, then measure incremental revenue against an existing baseline. Past action is measurable. For example, the goal of your brochure might be to convince your readers to call a toll-free number for more information. To measure the effectiveness of that particular tactic, simply record how many calls were placed as a result of the brochure, again, against a previously established baseline.

In Chapter 10, you read about an internal marketing project to convince employees to record their available skill sets, training, and experience so that the information would be available to team leaders as they decided future team assignments. We reported the result of that marketing project was a 60-percent increase in data entered into the system in one day. That certainly is a concrete measure of the action taken as a direct result of the marketing project.

You can design similar projects with built-in metrics that can be used to determine the effectiveness of your marketing efforts—response rates, cross-purchases, service add-ons, training completion. In the remainder of this chapter, we will review one option that you can use to evaluate the effectiveness of your own marketing projects. Don't lose sight of the goal of evaluation: to determine if your specific tactics did indeed accomplish your strategic goals.

Survey

Technical marketing communicators often use surveys to evaluate the effectiveness of their tactics. Dudnyk Advertising & Public Relations worked with a manufacturing client to communicate product information and general industry news to their end users. They chose to do that with a printed newsletter and coordinated audiotape program. Each communication was issued three times per year, alternating media so end users received a mailing every two months. Their management wanted an evaluation of the program to assess the value of each media vehicle and identify weaknesses.

Dudnyk Advertising & Public Relations developed a telephone survey to evaluate recall and satisfaction with various aspects of the newsletter and tape. They selected two segments of the audience for comparison: end users who were employees of large corporations and those who were independent consultants to the industry. They selected these names randomly from the newsletter and audiotape mailing list. They completed 15-minute interviews with 80 subjects from each segment. The subjects received no compensation for the interviews.

On the questionnaire, the telephone interviewer asked for the following information:

- Demographic information
- Recall of recent newsletters and audiotapes
- Recall of newsletters published by competitive manufacturers
- Typical amount of each issue read/each tape listened to
- Pass-along or retention value

- Identification with the sponsor
- Influence on opinions about the sponsor
- Scaled evaluations of various content aspects (range of 1 to 10, with 1 meaning "not at all satisfied" and 10 meaning "completely satisfied")
- Format preferences: printed newsletter versus audiotape

The results of the survey showed that the recall of the newsletter-audiotape communications was approximately 90 percent between both audience segments. Recall of newsletters published by competitive manufacturers was lower (a result somewhat biased because not all recipients received the competitive newsletters). The average recipient tended to skim most of the newsletter and read about half of it thoroughly. Typically, recipients listened to about three-fourths of the audiotape. More than half pass along the newsletter or audiotape to colleagues, and about half routinely save the publications for future reference.

As you would expect of an unsolicited direct mail vehicle, only a small core of recipients were "completely satisfied" with the newsletter/audiotape. However, a majority reported being "somewhat satisfied," and a small number placed the publications within the "dissatisfied" rankings.

A comparison of responses between the two audience segments revealed that each audience uses the publications differently. Specifically, corporate employees highly valued the research summaries presented in both the newsletter and audiotape. Independent consultants placed more value on information about product use techniques.

The majority of recipients were able to correctly identify the manufacturer as sponsor of the publications. About one-third believed their opinions of the manufacturer had been favorably influenced because of the newsletter and audiotape.

Recipients had equal preference for newsletter or audiotape format and approved of some overlap in content. Unsolicited comments captured by the interviewers showed that many recipients spend considerable time in their vehicles traveling among work sites. The ability to hear and read information offered valuable reinforcement for the message and provided flexibility in accessing the information.

Based on survey results, the technical marketing communicators made the following changes in the newsletter and audiotape content:

- More emphasis on information used to make product decisions (why product choices were made as well as testimonial results)
- More research reports
- More "how-to" guidelines

They also made the following changes in format:

- Made the newsletter easier to skim
- Shortened the tape to encourage listening to the full program

In addition, because recipients saw value in having an overlap of content between the newsletter and audiotape, each vehicle should cross-promote the other. In general, the newsletter provides details about a topic, and the tape provides "first-person" commentary.

This kind of evaluation can be helpful to determine the success of any kind of marketing endeavor and you'll need to budget adequate time and money.

Summing It Up

This chapter is your opportunity to look back over the process we have presented in this text. Does it make sense to you? You need to internalize the definitions of technology, communication, and marketing and to appreciate the joining of these terms to form a definition of this profession: technical marketing communication. The process begins with needs analysis, audience analysis, and establishing strategy. Branding and creativity permeate all you do. You make your tactical choices based on the strategic objectives, and you execute your plan. In this final chapter, we reviewed how important it is to evaluate and look back to record and apply lessons learned. Ask yourself what went well and what should not be repeated. Then immediately plug improvements into your forward processes and methodologies as you continuously hone and advance your craft. What does the future hold for technical marketing communication? Only time, you, and your customers can tell! This process will ensure a continuously improving marketing experience.

Applying What You've Learned

1. Plan a focus group to follow up on the *Hear-N-There* project presented in Chapter 11.
2. Plan a focus group to follow up on the marketing project for your university's technical marketing major.
3. Design and bring to completion two of the tactics you have identified in the marketing plan for your university's technical marketing major.

SMALL GROUP ACTIVITY

Write a short memo to a supervisor to describe whether the *Hear-N-There* project was a success. Answer the following questions:

- Did the employees understand the communication?
- Did the employees value the communication?
- Did the employees find the communication clear and actionable in its directions?

Give specific justification for your conclusions.

INDEX